JAMES THURBER

Literature and Life: American Writers

Selected list of titles in this series:

Complete list of titles in the series available from the publisher on request.

JAMES THURBER

Robert Emmet Long

A Frederick Ungar Book

CONTINUUM · NEW YORK

Austin Community College
Learning Resources Center
1988

The Continuum Publishing Company
370 Lexington Avenue, New York, NY 10017

Printed in the United States of America

Library of Congress Cataloging-in-Publication Data

Long, Robert Emmet.
James Thurber.

(literature and life series)
Bibliography: p.
Includes index.
1. Thurber, James, 1894–1961.   2. Authors,
American—20th century—Biography.   3. Humorists,
American—20th century—Biography.   4. Cartoonists—
United States—Biography.   I. Title.   II. Series.
PS3539.H94Z76   1988   818'.5209 [B]   87-19125
ISBN 0-8044-2546-9

For Mark Van Doren,
a brilliant teacher

Contents

Acknowledgments

In preparing this book on James Thurber, I have been fortunate in having had the cooperation, always graciously given, of Helen W. Thurber, who granted permission to quote from unpublished letters and other Thurber material; and of Joel White, who gave permission to quote from the Thurber-White correspondence at the Cornell University Library. Donald D. Eddy and Lucy B. Burgess, of the Cornell University Library, Department of Rare Books, were exceptionally helpful in providing access to the material in the E. B. White Collection, and in giving permission to quote from it.

I am pleasurably indebted to Burton Bernstein, Thurber's biographer, for the lengthy conversation I had with him about Thurber at his office at the *New Yorker;* and to Scott Elledge, biographer of E. B. White, for our conversation about Thurber and White. Rosemary E. Thurber was also especially helpful; and I am grateful to the novelist Brian Burland, for sharing his recollections of Thurber with me. I am indebted, too, to John W. Crowley for reading the manuscript; and to Malcolm Cowley, Jay Martin, Robert E. Morsberger, Walter Sutton, and Joseph Ridgely for advice on one matter or another.

Chronology

1894   James Grover Thurber born December 8, in Columbus, Ohio, to Mary Fisher Thurber and Charles L. Thurber, the second of family's three sons.

1901   In Washington, DC, where family has moved temporarily, is blinded in left eye by older brother William in bow-and-arrow accident.

1903–7   Frail and with weak vision, attends the Sullivant School, Columbus, Ohio, where family is taken in for a time by the mother's well-to-do parents, the William Fishers.

1908–9   Attends Douglas Junior High School, where he is recognized for his intelligence, and writes Class Prophecy, with himself as unlikely hero in active world.

1909–13   Enters East High School, elected class president in senior year, and graduates with honor.

1913–15   Attends Ohio State University, commuting from home; leads solitary, neurotic existence; in "lost" 1914–15 academic year does not go to classes, and fails all his courses.

1916–18   Begins sophomore year again at twenty-one, and meets Elliott Nugent, who introduces him to fraternity and social life. With Nugent is reporter for the college paper, the *Ohio State Lantern*, and becomes editor in chief of the *Sundial*, monthly humor and literary magazine. In 1918, at twenty-three, leaves Ohio State without completing his degree.

1918–20   Becomes code clerk for the State Department, first in Washington, DC, and then at the American Embassy in Paris, from November 1918 to February 1920.

1920–21   Returns to Columbus, and begins work as reporter for the *Columbus Dispatch;* between 1921 and 1925 writes and directs five musical comedies for the Scarlet Mask Club at Ohio State.

1922   Marries Althea Adams, Ohio State beauty with dominant personality, and prototype of future "Thurber woman."

1923   Attracts attention through his Sunday half-page column, "Credos and Curios," for the *Columbus Dispatch.*

1924   Resigns from *Dispatch* to try free-lance writing; is press agent for a time in Columbus.

1925   Goes to France to write a novel that does not materialize. Hired as reporter for the Paris edition of the *Chicago Tribune;* later transferred to the Riviera edition in Nice.

1926   Returns to America in June. Lives in Greenwich Village area, New York City, writing pieces that are rejected by the *New Yorker,* and a lengthy, unpublished parody of inspirational books, "Why We Behave Like Microbe Hunters." Finds work as reporter and feature writer for the *New York Evening Post.*

1927   In February, at Village party, meets E. B. White, who introduces him to Harold Ross. Hired immediately as editor-writer for the *New Yorker.* Shares office with White, and is a principal writer for the magazine's "Talk of the Town" department.

1929   First book, *Is Sex Necessary?*, in collaboration with E. B. White, published.

1930   His first cartoons appear in the *New Yorker.*

1931   *The Owl in the Attic and Other Perplexities* published. Daughter Rosemary, Thurber's only child, born October 7.

1932   *The Seal in the Bedroom and Other Predicaments* published.

1933   *My Life and Hard Times* published to highly favorable reviews. Hemingway calls Thurber's work "the best writing coming out of America."

1935   In May, divorces Althea Adams; and in June marries Helen Wismer. *The Middle-Aged Man on the Flying Trapeze* published.

1936   Goes to live in Connecticut. Leaves the *New Yorker* staff to free-lance, keeping contractual arrangement for his writing with the magazine.

1937–38 *Let Your Mind Alone!* published 1937. In spring 1937, travels to France and England, and has one-man show of drawings at the Storran Gallery, London. Rents a villa on the French Riviera, returning to America September 1938.

1939   *The Last Flower* published. Collaborates with Elliott Nugent, in Hollywood, on *The Male Animal*. "The Secret Life of Walter Mitty" published in the *New Yorker.*

1940–41 *The Male Animal* opens at Cort Theatre, New York, January 9, 1940. *Fables for Our Time and Famous Poems Illustrated* published. In 1940–41, has series of five operations for cataract, glaucoma, and iritis, following which is legally blind. In state of despair during Martha's Vineyard convalescence.

1942   Settles in Cornwall, Connecticut, and has prolonged nervous breakdown. Release of Warner Brothers film version of *The Male Animal*, with Henry Fonda and Olivia de Haviland. *My World—and Welcome to It* published.

1942   Moves to New York and, although barely able to see, does limited number of drawings with aid of Zeiss loop. *Many Moons* and *Thurber's Men, Women and Dogs* published.

1944   Critically ill with pneumonia and appendicitis. *The Great Quillow* published.

1945   *The Thurber Carnival* published to critical acclaim, and is best-seller for most of year. *The White Deer* published. Buys stately, white fourteen-room colonial house in Cornwall, Connecticut—"The Great Good Place." Has circle of literary neighbor friends, including the Mark Van Dorens and the Kenneth MacLeans.

1947   Hopelessly blind, is no longer able to continue with drawings. "The Secret Life of Walter Mitty," with Danny Kaye, released as motion picture.

1948   Active contributor to the *New Yorker*. *The Beast in Me and Other Animals* published.

1950   *The 13 Clocks* published. Receives Doctor of Letters degree from Kenyon College.

1951   Declines honorary Doctor of Letters degree from his alma mater, Ohio State University, in protest over its suppression of academic freedom. Death of the *New Yorker's* founding editor Harold Ross.

1952   *The Thurber Album* published. Revival of *The Male Animal*, with Elliott Nugent and Robert Preston, at the City Center Theatre in New York.

1953   *Thurber Country* published. Awarded honorary Litt D degree by Yale University. Thyroid condition heightens "rages" and erratic behavior.

1955   *Thurber's Dogs* published. After eighteen years, revisits Europe. Is feted in London. Mother, "Mame" Thurber, dies at eighty-nine at end of year.

1956   *Further Fables for Our Time* published.

1957   *The Wonderful O* and *Alarms and Diversions* published.

1958   Travels to Europe and England. Is first American since Mark Twain to be "called to the table" for *Punch's* Wednesday luncheon.

1959   *The Years with Ross* published.

1960   *A Thurber Carnival*, revue based on his writings and drawings, produced at the ANTA Theatre, New York. Joins cast in September, for eighty-eight performances, playing himself.

1961   *Lanterns and Lances* published. Revisits Europe in deteriorating health. In New York, stricken with blood clot on brain, October 4; dies November 4. Buried in Greenlawn Cemetery, Columbus, Ohio.

1962   *Credos and Curios* and *A Thurber Carnival* published posthumously.

1963   Two-volume *Vintage Thurber* published in England.

1966   *Thurber and Company* published.

1981   *Selected Letters of James Thurber* published.

1

James Thurber: The Life and Career

When one thinks of James Thurber, one thinks of the *New Yorker* magazine, where much of his writing first appeared and where his cartoons, at once comic and disturbing, were published prolifically. But Thurber was more than a *New Yorker* wit. He was beyond doubt the preeminent humorist and satirist of his age. Often compared to Mark Twain, he had, like the nineteenth-century humorist, a deep strain of pessimism that underlay even his most exuberant comic imaginings. His stories rely at times on parody and farce, yet they are also filled with dread and apprehension. His special theme was the unceasing combat between the sexes, sometimes enacted on a field of dreamlike strangeness. During his lifetime Thurber attracted a vast audience, both in America and abroad, but he also belonged to "high" culture and was admired by T. S. Eliot, W. H. Auden, and other writers and intellectuals who were fascinated by the peculiar mixture in his work of innocence and savagery, the real and the surreal. It is partly this interaction in him between the real and the dreamlike that makes Thurber an essential figure in the development of modern literary consciousness.

Although he spent most of his adult life in or near New York City, James Grover Thurber was an essential Midwesterner with deep roots in Ohio, where his ancestors on both sides of the family had migrated from the East in the early nineteenth century.[1] His mother's side of the family had especially colorful and eccentric forebears.

1

Judge Stacy Taylor, Thurber's step-great-grandfather on his mother's side, was a Virginian of English stock who went West in 1826, settling in Ohio and quickly prospering in the fur trade with Indian tribes. It was typical of his hardy spirit that he also read law every night until dawn with a lit candle balanced on his chest. Thurber's other maternal great-grandfather, Jacob Fisher, another Virginian of English stock who went west to Ohio, was a man of legendary strength and peculiarity. A man so strong that he could pick up horses in his blacksmith shop to move them from one place to another, he was a fervid anti-Jacksonian, and once broke the jaw of a man who sided with Jackson's policies, then generously nursed him back to health.

Jacob Fisher's son and Thurber's maternal grandfather, William Fisher, the owner of a prosperous wholesale fruit-and-vegetable commission house in Columbus, was also startlingly unconventional. In public places, he would announce "I am William M. Fisher, of Columbus, Ohio," and expect to be catered to; and he was given to walking through the streets of his native city with a red rose clenched between his teeth that he had capped in gold. William Fisher married Katherine Matheny Taylor, the first of whose six children was Mary Agnes Fisher, Thurber's mother. Mary Fisher, known as "Mame," was a spirited, high-strung girl with a gift for mimicry and an aspiration to go into the theater that was quashed by her family. In 1892, when she was twenty-five, she married Charles Thurber, a young clerk active in politics from Indianapolis. With his poorly paid job with the State Republican Committee, Charles Thurber was not regarded highly as a son-in-law by William M. Fisher. He did, however, buy the couple a small house in Columbus, and his wife, without his knowledge, helped them out with checks and food baskets. In the course of his career Charles Thurber was on the staff of two Ohio governors and for eight years was secretary to the mayor of Columbus. But he never succeeded beyond this middling level of clerkship employment, and in the eyes of many the Thurbers were the Fishers' poor relations.

The Thurbers' three sons were born in Columbus in the 1890s—William in 1893, James in 1894, and Robert in 1896. In 1901 Charles Thurber became secretary to a congressman from his Ohio district, which necessitated a move to Washington—a period made memorable by an injury suffered by James at six years of age that affected his later life profoundly. While playing with bows and arrows, his brother William struck James in the left eye with an arrow, resulting not only in the loss of the eye but also in a condition of "sympathetic ophthalmia" that spread from the left to the right eye and eventually led to Thurber's blindness. With the loss of one eye and impaired vision in the remaining one, James was kept out of school for a year. Handicapped and physically frail, he did not take part in sports and tended to withdraw into himself.

In 1903 the Thurbers returned to live, very nearly as charity cases, with Mame's family in their mansion on Bryden Road. As tensions in the house increased, James was farmed out to Aunt Margery Albright, sometimes for three or four days a week but sometimes for weeks at a time. Margery Albright was an extremely odd woman who practiced herbal and homeopathic nursing and took in boarders. Her house was primitive and unimposing, but young James preferred it to the large house on Bryden Road where William Fisher had taunted him and treated him cruelly. Between 1903 and 1907, James attended the Sullivant School, in a tough, working-class section of the city. Known as "Blinky" by his classmates at the Sullivant School, he was shy, nervous, and introverted. He was so given to daydreaming that one of his teachers thought he might be deaf.

When the Thurbers moved or were evicted by the Fishers in 1907, they went to live in a rented house in another part of the city, and James changed schools. At the Douglas Junior High School, he continued to be frail and neurasthenic, but was recognized by his teachers for his exceptional intelligence. In 1909 he entered East High School, the best of the city's secondary schools, becoming a "teacher's pet" whose writing and drawing abilities were encouraged, and he graduated with honors. Without the means or apparently the inclination to attend one of the private colleges in the East, he enrolled at Ohio State University in Columbus, commuting by streetcar from the family house. At the university, he astonished his professors by his phenomenal memory, but was otherwise an unkempt loner whom the fraternities all shunned. The university's requirements in science, physical education, and military drill, for which he had no aptitude, oppressed him; and in his sophomore year he stopped attending classes altogether, spending his time instead reading voraciously in the library, going to movies addictively, and becoming immersed in his own inner life and fantasies.

When Thurber begain his sophomore year over in the fall of 1915, at the age of twenty-one, he met another student, Elliott Nugent,[2] whose friendship lifted him out of his listlessness and melancholy. Nugent was everything that Thurber was not. The son of a theatrical family, he had already made his debut on the stage before entering Ohio State. Sophisticated beyond his years, he was good-looking, confident, and popular. He soon "adopted" Thurber, and arranged to have him admitted to his fraternity. In 1916–17 he and Thurber were reporters for the *Ohio State Lantern*, and in the next year were issue editors of the paper. Thurber also began to write for the *Sundial*, the monthly humor and literary magazine, and in 1917–18 was its editor in chief. Finally, Nugent introduced him to The Strollers, the campus dramatic society, awakening his interest in the theater.

But if Thurber managed to play a belated role in the undergraduate life, he eventually came to feel that he had been at the university too long. In 1918, when he was twenty-three, most of the able-bodied male students were away in the war. When Nugent left for the Great Lakes Naval Training Center, Thurber tried to enlist in the army, but was turned down because of his poor eyesight. He then learned of a code-clerk training program in Washington, DC, went there to apply and was accepted. After four months of training in encoding and decoding at the State Department, he was assigned to the American Embassy in Paris. He sailed for France in October, arriving at the seacoast town of Saint-Nazaire two days after the armistice was declared. His year and a half in Paris was seasoning he needed, but he was thrown into confusion by the experience. His letters to Nugent from Paris reveal that he suffered a severe nervous breakdown and was often depressed and melancholy. When he returned to Columbus in 1920, he continued to write to Nugent of his ideals and inner confusion. Passages from these letters printed in Burton Bernstein's biography give an impression of an odd and eerie immaturity. He poured out his feelings of hopeless yearning for two girls of his past, one from seventh grade, another from the university, putting them on pedestals; and one has the sense of his inability to come to terms with life or with sexuality.

In August 1920 Thurber was hired as a reporter for the *Columbus Dispatch*, work that brought him into contact with the city's other reporters, particularly Joel Sayre and John McNulty, who remained lifelong friends and were later contributors to the *New Yorker*. Another lasting friendship he formed was with Herman Miller, an English instructor and playwright-actor at Ohio State, and later head of its drama department. He met Miller when he became involved again with the theatrical groups at the university, especially the newly formed Scarlet Mask Club that staged original musicals. Thurber was coauthor of one of these productions, *Oh My, Omar!* in 1921, and was either collaborator or sole author of four later ones. None of these revues revealed unusual talent, but they were favorably reviewed in the Columbus press and attracted attention to Thurber locally. Indirectly they led to his sudden and surprising marriage in 1922 to Althea Adams, a campus beauty whose ambitions went far beyond the confines of Ohio. It may well have been, as Thurber's second wife later speculated, that Althea saw Thurber as her "ticket out of Columbus."[3] A tall, aggressive woman, she was a dominant female of the type Thurber would make famous in his drawings and fiction. He once confessed to a friend that she filled him with a "certain fear," and he told another that "sleeping with Althea is like sleeping with the Statue of Liberty."[4] The marriage was beneficial inasmuch as Althea gave him the direction and push he needed, but in other respects it was disastrous.

From February to December 1923, in addition to his work as a reporter, Thurber wrote a column called "Credos and Curios" for the Sunday half-page of the *Dispatch*. It was a miscellany of jokes, paragraphs, book reviews, personal reminiscence, humor pieces, and observations, and was heavily indebted to the successful columnists of the day, particularly Franklin P. Adams and the Ohio columnist Robert O. Ryder. Charles Holmes has described the overall impression of Thurber's "Credos and Curios" column as one of "immaturity and uncertainty."[5] Thurber was critical of Joyce and D. H. Lawrence for their sexual preoccupations, and recommended the more chaste and healthier-minded American writers Henry James and Willa Cather. At times he defended football and "the American Way," yet at other times assailed the philistine values of Columbus. No settled philosophy can be discerned in the columns, and only rarely do they contain flashes of the humor one associates with the mature Thurber.

When, through no displeasure with Thurber's column, the entire Sunday half-page was discontinued at the end of 1923, Althea decided that it was time for them to leave Columbus. They spent the summer of 1924 in the Adirondacks where Thurber wrote stories and humor articles that were rejected by magazines, and by the fall they returned to Columbus. But the *Dispatch* refused to take him back, and Thurber worked as a free-lance press agent for an amusement park, a movie house, and the Elks circus—until Althea decided that they should go to France. In Normandy, they rented a room in a farmhouse and Thurber began a novel about Columbus, but before long concluded that it was worthless and threw it away. Running short of money, they went to Paris, where Thurber was hired by the Paris edition of the *Chicago Tribune*, becoming a rewrite man on the night desk with Elliott Paul, Eugene Jolas, and William L. Shirer. In autumn 1925 he was transferred to Nice to work on the Riviera edition, an episode that, despite his disintegrating marriage to Althea, was one of the happiest of his life.

While Althea remained behind for a time, having, as Bernstein writes, "become attracted to one of the other members of the *Tribune* staff,"[6] Thurber returned to America, arriving in New York in June 1926 with ten dollars in his pocket. Living in a cheap, rented room on West 13th Street, he wrote stories and humor pieces that were rejected by the *New Yorker*, and an elaborate, unpublished parody of current best-sellers, "Why We Behave Like Microbe Hunters." In the fall, joined by Althea, he rented a basement apartment in the West Village, and earned a living as a reporter and feature writer for the *New York Evening Post*. By the end of the year, after rejecting twenty previous pieces, the *New Yorker* accepted one of Thurber's casuals, "An American Romance," about a little man who is whirled in the revolving door of a department store, setting a world's record and becoming suddenly rich and famous.

In February 1927, Thurber made perhaps the most important acquaintance of his career. He went to a party at the Village apartment of Russell Lord, who worked for the *New Yorker*, and there met E. B. White. White, who was already established at the *New Yorker*, arranged for Thurber to meet the magazine's editor Harold Ross, who hired him immediately. The meeting with Ross marked a turning point in the career of James Grover Thurber, who until then was wholly unknown and had been unable to find himself. Very soon thereafter he would find his vocation and his voice, his talents would come to a sudden full maturity and would flourish wondrously.

When Thurber came to the *New Yorker* in 1927, the magazine had been established for only two years and was losing money. A few of Ross's friends from the Algonquin Hotel's Round Table contributed, but most did not expect the venture to succeed and did not rush to be part of it.[7] Ross's editors and writers were generally young men whose reputations were still to be made, and at thirty-two Thurber was older than many of the others. It was his especial good fortune to be assigned to an office with White who, although five years younger than Thurber, was already an accomplished prose stylist.[8] White became not only his office mate but also his mentor, and his influence on him was significant, as Thurber was often later to acknowledge. He taught him how to write sentences that had clarity, precision, and conversational ease, and that glowed on the page; and it was through his example that Thurber discovered that observation and humor could be a demanding craft.

Those on the staff of the *New Yorker* in the late 1920s and early 1930s included Robert Benchley, Dorothy Parker, Russel Crouse, Clarence Day, Ogden Nash, and Clifton Fadiman; and its frequent contributors included S. J. Perelman, Ring Lardner, and John O'Hara. The magazine was directed by Ross, Ralph Ingersoll (its managing editor), and Katharine Angell (later Mrs. E. B. White); but its first string of staff writers were White, Thurber, and Wolcott Gibbs (who came to the *New Yorker* only a few months after Thurber). Gibbs sometimes filled in for White, wrote profiles, stories, and parodies, and was the magazine's acidulous drama (and sometimes movie) critic. White composed the "Notes and Comment" section that opened the magazine, and coached Thurber to write the "Talk of the Town" column. For a period of eight years, from 1927 to

1935, Thurber *was* the "Talk of the Town," and like Ross himself and White, he put in long hours, sometimes working late at night every night of the week. His personal life was lonely, since his marriage continued to founder, and part of the time Althea lived apart from him in Connecticut, with her kennel of show dogs, while Thurber holed up in New York hotel rooms.

One day in the late 1920s, Thurber and White discovered that they had each begun parodies of the same subject—the current rash of books that, with pseudoscientific nomenclature, explained sex and psychological adjustment to the layman. They decided to combine their efforts into a single book, writing alternating chapters. Their joint venture, *Is Sex Necessary? or Why You Feel the Way You Do*, was submitted to White's publisher Harper & Brothers, together with some humorous illustrations by Thurber. In the small office they shared, Thurber had often distracted himself by doing quick sketches that he then discarded. They littered the room, and the waste baskets were filled with them. While they were engaged in writing *Is Sex Necessary?*, White persuaded Thurber that some of his doodlelike drawings would be exactly right as illustrations for the book and asked him to do a set of them. Thurber then did some rapid pencil sketches that White inked in and took with him with the manuscript to the publisher. After White spread the drawings on the floor of the office, the publisher examined them and said hesitantly, "These, I take it, are the rough sketches from which the drawings will be produced?" Unruffled, White replied, "No, these are the sketches themselves." The book, which was published in November 1929, proved to be an immediate success with the public, selling fifty thousand copies in the first year and attracting attention to both its authors.

White continued to ink in more of Thurber's pencil sketches and submitted a set of them to Ross, who was at first perplexed and unable to know what to make of them. Prodded by White, however, he began to publish them in the magazine and to his surprise found that they aroused considerable interest. Some of these early drawings were included in Thurber's next book, *The Owl in the Attic and Other Perplexities* (1931), together with pieces he had published in the *New Yorker* between 1928 and 1930, most notably his brilliant cycle of Mr. and Mrs. Monroe stories. Appropriately, the introduction to the book, which established Thurber both as a writer and as an artist, was written by White, who had been among the first to recognize his talents.

It was quickly followed by *The Seal in the Bedroom and Other Predicaments* (1932), a collection of Thurber's cartoons taking its title from a drawing that became instantly famous when it appeared in the *New Yorker* in mid-1932. In this cartoon a barking seal is depicted on the headboard of a bed in which a couple have been roused from sleep, the incredulous wife exclaiming irritably: "Have it your way, then, you heard a seal bark!" In her introduction to the book Dorothy Parker remarked, "I revere [Thurber] as an artist," and noted especially the psychological obliqueness of the drawings in which "the women are of a dowdiness so overwhelming that it becomes tremendous style."[9] A Thurber cult began to come into being, with many writers and artists particularly being impressed by the surreal or dreamlike quality of Thurber's imagination.

Thurber's next book, *My Life and Hard Times* (1933) was the most nearly perfect of his career. In this collection of family sketches, Thurber gave full play to his gift for creating comic anarchy. Its effect was like that of a romantic excursion into irrationality and wonder. Reviews of *My Life and Hard Times* were exceptionally favorable. Dwight Macdonald called it the "best humor piece to have come out of the entire post–World War I period,"[10] and Thurber was repeatedly compared to Mark Twain. The book also impressed Hemingway, who told Dorothy Parker that Thurber's was "the best writing coming out of America."[11]

Thurber's personal life, however, continued to be troubled. He and Althea were briefly reunited, and Althea gave birth to his only child, his daughter Rosemary, in 1931. Yet before long they were again living apart, Althea with her infant daughter, circle of suburban friends, and menagerie of dogs, and Thurber in a bachelor room at the Algonquin Hotel. What his life at this time was like is recorded in his autobiographical story "One Is a Wanderer," about a man who prowls the city's nightclubs and speakeasies until dawn to return to a solitary hotel room and a painful loneliness. He had relationships with women, importantly with Ann Honeycutt, who moved in a circle of *New Yorker* writers and later married St. Clair McKelway; but they were often transitory or ended in quarreling, and one has the impression that he was poorly equipped to play the part of a womanizer. He was more mental than physical, and was often impaired by alcohol. Under the influence of alcohol, he behaved erratically and was subject to sudden rages. Yet at other times he was a delightful companion and raconteur who attracted many friends. John ("Jap") Gude, a radio executive Thurber met at this time, later became his theatrical agent and was an extraordinarily loyal friend to the end of his life.

Thurber's haunts included Tony's, a gathering place for such *New Yorker* staff members as Robert Benchley, Wolcott Gibbs, Robert Coates, and John McNulty; and Bleeck's, where Thurber knew John O'Hara and a group of other writers. But his favorite watering place was Tim Costello's speakeasy on Third Avenue, where he became known for his recitations and renditions of ballads, particularly "Bye, Bye, Blackbird," and where his friends included the actors Humphrey Bogart, Franchot Tone, and Burgess Meredith. Beginning in the winter of 1934–35, in fact, Thurber and Costello's became inseparably associated in the minds of many New Yorkers. When Costello decided to redo his plaster walls, Thurber volunteered his services as a muralist, covering the walls with his drawings. They became so renowned a feature of the establishment that when Costello later moved next door he had the wallboard carefully taken down and put up in the new bar.

In 1934 Althea filed for divorce and in the following year, when the divorce was completed, both remarried. Thurber's second wife was Helen Wismer, the daughter of a Congregational minister who had graduated from Mount Holyoke, and worked as an editor in New York. They met at a Village party, and from the first she was attracted to Thurber. As it happened, he could not have chosen more wisely, for Helen Wismer was a steadying influence he needed and despite his notoriously difficult personality she remained devoted to him. Soon after the marriage, Thurber published *The Middle-Aged Man on the Flying Trapeze* (1935), one of his best collections. Drawing in part on his unhappy first marriage, it revealed an expansion of range in his fiction, particularly in the stories in which male characters, in the discord of their marriages, are brought to the near edge of insanity.

Late that year the Thurbers vacationed in Bermuda, a favorite place they were to revisit often.[12] When they returned to New York in the late spring of 1936, Thurber decided to give up his staff position on the *New Yorker*, believing that he would be able to support himself as a free-lance writer. He kept a contractual arrangement with the magazine, however, which gave them first refusal on anything he wrote, and he remained one of its most frequent contributors. After renting a house in Connecticut, Thurber began work on a series of spoofs of current inspirational books that appeared first in the *New Yorker* and then, with other recent pieces, were included in his book *Let Your Mind Alone!* (1937).

The Thurbers traveled to France in the spring of 1937, and in Paris frequented cafés with Hemingway, Dorothy Parker, and a circle of others. In May they went to London to be present at the one-man show of Thurber's drawings at the Storran Gallery, which drew extraordinarily favorable reviews. "The hallmark of sophistication," one critic wrote, "is to adore the drawings of James Thurber."[13] Thurber's celebrity was increased by the attention given to the recent British edition of *The Middle-Aged Man on the*

Flying Trapeze, and he was sought after as a dinner guest and introduced to a number of notables, including H. G. Wells and David Garnett, the latter of whom wrote in the *Observer* that Thurber was "the most humorous and original writer living."[14]

In the fall, for a modest forty dollars a month, the Thurbers rented a villa at Cap d'Antibes that came with a cook named Maria and her ineffectual Russian husband Olympy, humorous sketches of whom would later appear in Thurber's European travel pieces. The Thurbers enjoyed their life on the French Riviera so much that they stayed for a year. They returned to New York in September 1938, on the eve of World War II—a fertile period in Thurber's creative life that began with the composition of *The Last Flower* (1939), a fable in drawings that, inspired by the dark events abroad, envisioned apocalyptic destruction and a renewal of life through the rudimentary force of innocence and love. Gravitating further to the parable form, he began a series of brilliant animal fables in the tradition of Aesop and La Fontaine that the *New Yorker* published eagerly and were later brought out to acclaim in *Fables for Our Time and Famous Poems Illustrated* (1940). "The Secret Life of Walter Mitty," from the same period, also has a fable quality. Published in the March 18, 1939 issue of the *New Yorker*, "Walter Mitty" proved to be not only Thurber's single most famous tale but also one of the most frequently anthologized stories in modern American writing. Mitty's name entered into the American vocabulary, and has become part of the American folk mind.

In the same year that Walter Mitty was born, Thurber was struck with the idea for a play and contacted his old friend Elliott Nugent, asking him to be his collaborator. Nugent was not enthusiastic about Thurber's idea for the play, already having commitments in Hollywood as a screenwriter-director, but eventually Thurber won him over. By the end of the year the Thurbers went to Hollywood, where Thurber and Nugent wrote a treatment of the play, *The Male Animal*, a domestic comedy centering on a Walter Mitty intellectual who teaches at a Midwestern university based on Ohio State, and becomes embroiled in a campus controversy involving the issue of academic freedom. First tried out in California, the play opened on Broadway on January 9, 1940, with Nugent in the leading role as Tommy Turner. *The Male Animal* was well received by reviewers, ran for 244 performances, and became one of the standard works in the American theater repertoire. Yet even while reaching this new pinnacle of success, Thurber was about to confront the most tragic experience of his life. Before long he would go blind.

His eyesight failing badly, Thurber vacationed again in Bermuda, then returned to Connecticut to submit to the eye surgery he dreaded. A cataract had obscured the vision in his only sighted eye, but with its removal Thurber's problems were far from over. A second operation was required for glaucoma and iritis, conditions that recurred after surgery was performed and necessitated further operations. During 1940–41 Thurber had five operations in all, following which he was legally blind, having only one-fiftieth vision in his right eye. At Martha's Vineyard to recuperate, he became despondent, believing that he would be unable to resume his career as a writer and artist. A story he wrote there, "The Whip-Poor-Will," about a man whose inner suffering and obsession with death lead to homicidal mania, suggests his anguished state of mind. He was able, however, to write the first of his celebrated fairy tales for adults, *Many Moons*, before suffering a prolonged nervous collapse. His breakdown was particularly severe in the winter of 1941–42 but lasted in all for five years.

At Martha's Vineyard, Thurber poured out his anguish over being unable to see to a new acquaintance, Mark Van Doren, the well-known poet, critic, and professor of English at Columbia University—a meeting that began another important, long-term friendship. In the spring of 1942, indeed, he became Van Doren's neighbor, renting a

house in Cornwall, Connecticut, where, in addition to the
Van Dorens his circle included Kenneth MacLean, professor of English at Yale, and his wife Sara, and Rose
Algrant, a French teacher at a local private school. Cornwall was a sanctuary for Thurber during the war years, but
he was not wholly immobilized by his blindness, for when
the film version of *The Male Animal* had its premiere in
Columbus in the spring of 1942, he attended the opening
with his "seeing-eye wife" Helen. He also managed to do a
small amount of writing, composing his pieces in a large
script on yellow pads, with relatively few words to the
page. He wrote one of his finest stories, "The Catbird
Seat," at this time and assembled his best writing of the
last five years in a new collection, *My World—And Welcome
to It* (1942).

In early 1943 Thurber learned of a device called the
Zeiss loop, a magnifying helmet worn by precision work-
ers in defense plants, and managed to obtain one. Using
the Zeiss loop he was able to draw detailed pictures in
bright light on twenty-four-inch-by-ten-inch paper. His
doctor permitted him to do only two drawings a day,
allowing no more than five minutes for each, since the
loop was an added strain on the little that was left of his
vision. By the end of the summer he collected enough
drawings for a new book, *Thurber's Men, Women, and Dogs*,
which appeared in 1943 with an introduction by Dorothy
Parker. In addition, the forgotten manuscript of *Many
Moons* was discovered, and was published to enthusiastic
reviews the same year. By the end of the year Thurber was
the subject of an article by Peter De Vries, "James Thurber:
The Comic Prufrock,"[15] which pleased him enormously,
and in April 1944 he accepted De Vries's invitation to speak
at the Chicago Arts Club. They quickly became friends,
and adopting De Vries as his protégé, Thurber introduced
him to Harold Ross, who hired him as a staff writer at the
New Yorker.

The last years of the war for Thurber were a mixture of
serious illness and good fortune. Influenced by the suc-

cess of *Many Moons*, he wrote two new fairy tales, *The Great Quillow* (1944) and *The White Deer* (1945), the latter of which became a best-seller and was praised by many critics, including Edmund Wilson. Then in the fall of 1944 Thurber fell gravely ill, and was reported in the press to be near death. He contracted lobar pneumonia, and had barely recovered when his appendix burst and peritonitis set in. Had the operation been delayed, he would not have survived. He survived, in fact, to reach a new peak of fame with *The Thurber Carnival* (1945), a collection of his best work over a fifteen-year period. Reviews, as Charles Holmes has remarked, "were unanimous in pointing out, sometimes with an air of surprise, that Thurber was not simply a clever *New Yorker* writer but a major comic artist."[16] William Rose Benet in the *Saturday Review*, which printed Thurber's likeness on its cover, hailed *The Thurber Carnival* as "one of the absolutely essential books of our time."[17] It was a huge popular success as well. Harper & Brothers quickly exhausted its first printing of fifty thousand copies, and the Book-of-the-Month Club chose it as a main selection and ordered a further printing of 375,000 copies. It was on the best-seller list for most of 1945, and its sales made Thurber so financially well off that he was able to buy a stately, fourteen-room Colonial house in Cornwall, the "Great Good Place" he had long sought.

In Cornwall, Thurber was the cynosure of a group of permanent and summer residents: Mark and Dorothy Van Doren, Kenneth and Sara MacLean, Rose Algrant, Marc Simont, an artist who admired Thurber enormously and illustrated his fairy tales, the Lewis Gannetts, and the William L. Shirers. His daughter Rosemary now also spent her summers there, sometimes acting in theatricals with the Van Doren sons. By 1947 Thurber's vision had failed so badly that he had to give up drawing altogether. But he led an active social life, entertaining friends at his home in the evenings and going with his wife to theirs. He also continued to be in the public eye. In 1947, for example, "The Secret Life of Walter Mitty" was produced as a film starring

Danny Kaye, adding to the already worldwide fame of Thurber's most famous escapist.

Thurber had by then begun to dictate his pieces, and in 1948 found an ideal secretary, Elfride Von Kuegelgen (known as "Fritzi"), who remained with him, off and on, for the rest of his life. Because of his phenomenal memory, he was able to compose a piece, then revise it in distinctly separate versions, in his head before "Fritzi" came at noon to take dictation. The method worked so well that Thurber was again contributing to the *New Yorker* regularly, and by the end of the year published a new anthology of his recent writing, *The Beast in Me and Other Animals* (1948). In 1950 the Thurbers vacationed once again in Bermuda, bringing along his secretary, and there he composed another of the fairy tales, *The Thirteen Clocks* (1950).

Later that year he was awarded a Doctor of Letters degree from Kenyon College, the first of several he received in the early 1950s (others coming from Williams College and Yale University). He was also designated as the recipient of an honorary Doctor of Letters degree from his alma mater Ohio State, but declined it in protest over the university's recently imposed "gag rule" that barred speakers on campus whose views were considered politically radical or controversial. Throughout this time, in fact, Thurber often spoke out against witch-hunts, blacklists, and other attempts to restrict the freedom of expression of writers and artists. In this atmosphere of political coercion the issue of academic freedom in *The Male Animal* assumed new relevance and in part prompted its revival on Broadway in the spring of 1952. Elliott Nugent once again starred as Tommy Turner, and Robert Preston played his football hero nemesis Joe Ferguson, in a production that enjoyed an even-longer run than the original one.

Out of tune with the present, Thurber began to look back increasingly to the past. In *The Thurber Album* (1952) he re-created the past of Columbus, at times sentimentally, in verbal portraits of his quirky ancestors, professors at

Ohio State, and those he knew as a young reporter in the city. The book was a popular success and a best-seller, but Thurber was in the reverse of good spirits. He developed a toxic thyroid condition that left him unable to concentrate or to write for a year, and his frequent irritability led to outbursts of uncontrollable anger. He would not permit a thyroidectomy, an operation that had left his brother Robert a listless invalid, and instead was treated with experimental drugs that took years to bring the condition under control. In the meantime those near him (in New York, Cornwall, and Bermuda) attempted to cope with his affliction with as much patience as they could manage. New books by Thurber appeared—*Thurber Country* (1953), an anthology of recent work, and *Thurber's Dogs* (1955), a collection of essays and drawings on the theme of canines—but they were not among his best. Generally, his new writing expressed a curmudgeon's alienation from everything contemporary. After the death of Harold Ross in 1951, Thurber had begun to feel alienated even from the *New Yorker*.

Restless, he traveled with his wife to Europe in the spring of 1955, and stayed for a time in Paris. In London he was invited to tea with T. S. Eliot, an ardent Thurber admirer, and was besieged for interviews. The particularly warm reception by the English was gratifying, but Thurber's return to America was darkened by the death of his mother. The Thurbers went to Columbus to be at her bedside, and were with her for a month while she lay in a coma following a stroke. "Mame" Thurber, who died a few weeks short of ninety, had been perhaps the most influential person on Thurber's life. He inherited her high-strung nature, compulsion to talk and "perform," and her salty comic talents that he called "the finest . . . I have ever known."[18] Although living apart from her, he still felt the presence of her personality. The conflict in Thurber between the mother's dominant personality and a rebellion against it and inability to assert his manhood fully, was a powerful element, one would think, of Thurber's creative life.

The mother's death coincided with his beginning another series of fables, most of which appeared in the *New Yorker* before they were collected in book form as *Further Fables for Our Time* (1956). Thurber also sent his final fairy tale, *The Wonderful O,* to the *New Yorker,* but when William Maxwell, the new fiction editor, did not take it for reasons of length, his bitterness toward the magazine increased. *The Wonderful O* (1958) was published in the same year as *Alarms and Diversions,* an anthology of his best prose since 1942 and of his drawings from as far back as 1931. *Alarms and Diversions* reflected the extent to which he had become antagonistic to prevailing trends in America, particularly the decline of language and communication and the near demise of humor.

But if *Alarms and Diversions* suggested an atrophy of Thurber's own powers as a humorist, he was granted an end-of-career success with his memoirs of Harold Ross, begun as a series for the *Atlantic.* The first of the pieces was published in the November 1957 issue, and additional installments appeared every month thereafter until August 1958. After finishing the last installments in Europe, Thurber traveled to England, where he was "called to the table" at *Punch* magazine's Wednesday luncheon—the only American since Mark Twain to receive such an honor. The Thurbers returned to America for the book publication of *The Years with Ross* (1959), which became a best-seller and a Book-of-the-Month Club selection, and of which Edmund Wilson wrote that both "as a literary portrait and a history of journalism it will certainly become a classic."[19] Thurber's exuberantly irreverent and comic portrait of Ross, however, offended the editors of the *New Yorker,* as well as Katharine and E. B. White, whose longtime friendship with Thurber became chilled and distant.[20]

In the mid to late fifties, Thurber's writing was frequently adapted for the stage,[21] screen,[22] and television;[23]

even operas and ballets were drawn from his work.[24] But in 1960, for the first time, a revue based on his writings and drawings was produced on Broadway. The revue, *A Thurber Carnival*, directed by Burgess Meredith, opened at the ANTA Theatre on February 26, 1960, and received generally good reviews.[25] When ticket sales began to fall off, Thurber stepped in to play himself and, remarkably, rescued the show. For three months audiences flocked to see the great blind humorist, seated in a chair that moved to center stage on a conveyor belt, recite one of his tales of comic confusion. Thurber had done recitations for his friends all his life, but never before had he performed before a theater audience. It was a role he relished, and it was as if, through her son, "Mame" Thurber's greatest ambition had been realized.

His performance in the revue, however, was Thurber's final triumph. *Lanterns and Lances*, a collection of new pieces with a jaundiced view of modern times, was published in 1961, but it was one of Thurber's weakest books. Then in Cornwall he suffered an apparent stroke that affected him radically. He was no longer a pleasure to be with, and the writing he dictated—misanthropic and obsessed with ghosts—was rambling and incoherent. He drank frighteningly and quarreled with everyone, even with Mark Van Doren whom, as Bernstein remarks, "he probably loved and respected more than any other man."[26] When he sailed to England on a brief, ill-advised trip to discuss the production of *A Thurber Carnival* planned in London, he had to be kept in his cabin, where he drank and raved constantly.

After returning to America, the Thurbers accepted an invitation to a party at Sardi's East, on the occasion of the opening night of the musical *Sail Away*, by their friend Noel Coward. Feeling shut out of the limelight by the attention being paid to Coward, Thurber demanded the microphone and began to sing "Bye, Bye, Blackbird," the ballad he sang at Costello's bar in the great days of his early fame. Part way through the song he lurched forward suddenly and collapsed. At the Doctor's Hospital in New York an operation was performed on his brain, and a large hematoma, or blood tumor, was discovered. There was also evidence of arteriosclerosis of the brain and of a series of small strokes that had occurrred within the last year. For nearly a month a deathwatch was held at his bedside, and practically his last words, before lapsing into a coma, were "God bless . . . God damn." He died on November 4, 1961, a month before his sixty-seventh birthday. His death was reported throughout the world, receiving extensive coverage in England, where he was compared to Mark Twain and Lewis Carroll. In America, E. B. White wrote a moving obituary of Thurber in the *New Yorker*;[27] and in the front-page story and obituary in the *New York Times*, William Shawn, Ross's successor at the *New Yorker*, called Thurber "a master among comic artists," and "one of the great American writers of our time."[28]

After Thurber's death, a collection of his pieces entitled *Credos and Curios* (1962) was published, and the *Selected Letters of James Thurber* (1981) appeared at the beginning of the 1980s. But there is still much Thurber material, including thousands of published drawings, that has never been collected in book form. The largest and most complete biography of Thurber is Burton Bernstein's *Thurber: A Biography* (1975), an unsparing account that emphasizes the tragic in Thurber. Thurber's work itself tends to be tragicomic, and it is filled with the self-contradictions and complexities of the man. A writer who turned reality into fantasy, Thurber loved elation and grotesquerie, but felt a deep, even terrible, loneliness at the heart of life. And it was appropriate at the end, when it came time to sum up, that he should have found the words to express his sense of the very mixed nature of the human condition, should on his deathbed have cried "God bless . . . God damn."

2

~~~~~~~~~~~~~~~~~~~~~~~~~~~~~~~~~~~

Thurber's Dreamscapes: The Drawings and Illustrations

Although Thurber was to achieve recognition on a vast scale for his writing, it was for his drawings that he first came to public attention. A Thurber cult, based on the drawings, came into being almost immediately, and was international in scope. These cartoons and illustrations reveal many essential features of Thurber as an imaginative artist—his spontaneity and high spirits, his gift for evoking laughter, as well as something almost sinister, in the conceptions that he struck off with such rapidity. The loss of his vision later in life was particularly tragic in that it destroyed an important outlet for his creative energy, removing him from the visual world in which he delighted. Because his work as a visual artist and as an artist in prose often overlap, revealing a common concern with physic anxiety and miniaturization, it might be well to begin with his drawings, the form in which Thurber first appeared before the world.

E. B. White once remarked that Thurber's drawings were "works of genius, greater than his writing."[1] They are not greater than his writing, but like the writing they reflect Thurber's lifelong preoccupation with dreamlike, inner experience. Thurber began to draw when he was seven years old, a habit he kept up while he attended various schools in Columbus and that coincided with his early efforts at writing. A school friend remembered that he "was constantly drawing and throwing the drawings away, as if he had no further use for them,"[2] and he did the same later as an undergraduate at Ohio State. At the university, however, he published some of these drawings in the *Sundial*, the literary and humor magazine of which he was editor in chief. Although the later drawings suggest that Thurber was wholly unfamiliar with conventional draftsmanship, his sketches in the *Sundial* reveal otherwise. They are carefully filled in, with cross-hatching and realistic detail, and reveal an art nouveau influence. An element conspicuously missing is Thurber's flair for idiosyncrasy and bold eccentricity.

Missing, too, is any strongly discernible indebtedness to the comic strip, of which, as Charles Holmes points out, Thurber was an early and avid reader. In a May 1923 "Credos and Curios" column for the *Columbus Dispatch*, in fact, Thurber called attention to the American comic strip as a significant art form."[3] He liked those particularly that dealt with the domestic American scene, such as Walter Hoban's "Jerry on the Job," which he praised for its "peculiar force of fantasy, a rare quality in American artists of any medium."[4] Like young E. E. Cummings, he was also attracted to the fantasy of George Harriman's "Krazy Kat" comic strips, and he liked the domestic turbulence and whimsy of Fontaine Fox's "Toonerville Trolley." Thurber took a trunkful of these comic strips with him when he went to live in New York, and their influence on his later drawings seems evident.

When Thurber joined the *New Yorker* in 1927, however, he did not think of himself as an artist but as a writer. In the office he shared with White, he drew quick sketches continually but chiefly as an outlet for his nervous energy. "Thurber could do two drawings in a minute," White said, "and they would both be very funny, even brilliant. Then, he would throw both away and do two more. There must have been thousands around that office at one time or another."[5] It was not even Thurber but White who proposed that he do the comic illustrations for their book *Is Sex Necessary?*, and who persuaded Harper and Brothers to publish them. In his "Note" to the drawings in the book,

White was also Thurber's first advocate as an artist. He describes Thurber's men as "badly frightened . . . fugitive beings," and observed that the drawings give a sense of the "serenity of life's mystery, as well as the charming doubtfulness of its purpose."[6] The fear of Thurber's men and insecurity of their world are the chief impression conveyed by Thurber's first professional efforts as an illustrator.

But this fear is as yet tentative. His men and women in *Is Sex Necessary?* are caricatured as crude figures in outline, but they have not as yet taken on the style of Thurber's more developed conceptions, are not as yet "Thurber men" and "Thurber women." In some of the sketches, in fact, Thurber was indebted to a conventional pictorial realism of the 1920s. One scene, for example, shows a pretty girl being embraced by a man in a bowler hat, and only the crudely drawn man in the background who looks on with anxiety and dread suggests Thurber at all. Thurber's profiles of Dr. Walter Tithridge and Dr. Karl Zaner, the putative sex authorities the book satirizes, are also rendered conventionally. They are made to seem rather sourly out of touch with life, but they are not actually grotesque. Two uncaptioned sketches of men seated in chairs and viewed from the rear are variations of an early Thurber drawing in the *Sundial;* and they add to an impression that Thurber was trying out a variety of styles rather than having as yet found his distinctive one.

Part of the interest of the drawings is that here and there they reveal Thurber's mature style as it is just beginning to emerge. A sketch of a dog is striking because realism has been rejected in favor of a technique resembling a child's drawing. A quality of distortion can be noticed since the dog's face resembles that of a fish, and the body is flat rather than two-dimensional, with a hind leg appended awkwardly to the figure. Another animal drawing depicts two small, piglike creatures with long bodies and short legs. But they cannot really be pigs, because their coats have striped patches. Comic figures, they stare at each other with a look of suspicion, an eye-balling of the opposite sex that is an oblique satire of human courtship.

Courtship is satirized more overtly in Thurber's men and women, who conspicuously lack stature and dignity. Types belonging to the middle class, these figures have not been filled in or fully delineated, and their unfinished outlines imply their incompleteness as people. Some of the women have only a small dot for an eye, but the faces of Thurber's harassed men suggest even less consciousness. In a revealing drawing a man is seated tensely at the edge of a hardback chair, his flipperlike hands resting on his knees as he stares with uncertainty and misgiving at a nude woman on all fours before him. She is examining a small flower, whose mating implications she is on the verge of grasping with an unsettling clarity.

A major influence on the drawings, despite the fact that the book spoofs analysts and other experts on sex, is Freud. Some of the sketches under the caption "Sex Substitutes" portray men engaged in sports or other activities at moments of intense physical and emotional stress. A man in a bicycle race, for example, his head bent downward to the low handlebars, is straining over his bicycle but could as easily be stretched over a woman. Two rudely outlined male figures shooting craps, the dice on the ground before them, have reached an emotional crisis comparable to a sexual one. The torso of the figure in the foreground is twisted tautly as his arms fly out and upward to form a silhouette of exaltation. A more startling use of Freud appears in a series of "unconscious" drawings that are sketched against a background of darkness to give the effect of dreams or sexual fantasies. "Unconscious Drawing, Plate I" shows the huge figure of a naked male who holds two tiny female figures in the palm of his hand. These women who are like inch-tall, featureless dolls have their legs spread wide, and one looks up into the man's eyes invitingly. Both they and he are phantoms, comic yet eerie, belonging to a night world of preconscious desire.

Another sketch, "Unconscious Drawing, Plate II," illustrates the repression of libido in a naked male figure seated on the ground while hunched forward with his head held despairingly in his hands. Standing before him is a featureless naked woman with a long, elongated body like that of a Giacometti figurine. She stands in front of his crotch and her arms are raised high in the air as if she were a priestess of desire. The childlike, crudely drawn figures give the sense of a dream state. "Unconscious Drawing, Plate IV," representing masculine "Ironic Detachment" supposedly rising superior to the "Love Urge," shows the torso of a huge male figure, rather like a phantom, against a jagged background of darkness belonging to dreams. A nude woman no larger than the man's hand walks away from him while turning back to look at him invitingly, and an amused smile of indifference plays on the man's rubbery face. The drawing is ironic, since the lines below explain that it was submitted by the "recently divorced" wife of the author of the sketch. It is apparent that the indifference of the male figure is an attempt to compensate for his lack of sexual confidence and know-how; and the name of the author, Walter L. Mouse, from Columbus, Ohio, is a fascinating anticipation of another Walter, Walter Mitty, who achieves competence only in his fantasy life. More generally, the drawings in Is Sex Necessary? are a forecast of Thurber's battle of the sexes, with woman— because of her greater affinity with instinct and biology— in the ascendancy, and man an unhappy victim torn between civilization and nature, and well adjusted to neither.

It is an astonishing leap forward, however, from the erratically brilliant sketches in Is Sex Necessary? to the mature drawings in The Seal in the Bedroom, published only three years later. That the drawings in The Seal in the Bedroom have an individuality belonging to Thurber alone was noted by Dorothy Parker in her introduction to the book. She was struck particularly by the unworldly nature of Thurber's men and women, who have "the outer semblance of unbaked cookies." There is about "all these characters, even the angry ones," she wrote, "a touching quality. They expect so little of life; they remember all the old discouragements, and await the new. They are not shrewd people, nor even bright, and we must all be very patient with them. Lambs in a world of wolves, they are, and there is on them a protracted innocence."[7] But they cannot simply be called innocent. The women at times are Amazonian and have a frightening quality as they overwhelm Thurber's small, passive men. In a drawing entitled "Stop Me!," which portrays skaters on a pond, the central figure is a tall, stout woman who has lost control of her skating and is about to collide with a male skater. Her hat has just blown off and her hair streams behind her, but what one notices particularly are her heavy arms and posterior and a certain manic glee on her face. The man with whom she is about to collide is, by contrast, small and meek. He has not had time even to react as he stares blankly at the apparition before him.

Another drawing, captioned "Will you be good enough to dance this outside?," is one of Thurber's fantasy situations in which a man is dancing with a large dog. The man's arms are wrapped about the dog's neck, and the dog has draped his paws over the man's shoulders. The man's wife, who has just advised them sternly to go outside, has little dwarflike legs and a face that is outlined by harsh or heavy lines. Below her pointed nose, a heavy line slashes into her face to indicate her opened mouth. The husband and dog have turned to stare at her, and the dog seems to be clinging to the man as for protection. In the embrace of the man and large dog there seems a hint of homosexuality, but homosexuality hardly enters into Thurber's world. His middle-class men cannot imagine options other than to feel the attraction of women and often to be horrified by them.

The fantasy element in the drawing of the man and dog dancing is a feature of many of the other cartoons having domestic settings. Another entitled "I don't know. George got it somewhere," shows two women conversing in the living room of one of them. Standing by the chair of one of the women is a penguin, an odd creature with a bald head and a plump stomach. Why its presence in the house is accepted as normal is as unexplained as how the seal came to be in the bedroom of the sleepless couple. In other drawings the irrational takes the form of an individual's hallucination. In "He Claims Something Keeps Following Him, Doctor," for example, a wife and physician stare at the woman's husband as he looks over his shoulder at a troupe of tiny elves approaching him. Not much taller than the floorboard, they wear stocking shoes and tall hats with tassels at their conical peaks. One is bearded and potbellied, the other moves with a low, slouching walk like Groucho Marx. No explanation is offered for the man's hallucination. Like the seal and penguin scenes, the drawing provokes laughter while declining to provide full release from the absurdist tensions of the situation. It acts on the nerves disquietingly.

The drawings in *The Seal in the Bedroom* are of various kinds, with one section devoted to "Parties." In this section, whether set in apartments or at speakeasies, alcohol flows freely and characters are captured grotesquely. In "Love," a man in a tuxedo bends over a couch to ogle a young woman. His head is egg-shaped, his eye darkly circled, emphasizing his lurid pallor. The woman to whom he is speaking has an eye that is indicated by a whirled line, a broad nose, and jagged lines for fingers. She has no chin. The idea of love between these unattractive inebriates is a joke. "Berserk" is set at another party at which a man at the center of the drawing (resembling Thurber himself) has lost control of himself. His arms fly out in wild, angry gestures, and the disheveled state of his hair and the distortion of his features make him seem like a crazy man. It is somehow not a *human* face. "The Fog," set at a party where the guests have been drinking heavily, focuses upon a man whose senses are reeling. Notes of music and the word "Ha-ha" in various parts of the drawing indicate that the party is well under way, but everything is seen through the inebriated consciousness of the man whose large eye is dark and horribly bloodshot. Not far from him a woman's head appears upside down in the air, and a woman next to him is represented as a vibrating, blurred image with three overlapping faces.

More often the drawings are concerned with married couples at home or at gatherings, settings of the stressful relationship of the sexes. In "Everybody Noticed It. You Gawked at Her All Evening," a couple are in bed, the man's face turned away from the viewer, his wife on the attack. The man is sketched with a few sweeping lines reminiscent of Matisse, with no attempt made to represent him realistically. He is not even fully a man but a "type," a comic Everyman of the wife-hectored husband. In "When I Realize That I Once Actually *Loved* You I Go Cold All Over," a tall woman addresses her much smaller mate. He has a middle-aged paunch and weak features, while she is chinless and has a sharply pointed nose. The jest of the drawing is not merely that the wife should browbeat her meek spouse over their faded love, but also that one cannot imagine love as having existed between them at *any* time. These people have no dimension and exist in a context of vacancy.

Characteristically Thurber's drawings of perfectly ordinary people turn them into grotesques. In "Your Wife Seems Terribly Smart, Mr. Bruce," a wife is angered by her husband's talking to another woman on a couch. But what strikes one most is that the man should be made to look so ridiculous. He is bald and unintelligent looking, a large nose and a dot for an eye his only features, and as a typical male he suggests a gruesome view of man. Thurber's women are more disturbing still. In one of the drawings, two women are speaking disparagingly of another who is surrounded by several admiring men. This "beauty," who sits with her legs crossed, is sensual in a rather heavy way, but her face rather than being attractive is almost frightening, with dark lines that accentuate her pointed nose and monkeylike lips. These creatures, captured in scenes that involve the attraction of the sexes, suggest a puritanlike distaste for sexuality itself.

In an essay entitled "The Admiral on the Wheel," published in 1936, Thurber wrote of the tricks played on him by his vision. He relates that while going outdoors without his glasses, he saw or thought he saw a happy-go-lucky old lady with a parasol walk through the side of a truck, and a bridge rise lazily into the air like a balloon. He acknowledged, however, that his disabilities also had their compensations, enabling him to experience life as improbable fantasy. One would wonder if Thurber's defective vision may not have affected his conceptions as visual artist, predisposing him to see life and people through a prism of distortion.

But the skewed vision of the drawings also seems indebted to avant-garde art of the 1920s, particularly the work of Picasso and the surrealists, to whom Thurber was repeatedly compared by critics. Picasso's foreshortened effects and the fantastic distortion in the faces of his men and women have an affinity at least with the techniques used by Thurber in his drawings, and as in Picasso there is a strong interest in fantasy and the unconscious. One of the sketches Thurber drew for "The Pet Department" series in the *New Yorker* during the same period as *The Seal in the Bedroom* shows a horse's head protruding rather crazily through the window drapery of a living room, and in its use of startling disjunction makes one think of a canvas by Salvador Dali. The dreamlike quality of the drawings is pervasive. Thurber's men and women, with their ludicrous shapes and faces, sketched with bold, primitive strokes, have the effect of a dream that has invaded the normal life of the middle class. But if the drawings have an affinity with the surrealists, they also make one think of the comic strips (particularly those like "Dagwood" and "Maggie and Jiggs," where the husband is humbled and even assaulted by his wife), and it is as if Thurber had discovered a means by which to unite the concern with the unconscious of the avant-gardists with the domestic comedy of American popular culture.

Thurber's bias toward fantasy also affects his conception of the famous Thurber dog, who makes his first appearance in *The Seal in the Bedroom*. This lovable creature has the large, comically sober face and great floppy ears of a bloodhound, together with the short, stumpy legs of a basset. An uncaptioned drawing shows men riding to these dogs, who have a blitheful expression belonging to a profound innocence. Two of the most delightful sets of drawings are devoted to this animal. In "The Bloodhound and the Bug" and "The Bloodhound and the Hare," he is revealed as charmingly ineffectual, easily frightened, and without valor. These dogs are all without guile, and are wholly free of the neuroticism that afflicts man.

One of the most arresting of the drawings that appear in a series of panels is "The Race of Life," which depicts a man and wife, together with their small son, in a footrace toward the celestial city. A parody in visual terms of Bunyan's *Pilgrim's Progress*, its humor lies partly in the ceaselessly demonstrated inadequacy of the male. The husband, wife, and child are all nude, and in their nudity and bald features are comic figures. The son, who looks something like a peanut, has a humorous resemblance to an adult or "little" man. The wife leads the race, her gaze set directly toward her objective, and she looks energetic, in contrast to her mate, who trails behind hunched forward and already enervated. They encounter hurdles and hazards, including a confrontation with a large, white Lewis Carroll rabbit and a menacing stranger in a villain's stovepipe hat whom the wife stares down, spreading her arms out and back as the protector of her child and feckless husband.

The traverse mountains and wastelands, with the husband typically lagging behind both wife and child, and at last view the celestial gates. The child begins to ascend the cliff leading to the celestial city, while the woman looks back to call to her husband, pointing toward the gates. The husband, meanwhile, is shown in the distance, wet and drooping under a rain cloud, his impassive face evoking the hopelessness of his reaching the goal. Constantly witty in its depiction of the three naked figures, "The Race of Life" is, in essence, a fable, and as such it foretells one of the distinctive features of Thurber's later work, not merely as an artist but also as the author of two volumes of fables and of concise, jewellike stories that have a very pronounced fable quality.

In their subject matter and distinctive techniques, Thurber's later drawings vary remarkably little from those in *The Seal in the Bedroom*. A vast number were eventually to appear in the *New Yorker*, but even while the early ones were appearing Thurber already attracted an international audience. One of his admirers was the English art critic Paul Nash, who called Thurber "a master of impressionistic line"[8] and compared his style to that of the early Matisse. While in the United States in 1931 as a judge of an exhibition of paintings, Nash was honored with a luncheon at the Century Club in New York and asked that Thurber, whom he regarded as one of the country's truly notable artists, be seated at his table. In the same year the German artist and caricaturist George Grosz said of Thurber's work that it "began where that of other cartoonists left off,"[9] and they were actually featured together in a joint exhibition at Smith College in 1933. That Thurber's drawings should have been considered appropriate to show with Grosz's would imply that an affinity was felt to exist between them; and both do, despite their marked cultural differences, evoke middle-class life as if it were a grotesque dream.

In the 1930s Thurber's drawings continued to be exhibited in America and abroad. A one-man show of his drawings at the Valentine Gallery in New York in 1934 was reviewed by *Time*, which noted that the pictures were "enormously funny, and like most lasting humor, are the products of an unhappy mind."[10] Some of them, curi-

ously, were as "indecent" as those by Grosz. They included a blasphemous "Thurber Madonna," a scene depicting the Three Wise Men as old lechers ogling the
Virgin, and a drawing of a girl lifting her skirts enticingly
before a mutilated war veteran who weeps helplessly. In
1936 a Thurber drawing was included in the Fantastic Art-
Dada-Surrealism exhibit at the Museum of Modern Art;
and in the following year an exhibition of eighty Thurber
drawings was staged at the Storran Gallery in London.
Winston Churchill referred to Thurber at this time as an
artist who was "insane and depraved,"[11] but art critics
compared him to Picasso, Klee, and Matisse. Bernstein
relates that the owners of the Storran Gallery telephoned
Matisse in France, hoping to arrange a meeting between
him and Thurber, but that his secretary told them Matisse
had never heard of Thurber or of the *New Yorker.* Bernstein
adds, however, that when an American visiting Matisse in
1946 asked him whom he considered America's leading
artist, he named Thurber.[12]

Although critical studies of Thurber have generally
ignored the drawings, Charles Holmes and Robert Morsberger have each included them in their discussions.[13]
One of their most striking features for Morsberger is their
quality of fluid movement. A number of the sketches portray figures in motion—skaters, tennis players, fencers,
boxers, or dancers; but a similar attention to body movement can be noticed in Thurber's crowd scenes and domestic confrontations. This attention to physical forms in
motion, however, is but one aspect of the dramatic nature
of the drawings. In each something has just happened or
is just about to happen, and the viewer is instantly involved. The drawings are like little moments of frozen
time in which stylized figures reveal the inmost truth of
their lives. Frequently eyes lock together at an instant of
crisis, and it is particularly impressive how much Thurber
is able to convey with a small dot for an eye. It can indicate
fright, uncertainty, fierceness, jealousy, anger, and a score
of other emotions.

Thurber's people are also revealed by their clothing. "For a while," Morsberger writes, "Thurber costumed his people in the styles then current, but [after] the mid 1930's, he deliberately drew them wearing the attire of the early 1920's—the ladies in flat hair styles, long formless gowns, helmet-type hats . . . ; the men with derbies, bow ties, and styleless suits."[14] Thurber's little men not only wear derbies that have sometimes just fallen off in a moment of astonishment, they also frequently wear spectacles indicated by a line across the bridge of their nose that emphasizes their sedentary natures. The long gowns of the women accentuate the shape of their bodies, their heavy legs and big rumps, and give them a comically dowdy appearance. Although sex is central to many of the drawings, Thurber's men and women are not sexually appealing, undercutting the idea of romance and the passions.

The humor of many of the drawings is indebted quite often to parody. Thurber's men and women parody the American couple, but specific incidents depicted also rely on parody for their effect. A drawing with the caption "It's a Naive Domestic Burgundy Without Any Breeding, But I Think You'll Be Amused By Its Presumption" shows two couples dining together and holding up their glasses. The words in the caption are not spoken, however, by a man of sophisticated appearance but by a bald, ordinary, even banal-looking man who is smiling fatuously. The others at the table have blank or dumb expressions and, like the host, reveal in their pretension to connoisseurship all that they are not.

"The War Between Men and Women" (1934), one of Thurber's best-known early parodies set in a series of panels, has been imagined with comic robustness. In the opening scene, set at a large estate, a man throws a drink in a woman's face, inaugurating a war between the sexes. A second panel, "The Battle of the Stairs," shows them in riotous conflict. Women pursue men with baseball bats, and some of their male victims are seen falling from the balustrade of the upper landing to the floor below. A multitude of figures engaged in the fracas on the steep staircase and along the upper landing evoke an unrestrained mayhem, in which the characters, both the fierce women with stringy hair and pointed noses and the bald men with bland faces, have been shorn of dignity. The third panel, "The Fight in the Grocery," moves the conflict farther out into the world as dozens of men and women skirmish in a grocery store, hurling cans of tinned food and bottles at each other. It is a crowd scene of comic anarchy and, as in some of Thurber's prose writing, exaggeration is exuberant and unrestrained.

Later scenes draw on the metaphor of armies and civil war. A group of men argue strategy at their battalion headquarters, which looks as if it had previously been used for poker games; and a group of women with war medals on their bosoms are shown at their headquarters that suggests a women's club. A number of comic scenes follow, but an unforgettable one set in the country, "Zero Hour—Connecticut," pictures men and women crouched along opposing sides of a wall of piled stones, some checking their wristwatches as the moment of pitched battle is about to begin. The long, tense line of figures with their eyes fixed on the enemy's over the edge of the wall is comic yet chilling, too, in the ferocious implications of its dreamlike imagery.

A later scene, "Gettysburg," is a fantasia of masses of men and women assaulting one another with fists and clubs—an epic battle leading to the rout of the women and their eventual surrender. The scene of the surrender is a parody of a great national armistice, with troops of men and women at either side of the drawing. In the center, their commanders have met on horseback, the general of the women's forces surrendering not a sword but a baseball bat. Yet one feels even at this climactic moment that hostilities may erupt again, that the tensions between the sexes have not been stilled. In some respects, "The War Between Men and Women" can be compared to Thurber's prose writing. The vignettes in *My Life and Hard Times*, for example, published a year before the series of drawings, are also parodies that build in a series of episodes in which fantasy is given full play, and in which the incidents and characters who figure in them have a cartoon dimension.[15]

Other sets of drawings of the 1930s are also pointedly parodistic. "James Thurber Presents William Shakespeare" (1935), for example, illustrates scenes from Shakespeare with a comically reductive effect. A sketch for *Macbeth* reveals a sleepwalking Lady Macbeth with the comic features of a modern Thurber woman. Another, comic yet repellent, shows Desdemona asleep in a large canopied bed while Othello crouches on the covers looking like a small, ugly black monkey. These drawings may well have inspired Thurber's illustrations of famous poems, collectively entitled "Famous Poems Illustrated" (1939) and published in book form in *Fables for Our Time and Famous Poems Illustrated* (1940). The drawings "illustrating" poems by a variety of authors ranging from Longfellow to A. E. Housman, all parody lyric sentiment or heroic romance. Walter Scott's *Lochinvar*, with its ballad hero and heroine, lends itself to deflation by Thurber. In the opening panel, Lochinvar gallops on a steed with mad-looking eyes toward Wetherby Hall, where the fair Ellen is being betrothed to another man. The fair Ellen is a Thurber woman with a tiny dot for an eye, a pointed nose, and straggling hair. Her bridegroom is a bald, mustached older man who is dressed very formally. In the next scene, Lochinvar has burst into the ballroom to announce that he will dance with his love, whose face now wears an inane smile, and the bridegroom stands stiffly to one side as if immobilized.

Their romantic dance is comic, Ellen's sacklike dress accentuating her heavy body, her hip swung out, her hair flying. In the following scene, Lochinvar has thrown Ellen on his steed, a look of amazement on her undistinguished face, her stringlike hair swept back in the wind. The bridegroom, meanwhile, continues to stand stiffly, merely staring. Mayhem follows, as the men at the wedding mount horses in a confused effort to pursue the couple—while the bridegroom, of smaller size than in the previous scenes, continues to stand stiffly, staring before him. He is the most delightful conception of the drawing, and his impotence complements the travesty of romantic sentiment in Lochinvar and Ellen.

Thurber's parody of Tennyson's *Locksley Hall* is even more scathing. In the opening panel, illustrating the line "in the spring a young man's fancy lightly turns to thoughts of love," a young man with a head shaped like a walnut and an unimposing face is seated dreamily on a rock. In a cloud above is the face of the woman of whom he dreams. It is a horrible face with stringy hair and a pointed nose. In the next panel in which Amy is "married to a clown who will drag her down," Victorian sentiment is "illustrated" in terms of modern American middle-class life. Amy, a housewife, stares with chagrin at her husband, a potbellied man who has fallen asleep in an armchair, a cigarette still in his mouth, a newspaper in one hand falling to the floor. Tennyson's dreamer is then roused by the sounding bugles of companions, and has a reverie of "taking a savage woman and rearing a dusky race." In Thurber's envisioning of this the hero retains his pathetic appearance and the woman at his side rather than being a savage beauty is a pedestrian housewife. The "race" of young athletes they will rear, their several small sons, are shown cavorting about and diving into the water. These diminutive figures are ridiculous: nude, bald, and with the blank faces of "small" adults. Incapable even of imagining wildness or savagery, the hero cannot escape from his banality. In the final panel, as a "mighty wind arises," he goes off supposedly to a life of action, but the derby he wears and the sheepish grin on his face expose his incapacities, his disqualification for action or for the achieving of any romantic ideal whatsoever.

In Thurber's drawings, no matter of what type, the male's failure is pervasive. Sometimes his inadequacy is emphasized ironically by the compliments women pay him. "You Were Wonderful at the Gardners' Last Night, Fred, When You Turned on the Charm" shows a wife speaking to her husband while the couple are in bed. Ironically, it is impossible to imagine the husband charming anyone. He is a small, slightly built man with spectacles who looks as if he works in an office and huddles under blankets as if turning inward upon himself. A rather similar drawing concerns a man and woman seated together on a sofa. The woman is telling the staid and pathetic-looking man "I think of you as being enormously alive." In other sketches the appearance of the male figure is also revealing. "Mush!" depicts a little spectacled man on a sled tugging at the reins attached to the collar of a Thurber dog who looks back at him quizzically. The situation belittles the man in every way. His child's sled is hardly a sled of the Arctic, and the Thurber dog has no resemblance to a team of huskies. His dogsled fantasy confirms what his slight appearance already suggests, that he is mild and ineffectual.

Ineffectuality is implied to be sexual as well in a drawing entitled "Well It Makes a Difference to Me." An assertive-looking woman who speaks these words is in bed, while her husband clad in pajamas stands next to the bed looking crestfallen and ashamed. In other cartoons Thurber's men engage in physical combat with large, overpowering women. In "Interior with Figures," a man and woman are dueling with rapiers, but while the man merely stares before him, as if paralyzed, the woman is in violent motion. Her sacklike dress reveals the contour of her heavy figure, particularly her legs that are outstretched in attack, her straight hair flying back as if charged with electricity. As she shouts, she makes formidable slashes of the air with her rapier, overturning a chair and floor lamp, and rather like the man in the drawing the viewer feels fear.

When Thurber's women are not vanquishing his men in combat or altercation, they pursue them menacingly. The well-known drawing on the cover of *The Thurber Car-*

nival portrays a man and woman on a carousel, he forward on a large rabbit (its long ears standing straight up, its legs leaping in flight), she just behind astride a hound. The man has turned back to look at his pursuer, and his eyes have just met and locked with hers in a moment of shocked intensity. The woman's expression is gleeful and perhaps a little mad; her wavy fingers are clawlike and her sharply pointed shoes look like spikes. Other drawings, including the unpublished ones in the E. B. White Collection at the Cornell University Library, are equally disquieting.[16]

Some of the sketches depict marital tensions at a point of impending violence. In "Have You Seen My Pistol, Honey-bun?," a little man with spectacles and a comb mustache twists back to glance at his wife as he searches through the top drawer of a bedroom bureau. His wife, seated on the bed, peers intently over the top of an opened newspaper, behind which she aims the pistol at her husband. Whether intended by Thurber or not, the drawing lends itself to a Freudian interpretation, the pistol the man cannot find being his male sexuality that his wife has taken from him. In other cartoons, the division between the sexes is projected in luminous images of a psychic nature. "Man in Tree" has a large tree in the center, with a woman beneath, her hand to her mouth as if calling out, a frown on her face. Far above, in a kind of surreal image, a man lies on his back on the mattresslike foliage of the treetop, seeking oblivion in dreams. This drawing, too, suggests Freud, since the tree is a phallic image and as such evokes the man's inmost conflict.

With its projection of psychic fear, "Man and Tree" is comparable to another drawing, "Home and Woman." "Home and Woman" falls into the category of what Thurber called his "unconscious" drawings, which came to him without premeditation. In the drawing, a tiny man clutching a derby and shaken with fright stands before the steps of a tree-shaded brick house, the back of which dissolves into the phantasmal face of a scowling woman with string hair and a hypnotic eye. Their eyes have met fixedly at the critical moment when the man is about to enter the house that, to refer to Freud again, is a readily identifiable female sexual symbol. The woman's power seems enormous, partly because of her gigantic size and voracious appearance, her arms reaching out along the roof and lower part of the house as if to seize and swallow up the minutely small man. If the home has been thought to be man's domain, Thurber's home in the drawing is a nightmare in which man has been rendered impotent. Interestingly, Bernstein noted in our interview that the face of the woman in the drawing is that of "Mame" Thurber and that the tiny man is Thurber's father, who wore a derby and inspired the figures of derby-wearing men who are crushed by their mates in many of the drawings.[17]

The battle of the sexes is one of the most persistent themes in the drawings, but a looming irrationality is a feature of others that have nothing to do directly with sex or marital discord. Couples return home to find their apartments occupied by loonies; a man is introduced to his fiancée's family, who are performing acrobatic leaps from circus rings suspended from the ceiling of their living room; a gentleman is shown to his new room with garishly striped wallpaper where the previous tenant had lost his mind. In a number of the sketches, Thurber's irrational images tease the mind for explanation. In one, "Perhaps *This* Will Refresh Your Memory," a defendant in a witness box looks over, startled, at a zanily grinning kangaroo to which the prosecutor is pointing. What can this mean? How can the mute kangaroo be brought forward as a surprise witness, and why does the man look guilty? One must laugh at this "nonsense" that strains the power of reason to its limits as a release from absurdist tensions.

The drawings were published in the *New Yorker* prolifically during the 1930s, but after his series of eye operations in 1940–41 Thurber was left all but blind, and his drawings appeared much less frequently. His last ambitious set of sketches, drawn in 1945 with the aid of the Zeiss loop, was "A New Natural History," a delightful collection of animal illustrations that reflect Thurber's interest in wordplay. The peculiar-looking animals in the sketches are witty approximations in visual terms of words in the English vocabulary that suggest them. Thus the hoodwink is an owl with dark hooded eyes, a spouse is a small rodent, the huff a parrotlike bird that looks offended as it perches on a bough.

A thesaurus, a prehistoric creature, has a ruffled mane resembling the opened leaves of a book, and a pair of martinets are long-beaked birds with high-stepping legs that give the impression of their marching erectly to martial music. One has its bill thrust haughtily in the air, and the other stares straight ahead with a testy expression. Included in the group, charmingly, are a trochee encountering a spondee. Part of the humor of the sketch is in the expression of the catlike creatures' eyes, the full-eyed spondee staring at the squinting trochee as if trying to make out what it is. In keeping with the metrical feet from which they take their names, the trochee has two short hind legs and two tall front ones, while the spondee has merely two legs, one in front and one behind.

Thurber's humor in the drawings ranges from the grotesque to the disarmingly innocent, as in his "parable in pictures," *The Last Flower* (1939). Composed on the eve of World War II, the sketches give the impression of having been drawn by a small child. Rather than being realistic, they are projections of fancy and have a quality of surprise and wonder. They begin with the collapse of civilization during World War XII, a time when life has been reduced to utter barrenness and desolation. In time a small flower springs up, primitive man and woman discover love, a pleasure in imagination comes into being and civilization is gradually rebuilt. Then political leaders supported by generals and armies appear, another war erupts, and civilization is once again destroyed. At the end nothing is left except a solitary naked man and woman and a small drooping flower, which has just sprung from the earth like a token of the power of survival of the human spirit. Oddly, a delightful humor plays through this doomsday parable. Thurber's crudely drawn characters are surprisingly expressive, and his satire of the demagogues on podiums being hailed by crowds (like Hitler) is as sharp and pointed as the bayonets his masses of lunging soldiers have mounted on their rifles. Particularly poignant are the finely imagined scenes where Thurber dogs desert their masters and a horde of large, voracious rabbits descend upon the remnants of humanity. A parable of survival in the face of the greatest odds, *The Last Flower* gives the impression of being surprisingly optimistic.

The work, however, has occasioned widely different comment. In his obituary of Thurber in the *New Yorker*, [18] E. B. White described it as his favorite Thurber composition, calling its "fresh" and "wiltproof" flower a testament of faith that could serve as his best memorial. But in a review of the book when it first appeared, W. H. Auden, although a confirmed Thurber admirer, was critical of its vision of the social and political life. More specifically, he referred Thurber's drawings to the use of the "icon" (with its universally relevant symbolism) and the "portrait" (with its detailed realism), which had existed harmoniously in art up to the middle of the sixteenth century. Thereafter this equilibrium was destroyed, and the realism of the portrait came to predominate over iconography, which was relegated to the cartoon. Thurber's spiritual father in this respect, Auden claims, was Edward Lear, whose scribbled drawings refer wholly to the "inner life." The icon for Lear and Thurber is "the average non-political man of an industrialized society" who views the social and political life as remote from himself, an absolute distinction that leads to distortion in *The Last Flower.* The parable, Auden remarks, "suggest[s] (1) that all politicians are equally evil, and (2) that all lovers are without error."[19] Evil is an absolute condition in *The Last Flower,* and so are love and innocence.

Thurber's insistence on the saving power of innocence and love creates a number of internal complications and makes the parable ambiguous. The appearance of the flower in a ruined world, for example, brings rejuvenation; yet this renewal in the cyclical pattern of the fable is sure to be followed by apocalyptic destruction. Moreover, the flower itself contains the seeds of this destruction, for from it will spring not only constructive creative energy but also all of humanity's power-seeking and aggressive drives. The flower is particularly troubling as a symbol of instinct, mating, and "love," since in Thurber's earlier drawings and writing sexuality is the source of his characters' neurotic suffering. Curiously, the drawing of the small flower is an exact likeness of the one in *Is Sex Necessary?* that begins the mating ritual and leads to an estrangement of the sexes.

The ambiguities of *The Last Flower* reflect on Thurber's career as an artist. The childlike draftsmanship of many of the drawings evokes a very striking quality of innocence, but the scenes they depict are pessimistic in their implications. Thurber's men and women are seen through a lens of distortion that makes them seem grotesque, and their relationships simmer with subterranean hostilities. They cannot enter into unions of understanding, nor can they achieve distinct personal identity. Such identity as they possess is determined for them by the mass culture to which they belong and which they express. Comedy and dread go hand in hand in the psychic landscapes of Thurber's drawings, constantly jolting the viewer's sense of a stable reality in which he might believe. Intriguingly, the same is true of his prose writing, and particularly his stories. They are entirely of a piece, the drawings like highly condensed little tales, the stories like vivid sketches haunted by the irrational. In each case they announce that life cannot be solidly defined, only evoked by fear and insecurity.

3

Ordeal in Fantasy: Thurber's Fiction of the 1930s

Thurber's fiction of the 1930s is anticipated in some respects by his first book *Is Sex Necessary? Is Sex Necessary?* is a spoof of the flood of recent books that had attempted to reduce sex to scientific explanation and to allay apprehension. But Thurber and White, while posing as sex experts, give the sense that sexuality is actually a cause for alarm, is profoundly irrational. The strong element of parody in the book is reflected in the roles assumed by Thurber and White as disciples of Dr. Walter Tithridge and Dr. Karl Zaner, "deans of American sex," who have clouded the subject with jargon and dubious formulas. As authority figures, Thurber and White prove to be even less competent and credible. Perhaps the chief influence on the book is Robert Benchley, who often posed as an expert on various subjects and used pseudotechnical terms to bolster his authority while betraying himself as a perfect fool. Thurber and White also introduce quasi-scientific terms as a form of foolery, and are Benchleyesque in their inability to grapple with their subject.

An unusual feature of the book is the even blending of their voices, making it difficult for the reader to know which of them had written which of the chapters. In one of the chapters the narrator refers to his colleague "Dr. White," revealing it as the work of Thurber, but otherwise there is no attribution of authorship. The authorship of the various sections, however, breaks down in the following way: the foreword, chapters 2, 4, 6, the first and final parts of chapter 8, "Answers to Difficult Questions," and the "Note on the Drawings" at the end are by White; the preface (as Lt. Col. H. R. L. Le Boutelier), chapters 1, 3, 5, 7, the middle part of chapter 8, the glossary, and of course the drawings, are by Thurber. The contributions of White are characteristically low-key and ironic. It is typical of him, for example, in the chapter entitled "How to Tell Love from Passion," that he should start out to make a clear distinction between the two, only at the end to admit that they are hard to distinguish. In the chapter entitled "The Sexual Revolution," he traces the migration of young women from the Middle West to New York City in search of liberation, but with such inner ambivalence that they finally choose concerts over sex.

But if the prose styles of Thurber and White are similar, their temperaments are not. White's effects are quiet and his mind is sane. Thurber, on the other hand, is more likely to be *in*sane, to let himself go, to favor comic exuberance. Partly because of this willingness to take risks, the great comic moments of the book belong to Thurber.[1] Chapter 3, "A Discussion of Feminine Types," is a good illustration of his love of the preposterous. In discussing the "Quiet Type," he relates that he had noticed a young woman of this type at a Sunday tea party and wondered how to approach her, fighting off a "baseless alarm." The studied casualness of his approach is marred by an "involuntary winking" of his left eyelid, to which he is "unhappily subject," and the young woman abruptly leaves the room. He observes another Quiet Type on a Fifth Avenue bus, and when he explains that he would like to make a "leisurely examination" of her, she slaps his face. He then attends a weekend party where, supposedly a detached scientist, he becomes tipsy, stands on a piano and falls, losing his glasses. When he bends over to search for them he is assailed by a touch of vertigo, "which runs in my family," and falls again. In his pretense that his interest in women is clinical, and that his dizziness is due not to his drinking but to a hereditary ailment, the narrator is obviously unreliable, and his credibility as a spokesman for science is destroyed. He is, in fact, a buffoon.

The party scene builds in a series of comic incidents. In the final episode, the narrator finds himself on a cliff by the edge of a lake. He is not sure how he got there, but apparently the young woman with him has assisted him and has a sexual interest in him. Soon he falls again, and in doing so clutches the young woman, bringing her down with him so that they become entangled together on the ground. Yet even at this opportune moment he is unable to act. His scientific attempt to, as he says, "get at" the woman is thwarted. The scene is replete with Freudian images—the jutting cliff a male symbol, the lake a feminine one; but although the narrator approaches the edge of the lake he cannot enter it, and in the latter part of the chapter he backs away from other female types. There is the "Buttonhole-twister" type, the "Don't-dear" type, and the "I-can't-go-through-with-it" type, all of whom are "best to avoid." Indeed, he has ruled out virtually all feminine types in his flight from contact.

The chapter entitled "The Nature of the American Male" looks forward even more clearly to the fiction Thurber would soon write. Commenting on the phenomenon of "pedestalism," he notes that sublimation has been the lot of the American male for generations and offers the case history of a certain George Smith. In 1899, at the age of twenty-nine, Smith formed an attachment to a virgin whose hand in the course of three years he has not even held. In 1902, still living with his mother, he had run frightened from a haberdashery in Indianapolis, where a middle-aged man, Herschel Queeper, had thrown a fit while sublimating with a pigs-in-clover puzzle. Thereafter Smith attempts to solve the puzzle himself, but after two months he, too, reaches a point of desperate frustration. He then rounds up stray dogs (eighty-two of them in all) to see if they might, through instinct perhaps, be able to solve the puzzle for him. But penning the dogs up in his house leads merely to a scene of comic bedlam when

Smith and the dogs engage in a tug-of-war with a carpet. In the struggle Smith is edged out of the house and then down the street for several blocks, until the fire department is called out and Smith is treated by an analyst. The analyst is of no help, but one day Smith drops the pigs-in-clover puzzle, breaking the glass, and discovers that he can *push* the balls into the slots with his fingers. Having cut the Gordian knot, he gains the confidence to propose to and marry the virgin.

Smith's "case history" is glaringly Freudian, its focal image of the pigs-in-clover puzzle that is finally solved by *pushing* the balls into the slots tantamount to intercourse achieved after a harrowing inner struggle. It also seems very personal, since Thurber had himself put women on pedestals well into his twenties, and had suffered a severe nervous breakdown in Paris when he had had his first sexual experience. Smith's case reads like an attempt to overcome a paralyzing idealization of women by, as it were, laughing it away. It is perhaps significant that Smith's ordeal occurs in Indianapolis, where his father had been born and raised, and begins in the 1890s when Charles and "Mame" Thurber married—establishing the background and origins of Thurber-Smith's traumas. It is also revealing that Smith lives with his mother (just as Thurber until his marriage had lived with his), implying the source of his pedestalism and inner struggle to become the sexual partner of another woman. The wild farce of the tug-of-war incident prepares for farcical domestic uproar of *My Life and Hard Times*, but the psychosexual conflict it involves is a foreshadowing of Thurber's irresolute man in the stories of the 1930s.

This type of man appears shortly after in *The Owl in the Attic* in the series of eight stories devoted to John Monroe. White's introduction to the book, a superb parody portrait of Thurber, is revealing. Evoking Thurber as a modern Lord Jim, White pretends to have glimpsed or heard of him at various times in the Orient. He "kept bobbing up," White relates, " . . . in the port gossip of those seas, and although the news was always fragmentary, the Thurber legend was, I later realized, steadily building in my mind."[2] The legendary Thurber barely escapes death when he unwittingly violates the etiquette of a tribal ceremony in the Far East, and later blows up a ship's galley while cooking a breakfast into which he has carelessly mixed gunpowder. A man with a romantic vision but ineffectual in all practical matters, Thurber turns up in New York in 1926 "trailing a thin melancholy and leading a terrier bitch." He is alarmed by the "thrumming" of sex in the metropolis, and in the quandary of marriage "reads a droll sadness." John Monroe, too, is a failed romantic, a man caught tightly in the coils of marriage.

The first of the Monroe stories, "Tea at Mrs. Armsby's," is spare to an exceptional degree and concerned more with the nuances of psychological atmosphere than with fully detailed characterization. The Monroes are a young couple who arrive for Sunday tea at the apartment of older acquaintances after having attended a cocktail party. Mrs. Monroe is tipsy, and begins making alarming statements. She tells Mrs. Armsby that her husband collects pencils, and has "eight hundred and seventy-four thousand" of them. Other strange remarks follow, and before long Mr. Monroe hurries his wife away from the tea party, hailing a cab hastily in the street. It is hard to know what to make of this story, with its extreme understatement. The polite and somewhat formal occasion is disrupted by intimations of the fantastic, no communication exists among any of the parties involved, and one is left wondering what can be wrong between the couple for Mrs. Monroe to have made such wild statements about her husband's collecting mania. It seems likely, however, that she has blurted out the truth. Mr. Monroe is methodical and odd, she is annoyed, and in her tipsy state her perception of her husband as a comic little man comes out.

In "The Imperturbable Spirit" one sees the Monroes at a later stage of their lives. Mr. Monroe is shown in a shop in New York fingering some canes, which he likes to think of as being "imperturbable," overlooking their function in propping up the infirm. He has been reading a book on God, ethics, and morals, but since he has to look up such words as eschatology, he cannot have much expertise on the subject, and his very concern with imperturbability suggests that he is uncertain. His uncertainty is dramatized by the arrival of his wife on a ship ominously named the *Leviathan*. "Little" Mrs. Monroe appears on the pier with her luggage into which she has smuggled bottles of Benedictine. When she sends him to the luggage platform to pick up her hatbox containing several more of the bottles, he grows pale with fear. He even lapses, like Walter Mitty, into a reverie in which he stands trial in a courtroom. At first fleeing in panic from the baggage area, he creeps back, snatches the hatbox and runs panting with it for several blocks. At the end Mr. Monroe is shown at home reading to his wife in a "deep, impressive voice" from a book on God, ethics, and morals. Flayed with irony, he becomes the very type of the weak Thurber husband.

Other stories in the series parade his weakness and subject him to further humiliations. In "Mr. Monroe Outwits a Bat," he runs from a bat that has got into his room at night and comes tapping on the door of his wife's bedroom. She asks if he would like to get into bed with her, as she might to calm a small child who has been frightened by lightning, but he pretends that he is merely looking for something with which to kill the bat. Instead of returning to his room, however, he slams a folded newspaper loudly against the outer side of his bedroom door, as though battling the bat, and sleeps on a couch in the corridor halfway between his room and his wife's. At dawn he enters his bedroom and, finding the bat gone, returns to his bed and goes to sleep. It is perhaps revealing that the couch should be halfway between their rooms, as if he were still clinging to Mrs. Monroe, who seems as much a mother figure as a wife. Mr. Monroe is revealed as a child-man, too, in "The 'Wooing' of Mr. Monroe," a story in which his wife has learned of an extramarital affair and calls confidently on the other woman. She tells her that she will have to be prepared for John's ineptness with mechanical devices, relating an incident when he had filled their apartment with steam after turning on the hot-water faucet of a shower. Unable to reach in through the scalding water to turn off the faucet, he had cried, "Woo! Woo!" helplessly. The other woman understands, and with suave irony it is apparent that the affair is at an end.

In "Mr. Monroe and the Moving Men," "The Monroes Find a Terminal," and "Mr. Monroe Holds the Fort," Mr. Monroe is dominated by his little wife, unable to act decisively, and often at the mercy of his inner fears. Large, muscular moving men call him "sonny," and when he is alone in the house faint noises in upstairs rooms alarm and unnerve him. But he is captured most memorably in the final tale called "The Middle Years," after the story by Henry James. Now thirty-five, Monroe meets a lady at a party while his wife is away on a trip to Bermuda. He would like to have an affair with her and wonders how best to approach her. As he remembers another alluring woman, however, who had seemed to be interested in him but had not been after all, and as the face of his wife looms up at him with a satirical smile, he postpones doing anything immediately. He reads a Henry James novel that before long makes him feel drowsy, and decides to rest for a while. He sets his alarm clock for midnight, an ideal time, he thinks, to drop by at the woman's apartment; yet when he is awakened by the alarm clock he turns it off and goes back to sleep. As in the earlier stories, Monroe rationalizes his failure to act. His notion of calling on a woman he has met only once at her apartment at midnight, for example, is so grotesquely inappropriate as to indicate that he does not really want to go at all. More a Jamesian "inner" man than one effective in the active world, he is paralyzed to assert himself sexually.

What is striking about the Monroe stories is their chiseled quality, their spareness and concern with form.

Thurber's sentences are unusually simple, with no words wasted, and motifs are woven through the stories expertly. The chief device is irony, leading to a deflation of Monroe's illusions of being in control of his life when he is in fact at the mercy of everything—more rugged men and, whether wife or would-be lover, of women. The stories are influenced, one would think, by T. S. Eliot's J. Alfred Prufrock and James Joyce's *Dubliners* stories. Thurber's short, declarative sentences, the inevitability of his endings, which have the form of little epiphanies of humiliation, are reminiscent of Joyce's concise portraits of thwarted lives. Monroe could be compared, indeed, to Gabriel Conroy in "The Dead," a man whose illusion of importance is shattered by the final revelation of his overriding fear of life.

The Monroe stories are satirically skillful, but as a sustained sequence are perhaps too much alike. In the stories that follow, Thurber deals with little men whose experience is more emotionally charged than Mr. Monroe's. Two of the early ones focus upon a "little" man's limitations through his ineptness with cars. In "Mr. Pendly and the Poindexter" (1922), the hero, Mr. Pendly, has weak vision and gnawed by a feeling of inferiority sits in the passenger seat of the family car while his wife drives. Sometimes he escapes into inner reveries, imagining himself a man of bold masculinity who descends on a garden party in an "autogiro" to pick up his wife. One day his wife, who is exceptionally competent with cars, takes him with her to the Poindexter Sales Company to look at a new model. There he is ignored by the salesman, "a large, vital man," and condescended to by a mechanic. Again he escapes into his inner life, imagining himself impressing the mechanic by making a repair that had baffled him, only to be rudely awakened by his wife as she exclaims: "What's the matter; are you in a trance or what?"

Like "Mr. Pendly and the Poindexter," "Smashup" (1935) is a very carefully written story. Its hero, Tommy Trinway (note his little boy's name) has had an accident driving the family surrey while in his midteens, and has not been allowed to drive it again. A bookish boy who wears glasses, he becomes a young man of thought rather than of action. Later, a woman named Betty Carter, deciding that he has a future, falls in love with him; and when he is twenty-eight, "she married him." Tommy and his wife seem modeled after Thurber and his first wife, Althea Adams, and the story concerns the tensions of their marriage that were similar to those of the Thurbers. Mrs. Trinway is commanding, and a capable driver; Tommy, although he dreams at night of driving at high speed with his cap on backwards like Barney Oldfield, is not.

When they have been married for ten years and are about to leave on a trip to New York, Mrs. Trinway sprains her wrist and Tommy begins practicing on a country road so as to be able to drive them to the city. He drives at a fast speed while humming a tune that intimates his resentment of his wife, and sensing what he is thinking she laughs that he must be very sure of himself. "Their laughter," Thurber remarks, "was a little strained, like the laughter of two people who had just met." Tommy's birth into manhood is evoked in the course of the trip, particularly when they reach the Bronx and he is able to negotiate his way through congested city traffic. In Manhattan a woman darts suddenly into the path of the car, Tommy swerves and at the same time avoids crashing into the pillar of an elevated subway. A traffic cop congratulates him on his quick reflexes, and Tommy feels like a new man.

In the lounge of the hotel where they stay, they have Scotch and sodas, and a small, fine scene ensues between them. Mrs. Trinway lights her cigarette, and over the flame of her match stares at her husband. No words pass between them but much is implied. At the end, Tommy orders single rooms for them and walks buoyantly away. The understatement of the ending is reminiscent particularly of Hemingway. One thinks of Hemingway when Mrs. Trinway asks her husband if anything is the matter and he replies tersely, "I'm fine." They are like the couple in "Hills Like White Elephants," whose marital tensions are evoked through the understatement of their clipped conversation. Hemingway's husband in the story even asks his wife if anything is the matter, and like Tommy she replies, "I feel fine." "Smashup" also anticipates Hemingway's story "The Short, Happy Life of Francis Macomber," in which a man dominated by his wife achieves a brief but all-important breakthrough into manhood.

Other stories of the period, too, concern couples whose marriages involve a competitive struggle of wills. "A Couple of Hamburgers" (1935) depicts the long-distance auto trip of a couple who are temperamentally at odds. The husband is loud, the wife squeamish and refined. When the husband stops at a diner, his wife is offended by the waiter's wiping the counter with a cloth and goes out to wait in the car. As they continue on, the husband begins a boisterous rendition of the song "Harrigan That's Me." "It's a name that *shame* has never been connected with," he roars as his wife hears a small sound, like that of tiny pins jingling in a thimble. Noting this warning that the transmission of the car is burning out, she settles back to await her husband's humiliation. The husband is a comic study in *hubris:* ironically, it is his "delicate" wife who notices the noise that will undermine his bluster and false sense of mastery. The image of the pins also evokes the nature of her relationship to him, the pinpricks of her gentility that drive him ever further into boisterousness and a loss of control. The story is humorous but also piercing, since one recognizes that the couple will continue to goad one another in never-ending combat.

"The Breaking Up of the Winships" (1936), written a year later, is a more ambitious exploration of a similar theme. It employs a Jamesian narrator who is both a personal friend of Gordon and Marcia Winship and a detached observer. He begins by relating that the Winships' separation has lasted for six months and seems likely to be permanent, and then goes back to the incident that had started them quarreling. After having seen *Camille,* the Winships have dinner with another couple and fall into an

argument over Greta Garbo. Marcia declares Garbo's abandonment to passion incomparable, while Gordon, preferring detachment, is unimpressed. Pressed by Marcia to
name a male actor greater than Garbo, Gordon names
Donald Duck. The absurd argument continues until Marcia returns home alone in a taxi and Gordon goes to his
club to spend the night.

When they go to a cocktail party a few days later,
Gordon brings up the Garbo-Donald Duck incident good-
naturedly to a lady novelist, who tells him (without necessarily being serious) that she is on his side. Overhearing
their conversation, Marcia believes that her husband has
deliberately humiliated her in public. In the taxi on the
way home she slaps his face, and the next day he moves
out of the house. Their differences presumably could still
be made up, but by now the quarrel has become an obsession to each of them. The narrator is reminded ironically of
Gordon's former detachment when he visits him and
notices a wild light in his eyes, and when he calls on
Marcia finds that she has put the quarrel on an abstract
level of integrity that cannot be compromised. In their
strife the principles over which they fought become confused. Gordon loses his detachment, becoming ruled by
his emotions, and Marcia, who defended passion, becomes governed by a purely intellectual conception of
their relationship.

The obsessions that keep them apart are underscored
by the presence of the dispassionate narrator, who at the
end also becomes the story's interpreter. After their quarrel has "tunnelled" into the narrator's "subconscious," he
has a dream in which he is out hunting with the Winships.
As they cross a snowy field, Marcia spots a rabbit and
taking quick aim brings it down. They run across the snow
to the rabbit, and the narrator is the first to come upon it.
What fills him with horror is not that it is dead but that it is
a white rabbit wearing a vest and carrying a watch. The
dream at the end is left unexplained, but clearly the Lewis
Carroll rabbit implies the free play of imagination that the

Winships have murdered in the constriction of their fixations. "The Breaking Up of the Winships" is one of
Thurber's marvelous stories, intricately crafted and by the
end poetic; and it is especially impressive in its use of the
unconscious and dream symbolism to focus the force of
the irrational in the marital conflict.

"The Indian Sign" (1933), a partly humorous story,
also examines the inner stresses of a marriage. The
Bentleys have been set at odds by the wife's obsession with
a seventeenth-century ancestor, a Cora Allyn, after whom
the firstborn female in every branch of the Allyn family,
and their own daughter (their only child), have been
named. The wife collects clippings about her ancestor
until the husband becomes exasperated, for the matriarch
is a constant reminder to him that he lives under the
thumb of women. Cora Allyn, moreover, is distinctly
threatening, a woman who in dimly authenticated accounts had slain nineteen Pequot Indians single-handed.

As a fiercesome colonial matriarch, Cora Allyn's associations are reinforced, although Thurber does not refer to
it, by an actual woman of her period, Hannah Duston. In
1697 the Duston family, dwelling in the English settlement
at Haverhill, Massachusetts, had been set upon by a band
of Indians. Gathering up seven of their eight children,
Duston had fired several shots and run off, leaving his
wife Hannah, who had just given birth, to her unhappy
fate. Hannah Duston, her infant, and nurse were led into
captivity by the Indians, who dashed out the infant's
brains against a tree and made it clear that Mrs. Duston
would be scourged and made to run the gauntlet. One
night while the Indians slept, however, Hannah Duston,
with the nurse and a boy also being held captive, fell upon
the Indians and dispatched them. Hannah Duston then
scalped the ten Indians, tied their scalps to her belt so as to
collect a bounty and, only a week after giving birth, trek-
ked 150 miles through the wilderness to her settlement.

Hannah Duston's exploit was chronicled, among
others, by Cotton Mather in *Magnalia Christi Americana*,

and later, with masculine indignation, by Hawthorne and Thoreau. More recently, in *The Return of the Vanishing American* (1968), Leslie Fiedler has devoted a chapter to her as an exemplar of the "anti-Pocahontas myth." "As late as June 17, 1874," he writes:

a statue was being unveiled, with appropriate ceremonies, in Haverhill, Massachusetts: the stone figure of a long-skirted, sunbonneted woman with a tomahawk raised aloft in her delicate hand—so like the standard Freudian dream of a castrating mother that it is hard to believe it has not been torn down long since by some maimed New England male just out of analysis.[3]

It is likely that Thurber had read or heard of Hannah Duston, but whether he had or not his Cora Allyn is of her time and type, and carries a similar threat. Thurber speaks of her "prophetic" figure poised against the sky, "with her matchlock or hunting knife . . . so outrageously and significantly triumphant." As the story proceeds and Mrs. Bentley refuses to relent in her fixation, tension mounts between the couple. Then one night while Mrs. Bentley is sleeping her husband steals into her room. She awakens and in the stillness and darkness of the room calls out, "Henry!" in a frightened voice. Finding release at last from his pent-up emotions, Bentley puts the fingers of his right hand to his lips and shouts, "Aha-wah-wah-wah-wah-wah-wah!" The scalping fantasy is directed toward his wife, but the ultimate source of his anger is the powerful mother figure who stalks many of Thurber's stories, often in the form of marital partners.

Mr. Bentley's symbolic murder of his wife is comic, but in "Mr. Preble Gets Rid of His Wife" (1933), written in the same year, the theme becomes rather-more sinister. Mr. Preble is a middle-aged lawyer in Scarsdale who jokes with his stenographer about running away with him. One day the stenographer laughs that he will first have to get rid of his wife. That night Mr. Preble asks his wife to accompany him to the cellar. When she asks why, he tells her that he wants to get rid of her so that he can marry his stenographer. Humoring her husband, she tells him that she will go down into the cellar with him if he will then "shut up" and give her some peace. They then descend the stairs to the basement where Mr. Bentley will "bury" her.

In the cellar Mrs. Bentley chides her husband for his crude plan to hit her over the head with a shovel, which would leave clues. She tells him, rather, that he should go out to obtain a piece of iron or some other implement that does not belong to him; and she reminds him that it is cold in the cellar so that he should hurry and not stop along the way at the cigar store. "And shut that *door* behind you!" she screams at the end. "Where were you born—in a barn?" The weirdness of the story depends partly on the matter-of-factness of the narration, and the wife's refusal to take her husband's homicidal plans seriously. One has to ask oneself if the scene between the two is really happening. The dream quality of the story is balanced by a strong sense of actuality, and actuality is challenged by a strong sense of dream. One of the finest features of the story is its psychological atmosphere, its quality of hallucination in the cold, murderous cellar where Mr. Bentley's subterranean life has been projected dramatically.

Realism and fantasy are interwoven in another marital story "The Unicorn in the Garden" (1939). Although one of Thurber's fables, it has the qualities of a short story severely condensed, and everything essential about the couple's life together is contained within its small compass. The husband and wife spring to life immediately by the precision with which they have been imagined and are fully believable. The time period of the story is limited to a single morning that begins with the husband looking up from his scrambled eggs to see a unicorn quietly cropping roses in the garden. He goes upstairs to tell his slumbering wife, who opens a hostile eye, tells him that a unicorn is a "mythological beast," and turns her back on him. The husband then returns to the garden, feeds a lily to the unicorn, and returns with an account of what has just occurred to his wife, who tells him that he is a "booby" and that she is going to have to put him in a "booby-hatch." When the husband returns to the garden he finds the unicorn gone, and before long goes to sleep among the roses. As he sleeps his wife, with a "gloat" in her eye, calls the police and a psychiatrist, telling them to come immediately with a straitjacket. When they arrive she tells them that her husband has seen a unicorn in the garden and, at a "solemn signal" from the psychiatrist, the policemen leap from their chairs and tie her into the straitjacket. The husband appears in the living room, but denies having seen the unicorn, and the wife is taken away raving to be shut up in an asylum.

Not only is the unicorn mythological, so too is the tale. Only in a mythological world could the unicorn make its surprising appearance or the wife be gotten rid of so obligingly by the policemen and psychiatrist. The tale is comic but its tensions are characteristic of Thurber's other stories of marital conflict. In this case, the wife is almost purely "evil," the husband long-suffering and "good." The difference between them is signified by the symbolism of the garden and the bedroom, in the former of which, where woman is conspicuously absent, innocence and beauty can exist or be imagined, and in the latter of which only strife exists. The imagery of the husband sleeping among the roses associates him with spiritual beauty and love, but the wife's mean nature precludes the possibility of selfless love and communion. In some sense, the wife *is* insane, since her ordering of life is informed purely by aggression and makes no provision for gentleness, imagination, and innocence. She has no sense of fantasy, and ironically not only does the husband take revenge upon her but so also does fantasy. She is taken out of the world to be confined in an institution by fantasy policemen and a fantasy analyst. "The Unicorn in the Garden" is one of Thurber's "happy" hallucinations, in which the mild husband is rewarded with peace, but he is a fortunate exception. Other husbands are more often broken by the women they marry.

Such a figure is depicted in one of Thurber's most powerful stories, "The Curb in the Sky" (1931). It is related by a third-person narrator who remarks at the beginning, with ominous foreshadowing, that when his friend Charlie Deschler announced that he was going to marry Dorothy it was predicted that he would lose his mind. Dorothy is attractive and has many suitors, but her habit of finishing their words for them while they are in midsentence soon wears them down and they drift away. Deschler is impetuous, however, and marries her soon after they meet.

A widely traveled man, he is an excellent raconteur, but Dorothy soon begins correcting him as he relates his stories. He becomes, indeed, a prisoner of her interventions, which ignore the spirit of what he is saying and fasten upon minute details, such as the exact number of miles they had traveled by car on a certain trip. Dorothy is not described in detail, but one *feels* her presence horribly, her mindlessness and determined undermining of her husband. The narrator visits the couple at various times, in the course of which he notes his friend's steady deterioration. Near the end Deschler takes refuge in his dreams, which he can relate, seemingly, without fear of being corrected by his wife. They become his *only* life, but, as the narrator points out, one cannot live with one's dreams day in and day out and remain sane. Before long he has to be sent to an asylum. A friend who visits Deschler writes to the narrator that his eyes "look better," no longer have their wild, hunted look. "Of course," he adds, "he's finally got away from that woman."

When the narrator drives to the asylum to see Deschler, however, he finds Dorothy beside him. He looks quite mad. As they talk, Deschler repeats the story of a dream in which he flies to the moon in an airplane made of electric wires, but when he tells that he pulled over to a "curb" in the sky, Dorothy cuts in to remind him that he had pulled over to a "cloud." "He always gets that story wrong," she remarks with a "pretty smile." At the end Deschler is denied sanctuary even in his dreams. Dorothy is appalling precisely because she cannot dream or imagine, she lacks consciousness and is utterly sterile. In constricting her husband's life ever further until at last it is wholly without substance, in reducing him to dependency and rendering him helpless, she is, in effect, his castrator. The force of the story derives partly from its mingling of realistic and romantic elements. Dorothy is only too real, but she is romantically conceived, too, in her possession of an absolute power over the male, and there is about her a dark quality of fairy-tale bewitchment.[4]

The theme of a breakdown of identity also appears in a number of Thurber's other stories. "A Box to Hide In" (1931) is a brief tale with hardly any plot. A first-person narrator who significantly has no name goes into a grocery store to ask for a box to hide in. When the grocer asks him what he means by wanting a box to hide in, he explains that it is a "form of escape. . . . It circumscribes your worries and the range of your anguish." A closet would not do. People might open the door and be startled to find him there, and he does not want to see people. Later he asks his cleaning woman if she has a large box he can hide in, and when she answers with dull incomprehension, he murmurs, "It's a form of escape." At the end his overpowering urge to hide in a box has not gone away, and one has the sense of his living helplessly with his obsession. His compulsion suggests a desire to return to unconsciousness in the darkness and enclosure of the womb, but his anxiety and fear are not defined specifically and are thus all the more suggestive. In its concise, allegorical form, "A Box to Hide In" makes one think of the existential parables of Camus and of Melville's "Bartleby the Scrivener," which ends with the hero's psychic withdrawal from life. But it is also similar to Hemingway's early stories in its evocation of the hopelessness of finding sanctuary from the threat of life, and it has Hemingway's spare economy.

"The Private Life of Mr. Bidwell" (1933), a haunting tale that anticipates certain stories of John Cheever, deals with another male character at the point of breakdown. At the beginning the suburban Mr. Bidwell is seen holding his breath in a ludicrous attempt to escape from his life. When his wife notices him holding his breath at a party shortly afterwards, she tells him that he is embarrassing her, and she berates him as they drive home. As time goes on, his obsession grows even stronger, so that he begins holding his breath even in his sleep. Later his fixation takes new forms, and at another party his wife finds him multiplying numbers in his head.

At the end the narrator remarks that Mrs. Bidwell has now left her husband and remarried. Ironically, however, even when the marriage has ended his trauma persists. He lives alone, no longer goes to parties, and is rarely seen by his old circle of friends. The last time any of them has seen him he was walking alone along a country road with the "uncertain gait" of a blind man, trying to see how many steps he could take without opening his eyes. Mr. Bidwell's attempts to escape are comic, but he is also poignant in his loneliness. In the course of the story his isolation merely increases. Seen at the beginning with his wife and in the ambiance of parties, he is glimpsed at the end as a roadside solitary, a would-be blind man who attempts to close out the world. He becomes finally like the narrator in "A Box to Hide In," a character who can no longer manage his anxiety.

Thurber's escape theme appears again in the extraordinary story "The Remarkable Case of Mr. Bruhl" (1930). Samuel O. Bruhl, the treasurer of a syrup-and-fondant company, lives in Brooklyn with a large, devout wife and two "tractable" daughters. His comings and goings are colorless, his manner mild, the stature of his dreams small. Then one day the newspapers carry the story and the photograph of a gangster who has been admitted to the hospital after being shot by members of a rival mob. The man, George ("Shoescar") Clinigan, looks remarkably like Mr. Bruhl, even having the same shoe-shaped scar on his left cheek. When Mr. Bruhl learns that his look-alike has left the hospital and is being sought by other gangsters, he grows pale with fear. He takes a different route to his office, becomes fidgety, and begins to lose weight. One evening he receives a phone call from a man who tells him that he is "cooked" and hangs up; but the call turns out to be merely a prank of a man at the office. The stories about Clinigan die down, and Mr. Bruhl gradually becomes less nervous.

Then Clinigan's picture appears in the papers again. The leader of the mob that had vowed to get him has been shot, a gang war seems about to erupt, and the article predicts that Clinigan is "cooked." After reading the account, Mr. Bruhl goes to pieces once more. Yet a week later something extraordinary happens to him. He has a personality change. His manner becomes unaccountably rough, almost brutal, and he speaks out of the side of his mouth. One evening when friends come by to play bridge, Mr. Bruhl appears from his bedroom gripping a revolver, and shoots out the mantelpiece clock. As Mrs. Bruhl screams and the friends faint, he growls, "What's the matta you? Ya bunch of softies?" A doctor who is called in explains to his wife that Mr. Bruhl has a "psychosis," and before long Mrs. Bruhl takes her husband on a restful trip to a mountain inn. While Mr. Bruhl is alone in the dining room of the inn, however, four sinister men appear, take out guns from cases for musical instruments and shoot him. When the commissioner of the New York City police interviews him at the hospital, Bruhl snarls that he isn't talking to "cops," and the commissioner sighs that they are "all like that. . . . They never talk."

In his transformation (at least in his own mind) into a hardened criminal, Bruhl becomes all that he is not—a figure of daring and virility. His life can be measured by his safe routines and his enclosure within the middle-class

Brooklyn house with his large wife and daughters, a femi-
nized world where he suffers acute sexual anxiety. His
fantasy life, on the other hand, places him in an outward,
public world of men who possess power, even unlawful
power. His miraculous transformation occurs, it should be
noticed, when he is napping. When he wakes, wearing
bold scarlet pajamas, he wields a phallic revolver. His
initiation into his new self occurs, as it were, in his unconscious, with Clinigan, his doppelgänger or repressed self,
emerging from his dream life. The shoe-shaped scar on his
cheek is itself foreshadowing and symbolic of this other
self; is like the brand of Cain, and evokes the idea of brutal
assertion.

Ironically, however, Bruhl (his name rhymes with
"fool") comes no closer to possessing an authentic identity.
It is significant that the exploits of the comically named
Clinigan have a comic strip or gangster film quality. The
scene particularly where the four silent men in overcoats
appear at the resort carrying weapons and line up to fire at
him; the cumulative roar and series of flashes; their leaving
in single file without speaking—all of this is drawn from
gangster films of the thirties, which were themselves a
form of escape from pedestrian reality. In turning into
Clinigan, Bruhl becomes nothing real. Even Bruhl's apparent death in the hospital is unreal, since he is immersed in
fantasy, dying as someone other than himself. The touching and finally terrible thing about Bruhl is that he should
come to feel his anonymity and unimportance so acutely,
and should have only illusion to shield him from their
threat. In this respect he anticipates by nine years
Thurber's most famous escapist, Walter Mitty.

Although a story of only 2,500 words, "The Secret Life of
Walter Mitty" (1939) took Thurber eight weeks to write,
"working day and night," as it passed through fifteen
separate drafts.[5] Interestingly, in a dream sequence in one
of the early drafts, Walter Mitty had interceded between
Ernest Hemingway and an opponent in a Stork Club scuf-

fle, a scene Thurber removed after concluding that the story should contain nothing topical.[6] The final version places Mitty in a Connecticut town during part of a single day, and the story begins and ends with episodes from his fantasy life. In this way the story has a circular movement that encloses Mitty within the world of his dreams.

Those who knew the Thurbers have speculated that the model for Mitty was Thurber's father, whereas others have claimed that he was inspired by Thurber's older brother William. Among other impractical schemes, William had wanted to prospect for uranium in Alaska, and he enacted fantasies before mirrors, once assuming the role of a police officer arresting his grandfather Fisher ("I'm going to take you in").[7] But, in fact, Mitty had already been anticipated in Thurber's earlier writing. He had been predicted even in the class prophecy Thurber wrote when graduating from the eighth grade at the Douglas School In Columbus. In the prophecy-fantasy of the fourteen-year-old Thurber, a certain Harold Young takes the class on a trip to Mars in a Seairoplane. When a rope becomes caught in the "curobater," the passsengers fear for their lives—until James Thurber calmly saves the day by walking out on a beam and extracting the rope. The paraphernalia of the Seairoplane and curobater and the heroics of young Thurber look forward to Mitty's fantasies quite strikingly. But one finds foreshadowings of Mitty, too, in the line of protagonists in Thurber's stories of the 1930s, men who attempt to escape from their ineffectual lives. Both Mr. Monroe and Mr. Pendly have Mittyesque episodes of escape into daydreams until their wives' scolding voices bring them back to reality; and Mr. Bruhl is a self-dramatizing escapist who in shooting out the mantelpiece clock stops time and reality so that he may enter his dream life. Coming at the end of the 1930s, Mitty is the essence and distillation of all these men.

The opening phrase of the story, "We're going through!," introduces its theme of an attempted breakthrough into larger life, an attempt constantly thwarted by the sound of Mrs. Mitty's voice reminding her husband that he may need to see his doctor about his tension, that he is no longer as young as he used to be, that he must be careful to wear gloves in the cold weather. In the first fantasy episode, instead of being tense Mitty is cool under pressure and astonishingly capable. He lives in a man's world of action as Commander Mitty, in charge of a huge, hurtling eight-engined Navy hydroplane. Confronted by the worst storm in twenty years of navy flying, he instructs the crew, who marvel at his fearlessness, to rev the engines to full power. The dream sequence dissolves suddenly into a scene in which Mrs. Mitty scolds him for driving the car too fast. The episode and its aftermath have the quality of a comic strip, in which a panel of heroically imagined action is immediately followed by one showing the hero as a little man tied to the apron strings of his wife.[8]

After Mitty drops his wife at a building where she is to have her hair done, a traffic cop orders him curtly to "pick it up, brother!" and he is plunged into another self-aggrandizing fantasy. Passing a hospital, he becomes the renowned surgeon Dr. Mitty, asked by a team of specialists (one of whom has flown in from London) to advise them in a hazardous operation. The patient is one Wellington McMillan, a millionaire banker and close personal friend of President Roosevelt. When the "anesthetizer" fails, Mitty imperturbably replaces a faulty piston with a fountain pen that will keep the machine going for another ten minutes. Then "coreopsis" sets in and the specialists, losing their nerve, ask Mitty to take over. The dream ends suddenly with a parking lot attendant's shouting to Mitty that he has driven into an exit lane. Far from being an expert with machinery, he drives the automobile so poorly as to endanger his life.

In the following episode, Mitty imagines himself on trial for murder in a sensational case that has made newspaper headlines. Throwing the courtroom into an uproar, he announces that he could have shot Gregory Fitzhurst at three hundred feet with his *left* hand, even if his right hand had not been sprained. In a cinematic "cut" to the real world, Mitty is then seen on the street muttering, "puppy biscuit," which he now remembers his wife had asked him to pick up, and hearing his words a woman passing on the street laughs at him. In the hotel lobby where he waits for his wife, he glances at a copy of *Liberty* magazine and escapes into a war fantasy in which, as Captain Mitty, he tosses off a brandy and goes off to fly alone over enemy lines to bomb an ammunition dump. With another sudden transition, however, Mrs. Mitty finds him "hiding" in a lobby chair. In the final sequence, he stands alone before the blank wall of a drugstore into which his wife has darted on an errand, refusing a handkerchief as he faces a firing squad in a cool defiance of death.

Robert Morsberger has noted an intriguing resemblance between this ending and the conclusion of Conrad's *Lord Jim*, and compared the phrasing of the closing passages:

Conrad	Thurber
Jim stood stiffened and with bared head. . . . They say that the white man sent right and left at all those faces a proud and unflinching glance. Then with his hand over his lips he fell forward, dead. . . . He is gone, inscrutable at heart.	He put his shoulders back and his heels together. . . . He took one last drag on his cigarette and snapped it away. Then, with that faint, fleeting smile playing about his lips, he faced the firing squad; erect and motionless, proud and disdainful, Walter Mitty, the Undefeated, inscrutable to the last.[9]

Thurber's parody of Lord Jim seems the more likely in view of Thurber's mock association with him in the early 1930s. In his introduction to *The Owl in the Attic*, White had pictured Thurber humorously as a modern-day Lord

Jim, bound on a romantic quest yet balked by the ordinary events of life and the quandary of marriage. Allusions to Lord Jim also appear in Thurber's own early writing, particularly in his epilogue to *My Life and Hard Times*, in which he complains that although he sits on the terraces of cafés wearing a pith helmet, a muscle in his jaw twitching as he stares straight ahead, his identification with Lord Jim is thwarted by his Ohio accent and the frequent need for visits to his oculist and dentist.

But the firing-squad episode is also a parody of romantic adventure films that provide escape for the masses. All of Mitty's fantasies, in fact, are indebted to movie heroics, and as such they undercut his attempt to establish an authentic identity. He is trapped not only by his confining circumstances but also by his inability to imagine heroic stature other than through clichés provided by the media. The episode in which Captain Mitty prepares to fly alone behind enemy lines was inspired specifically by the recent film *The Dawn Patrol*,[10] and in it Mitty assumes an English nonchalance in the face of danger to the point of triteness. When his dugout is shelled, Mitty remarks carelessly, "A bit of a near thing," and leaves to meet the enemy in the skies with a nerveless "cheerio!" Mitty is like a small boy before a mirror striking the poses of admired adults, and is constantly evoked as ineffectual and childlike.

In some respects, "Walter Mitty" has affinities with Joyce's *Ulysses*. Both works—one immense, the other minute in scope—are concerned with men of an unheroic age who feel inadequate and estranged. In the course of twenty-four hours in *Ulysses*, and part of a day in "Walter Mitty," they are followed in their wanderings, the narrations weaving back and forth between inner reverie and outward event. Although married, Leopold Bloom is essentially alone, a Jew in turn-of-the-century Dublin, and the large section devoted to him is filled with a sense of his lonely isolation. Walter Mitty, in his Connecticut town, is also isolated from others (his wife, the parking lot attendant, and the traffic cop are in fact no more than "voices"), and is driven inward upon himself in fantasy. Fantasy, satire, and parody all enter into *Ulysses* and "Walter Mitty" as their antiheroes attempt to cope with their marginality and lack of importance.

In both works their inner and outer experience is linked by an associational psychology, whereby a word may set in motion a chain-reaction response in their inner musings or return them suddenly to everyday reality. In the dream sequence in the courtroom, for example, Mitty strikes the district attorney, calling him a "cur," and immediately after is seen on the street muttering, "puppy biscuit"—a reminder of his status not as a hero in the outer world of events but as a domestic child-man. The works also employ refrains and leitmotifs to call attention to the protagonists' situation. Plumtree's Potted Meats recurs in *Ulysses*, for instance, as a continual, mocking reminder of Leopold Bloom's cuckold state. In "Walter Mitty," the leitmotif of the hydroplane's engines, "Ta-pocketa-pocketa," recurs in sequences in which Mitty imagines himself as being masterful with machinery, although he is actually helpless before anything mechanical. Another leitmotif in the story is the word "hell," which appears at several points and in a muted way evokes the anguished truth of Mitty's incapacities and sense of failure.

Freud is relevant, too, since the story reflects an exceptional concern with the unconscious, the source of Mitty's imaginative life. His "secret" life is subterranean, and from it he calls up images that reveal his neurotic fixations. The dream sequences are, in effect, power fantasies having a sexual implication. Mitty is associated, for example, with phallic revolvers—in the courtroom scene where he is on trial for having shot a man with a Webley-Vickers automatic, and again in the episode where, strapping on a Webley-Vickers automatic he goes off to engage the German air force. In this scene and in the one aboard the hydroplane Mitty is also associated with flying, which in Freud's dream lexicon connotes sexual experience. Mitty's

constant anxiety underlying these fantasies of power suggests more than anything a fear of impotence.

Mitty's anxiety of impotence also makes Thurber's
story relevant to the work of Nathanael West, another
satirist and parodist of the 1930s having a remarkable
interest in fantasy. West's *Miss Lonelyhearts* can be compared to "Walter Mitty" in a number of respects. Both
depict the psychic distress of a modern man who feels
helpless and alone, and seeks escape in fantasies that have
a cartoon quality.[11] In a series of cartoon panels, Miss
Lonelyhearts is constantly brought down from his lofty
envisionings of transcendence to the brutal reality of life,
and Mitty has a kinship with him as a fellow clown. Both
are trapped by their philistine environments, nervous anxiety, and sexual insecurity; and cannot find a way out of
their isolation to achieve a sense of coherent identity.

In essays on Thurber, Otto Friedrich and Robert Elias
have commented on Walter Mitty as a figure who, in his
dream life, does find a measure of triumph over a hostile
world. Friedrich remarks that "Mitty's daydream life is a
triumph not only over the humiliation of the moment but
over all of life";[12] and Elias regards the final episode of the
story a vindication of the dreamer. "When Mitty faces the
firing squad, 'Undefeated, inscrutable to the last,' " Elias
writes, "the victory has its limits. It is not only private
. . . ; it is ridden by the clichés of pulp romances. . . .
Nonetheless, it is a victory, even if qualified, that contrib-
utes to his self preservation."[13] But these readings are
absurd, and can be entertained only by disregarding the
text.

Mitty is not inscrutable at the end but perfectly trans-
parent.[14] Nor does he exercise control over or in any sense
direct his dream life. It controls him. The smallest incidents of humiliation set him helplessly dreaming, and
even in his dream imaginings he commits a series of blun-
ders that destroy his authority. His hydroplane is
equipped with too many engines to fly; the "coreopsis"
that sets in during the operation actually denotes a genus

of plant; and as Captain Mitty he flies off to oppose the "Archies" rather than the "Jerries." A death motif runs through the fantasy sequences, too, with an effect that undercuts Mitty's ability to assert himself even in his dreams. In the opening episode he braves death as an intrepid naval commander, and in the second he attends to life-and-death decisions as Dr. Mitty; but by the third, when he is on trial for his life, he makes his conviction certain by shouting impulsively that he could have committed the crime with his left hand. In the following sequence he prepares to fly off alone, in a plane requiring two pilots, on what is really a suicide mission; and in the final one, as he faces death by a firing squad, he is wholly powerless. The series of episodes suggest a kind of death wish that is similar to that of Mr. Bruhl when he identifies with a man certain to be killed. Mitty's failure is final, and ends with his imagined death.

The enduring interest of "Walter Mitty" owes much to its grounding in the American mythic imagination, as Carl M. Lindner has noted in his essay "Thurber's Walter Mitty—The Underground American Hero." Tracing Mitty's ancestry back to Rip Van Winkle, he observes that, like Rip, Mitty has a wife who embodies the authority of a society in which he cannot function. "The husband," he remarks:

is often reduced to the status of a naughty child . . . ; and he attempts to escape rather than confront a world symbolized by a wife who, more often than not, seems a mother-figure rather than a partner. Because of the threat which the wife-mother poses to the American male psyche, Rip must go hunting, Deerslayer cannot marry and dwell in the town, and Huck seeks the river rather than be *sivilized*. [15]

It should be noted, however, that by the time of Walter Mitty the protesting male has no woods or river to which to escape. Mitty is wholly encapsulated within illusion and has no identity whatever (nothing concrete about him, not even the work he does, is ever revealed). Reproved by his wife-mother for his own good, he is like a small child (his name suggests a child's "mitten"); he cannot act effectively because he cannot achieve adulthood. His dream life is, finally, a form of hysteria, and the story shows him at a point of nervous breakdown.

As a figure immediately recognizable and belonging to the American folk mind, Mitty can be compared to Sinclair Lewis's Babbitt. Less a distinct individual than an embodiment of the middle-class American salesman and businessman, Babbitt too is an escapist. He seems, with his "pink cheek pads," almost an infant, and he is infantile in his attempts to find himself or to establish any pattern of meaning in his life. Trapped by conformity, fearful of the disapproving opinion of others, he is a lodge member, a joiner, and a booster; but none of these garish activities gives him any genuine pleasure or sense of satisfaction. The strongest love he feels is toward another man, the sensitive Paul Riesling with whom he attended the state university and who feels his entrapment in Zenith to the point of desperation. Riesling's attempt to break out of the constriction and deadness of his life ends with his shooting his wife, an utterly mindless and repellent woman, and a term in the penitentiary. After Riesling's imprisonment Babbitt attempts to rebel but without having the equipment to alter his life. He goes to the Maine woods without establishing any contact with nature or manliness, and he has an affair with a pretty widow whom he views gauchely as romantic. Babbitt dreams of a fairy child who comes to him while he sleeps, but he does not possess a romantic imagination, is merely naive. When his wife has an operation, he is brought back to where he was at the beginning, to his responsibilities and a claustrophobic entrapment. In his ineptitude and helplessness, Babbitt is a parodied child-man like Mitty. They do not possess and cannot find any identity, and are tremendously threatened by an external world that they do not understand and that fills them with fear.

One difference between *Babbitt* (1920) and "Walter Mitty" is that Mitty's alienation is more radical. Lewis surrounds Babbitt with a sociologically detailed world and permits him some small, weary consolations, but Thurber allows Mitty no space at all in which to move or interact with others. Mitty belongs wholly to private experience, and the same can be said of Thurber's other men in the early stories. They cannot meet the world boldly but instead become figures of isolation and anxiety who take refuge in dreams. Thurber's conceptions may begin with Benchley's humor of helplessness, but it would be inconceivable to imagine Benchley writing "The Breaking Up of the Winships," "A Box to Hide In" or "The Private Life of Mr. Bidwell." He did not possess the mind or imagination that would have enabled him to do so. It was Thurber's achievement in the 1930s to have reshaped Benchley's comic themes into a serious literature of humor-terror, in which Walter Mitty and his kind sound the authentic note of existential suffering.

4

~~~~~~

The Further Range:
Thurber's Other Stories

Thurber's tales of the "little man" culminate in "Walter Mitty," but this type of story does not disappear exactly with the end of the 1930s decade. Shortly after the onset of his blindness in 1941, Thurber published two other stories, "The Catbird Seat" (1942) and "The Lady on 142" (1943), that are of a similar nature and are among his best. "The Catbird Seat" is in some respects a more ample version of "The Unicorn in the Garden," and like the earlier fable combines humor with fantasy. Erwin Martin, the story's hero, is the epitome of the little man, a timid clerk who has worked for the same company for years and has become head of its filing department. One day, however, a Mrs. Ulgine Barrows is hired by the president of the firm, Mr. Fitweiler, as an efficiency expert. An aggressive, dominant woman, she fills Mr. Martin with apprehension and fear. Eventually, when she plans radical changes in his department, he realizes that he must act to save himself. Drinking his habitual glass of milk before retiring, he plots to murder her.

In the original draft, Martin had gone to Mrs. Barrows's apartment and carried out the killing, but Thurber was dissatisfied with this version because Martin does not really seem capable of murder. In the published version, he goes to the apartment taking care not to be observed by others, but when the critical moment arrives cannot act and instead flaunts concocted vices before Mrs. Barrows— secret smoking of cigarettes, drinking, and use of cocaine, and abuses his employer Mr. Fitweiler as a "windbag." Mrs. Barrows orders him out of her apartment and the next morning reports him to Fitweiler. Fitweiler, however, fully conscious that Martin's abstemious habits are legendary in the firm, concludes that Mrs. Barrows has lost her mind. After conferring with a psychiatrist on the telephone, he has her forcibly removed from the office and his employment. She is expelled screaming and imprecating, never to return, and Martin's fantasy of revenge upon the powerful Ulgine Barrows is realized.

Although possessing a veneer of realism, "The Catbird Seat" is essentially a fable or fairy tale, and in many ways is a retelling of "The Unicorn in the Garden." Mr. Martin and Ulgine Barrows are not husband and wife like the couple in the fable, but they are similar to them as combatants in a male-female power struggle, Mrs. Barrows large and intimidating, Mr. Martin meek and enfeebled in his masculinity. Rather like the wife in "The Unicorn in the Garden," Mrs. Barrows plots against the hero and looks forward to his removal from his special sanctuary where he finds security and peace, but is outwitted by him. Mrs. Barrows is not removed to an insane asylum, but is shut out of Mr. Martin's world forever and shorn of her power. Her explusion from the office, like the wife's from the home in the fable, involves the collective action of men, notably including a psychiatrist, against her.

One feels, moreover, that her expulsion is warranted. Her officiousness has already cost a number of inoffensive people their jobs at A & F before she lays plans against Mr. Martin, and she has no compassion and no pity. A strictly mental and self-centered type, she is out of touch with the natural rhythms of life and everything about her is made to seem repellent. Even her name Ulgine is an approximate anagram of "ugly." She has a loud, brassy voice and "brays" rather than talks. Her expressions, like "tearing up the pea patch" (for going on a rampage) and "sitting in the catbird seat" (for sitting pretty, like a batter with three balls and no strikes on him) are taken from the sportscaster Red

Barber when he covered the baseball games of the Brooklyn Dodgers. Her frequent use of these expressions suggests that she regards life in terms of struggle and competition, and there is poetic justice in her being ousted and losing authority over others. On a deeper level of emotive response, she is an ogre or witch, whom Martin slays in order to restore peace and amity to the world. The fairy-tale happy ending, however, is ironic in some ways. In the real world Ulgine Barrowses are not so easily disposed of, and Mr. Martins do not normally slay Goliaths. Moreover, Martin's triumph is more problematic than that of the husband in the fable whose unicorn and rose-garden affiliations were with ideality and spiritual truth. Mr. Martin at the end merely returns to his safe but sterile filing system that will shield him from self-recognition.

If "The Catbird Seat" revives the situation in "The Unicorn in the Garden," "The Lady on 142" is in some ways a retelling of "Walter Mitty." It is narrated in the first person by a man who is nameless and is accompanied by his wife Sylvia as they take a trip by train from Cornwall, Connecticut to Gaylordsville, about twenty minutes away—a tiny excursion. His wife has her feet firmly on the ground while her husband, who searches ineffectually for Chiclets in his pockets yet enters into romantic adventure in his daydreams, does not. On the hot, sticky midsummer afternoon, as they wait for the train, he hears the station master on the phone saying that conductor Reagan has the lady "the office was asking about," and tells his wife that he feels there is some deep mystery about her. It is wartime and he feels that she may be a spy, a notion at which Sylvia scoffs.

As he leans his head against the back of the seat and closes his eyes, he falls into a kind of reverie in which he and his wife, because they "know too much," are snatched off the train by the lady and taken to the lair of her sinister associates. At the point at which they are about to be killed, he wakes to the reality of their arriving in a totally normal way at Gaylordsville. At the station, they are met by a female friend to whom Sylvia tells her husband's suspicion of the "lady on 142" as a German spy, and the women laugh at him. The dream sequence is introduced so quietly that the reader does not recognize at first that it is only a dream; only later, with their arrival at Gaylordsville, does it become apparent that the events described belong wholly to the narrator's romantic dreaming—dreaming that ends in anticlimax and humiliation, just as it does in "Walter Mitty."

One of the special features and delights of "The Lady on 142" is Thurber's use of parody. Early in the story when the narrator speaks of spies, his wife tells him that "Alfred Hitchcock things" don't happen on the New York, New Haven & Hartford railroad. But it is exactly Hitchcock that one is made to think of in the "dream" appearance of the lady with the pearl-handled derringer who spirits the narrator and his wife off the train to be met by a long black limousine with a heavyset foreigner at the wheel; in their sequestration in the remote house in the country where the group of spies gather; and in the suspense, huggermugger, and intrigue having the distinct styling of 1930s mystery films.

At the same time, Thurber parodies Dashiell Hammett's mystery novel *The Maltese Falcon*. The work is even alluded to quietly at the beginning when Sylvia tells her husband jestingly that the conductor on the train looks as if he knew "where the Maltese Falcon is hidden." As in Hammett's novel, the characters in the dream sequence are all strongly typed. The heavyset foreigner with "cruel lips and small eyes" is a stereotype, as is the lady from the train as she paces up and down at the house smoking a cigarette in a long black holder. The group includes a tall man with heavily lidded eyes and a lean young gunman with a "drawn, sallow" complexion and cigarette hanging from his lower lip who looks at the others "incuriously." The role played by the narrator in the dream sequence proves to be antiheroic. When he foolishly and self-destructively tells the tall man that he recognizes him as a tennis star who had lost to Tilden in Zagreb in 1927, he seals his own fate. The gunman hands his automatic to the tall man, who remarks, "I theenk I bomp off thees man myself," and the narrator wakes from his reverie "moaning." Yet he is not as radically estranged as Walter Mitty, and the story is a gentler, less disturbing version of a Mittyesque escape into fantasy.

"The Catbird Seat" and "The Lady on 142" are the last in Thurber's series of stories dealing with such men. Other stories do not fall into any single pattern and are of unpredictable types. "The Topaz Cufflinks Mystery" (1932) opens upon the scene at night of a man on his hands and knees before the headlights of a car while he barks like a dog. A motorcycle cop pulls up "out of Never-Never Land" to ask for an explanation, and it comes out that the husband and wife have been arguing about whether a man's eyes can be seen in the dark like a cat's, and that the husband has attempted to prove they can by placing himself on all fours by the side of the highway before the headlights of their car. There is no great point to the story: in a fantastic way the "bewildered, sedentary" husband has merely managed to make a fool of himself before his wife and the policeman. The situation, with its lunar quality, is reminiscent of Thurber's cartoons depicting men who have been shorn of sense and dignity.

In a later, frequently anthologized story, "The Figgerin' of Aunt Wilma" (1950), Thurber deals with a woman who, like a gallery of others from his Columbus past, is an oddity and an eccentric. Set far back in the Columbus past to 1905, when John Hance had run a neighborhood grocery store, the tale draws on the tradition of local color. The look and atmosphere of the store, the customs and manners of the people who gather there, are meticulously and exactly rendered. But the local color element is introduced partly to give verisimilitude to what is essentially a tall tale. John Hance and Aunt Wilma Hudson, to whom thrift is a religion, are both notoriously close with money. When they come together to settle a grocery bill of ninety-eight cents, a male-female duel ensues that becomes a family legend. It is authenticated and witnessed by the narrator, then a boy of ten. The problem comes about when Hance discovers that he has no pennies in his till, and proposes that Aunt Wilma give him a dollar plus three pennies and that he give her a nickel. Aunt Wilma is immediately suspicious, and becomes increasingly flustered by the mathematics of the complex transaction.

Hance's frustration and Aunt Wilma's confusion escalate as the tale continues; and when the boy returns to the Hudson house with his Aunt Wilma he cannot resist telling his uncle of Mr. Hance's ordeal. His uncle, who is implied to have been mismatched with his wife, at first chuckles and then breaks into "full and open laughter," part of a chorus of derision since male loungers in the store have smirked at Aunt Wilma too. His laughter convinces her that men cannot understand anything and are in league against her. One of the notable features of the story is the care with which all the characters, however incidental, have been drawn. But the most perfectly drawn is Aunt Wilma herself. She is similar in type to Aunt Ida in Thurber's reminiscent sketch "A Portrait of Aunt Ida," since her enclosure in settled feminine biases and deep suspicion of life beyond the narrow scope of her experience prevent her from recognizing her own confusion. "The Figgerin' of Aunt Wilma" is particularly revealing when placed against "The Topaz Cufflinks Mystery," the comic vision of which is distinctly urban, while the humor of "Aunt Wilma" belongs to regional or small-town literature. The stories could have been written by two entirely different authors.

Thurber's short fiction is especially puzzling in its diversity, its lack of any consistent approach or predictable subject matter. "The Black Magic of Barney Haller" (1932) is so original that nothing else exactly like it exists in American fiction, or even elsewhere in Thurber. The story is narrated in the first person by a man who lives in the country and has a hired man, Barney Haller, whose thick

Germanic accent distorts what he says so that it seems ominous. Moreover, whenever he appears he is followed by lightning that alarms the narrator and makes him feel that Barney Haller trafficks with the devil. When the story opens on a hot, sultry summer morning, Barney appears at the narrator's house with lightning playing about his shoulders and tells him that "bime by, I go hunt grotches in de voods." What he means by this is that he will look for forked branches or crotches to use as supports for saplings. But the narrator, who has an excitable imagination, can only envision "grotches" horribly as ugly little creatures "covered with blood and honey and scrapings of church bells." He goes with him to the woods, frightening himself by imagining Barney in the "voods" shedding his farmhand's garments and incanting diabolical phrases to conjure up "grotches." At the edge of the woods lightning suddenly slashes across the sky, thunder booms menacingly, and the narrator turns and flees while Barney stands impassively, staring after him.

That evening at six o'clock, while alone in the house and napping in an upstairs room, the narrator is awakened by the sound of rapping at his door. It is dark for six o'clock, with heavy rumblings of thunder and flickerings of lightning in the sky. The narrator is now convinced that the hired man has come to "get" him, even imagining him at the other side of the door standing barefoot with a "wild animal's skin" slung over his shoulder. Opening the door, he finds Barney at the other side, with lightning at his back. When Barney remarks, "We go to the garrick and become warbs," by which he means that it is time to clear the garret of wasps, the narrator is terrified. He has no intention of accompanying the eerie hired man to a garrick to become a "warb," and acting on a wild impulse quotes lines from Lewis Carroll, apparently hoping to ward off Barney's black magic. "Did you know," he says, "that even when it isn't brillig I can produce slithy toves? Did you happen to know that the mome rath never lived that could outgrabe me?" Barney backs slowly away from the porch, his eyes staring wide, and never returns to work for the narrator.

Part of the humor of the story involves the recognition that the hired man finds the narrator as strange as the narrator finds him. The narrator, a reader rather than a doer and a man of high-strung nerves, projects onto Barney all manner of fearsomeness. It is no coincidence that he reads Proust, and is disturbed from his dream of Proust's characters by the appearance of Barney at his door in the early evening. Proust's delicate nerves were so agitated by the slightest impressions, such as the taste of madeleines dipped in tea, as to set in motion a whole world of his imagining; and the narrator's nervous susceptibilities cause him to "imagine" things about Barney. Barney is in fact a simple man—stolid, slowly competent, and amiable. Almost nerveless, he walks about when there is thunder and lightning, unconscious of any danger. His indifference to thunder and lightning makes him incomprehensible to the narrator, who is as civilized as, to his mind, Barney is pagan. Barney Haller's name, which has the connotations of "barn" and "hell" (a word evoked quietly at the beginning) suggests a dual identity, half familiar and half weird. Ironically, Barney possesses no black magic, indicated in the story's title; it is the narrator who by the end becomes a sorcerer, fending off Barney's supposed threat to him by incanting fantastic phrases from his reading—the desperate gesture of a man without defenses. "The Black Magic of Barney Haller" is one of Thurber's superb stories, strikingly original and finely crafted.

But it is one of a kind. Nothing quite like it appears again. Instead one finds stories reflecting an almost bewildering virtuosity. "Am I Not Your Rosalind?" (1947) is a quintessential *New Yorker* story. Lucid and highly polished, it deals with familiar America as represented by two married couples, the Thornes and the Stantons. When the Stantons spend an evening at the Thornes, it comes out that their wives had each played Rosalind in *As You Like It* in senior-class high-school plays. They were born in the same year and had played the part at the same time. George Thorne insists that they recite some of Rosalind's lines into his tape recorder and they finally do so, overcoming their reluctance with additional cocktails. Each of the women praises the other's reading, modestly deprecating her own. Yet when the evening is over and the couples are alone, each scoffs at the other's reading and laughs with her husband over the hopelessness of her rival's physical appearance and various pretensions. As Thurber notes at the beginning, Rosalind had been one of the first "aggressive ladies in literature," a forecast, it would seem, of inmost aggression in the wives. "Am I Not Your Rosalind?" is a suave story, coolly amused and acidulously ironic.

"The Man Who Hated Moonbaum" (1940), on the other hand, has an almost surrealistic quality. Thurber's only Hollywood story, it was written after he had visited Elliott Nugent in Hollywood to work on the first draft of *The Male Animal*, and been introduced to various producers and directors in the film industry. The story has only two characters, a Hollywood producer who is unnamed and always referred to as "the little man," and a man named Tallman. Strangers to one another when they met over drinks at the Brown Derby, the producer had invited Tallman back to his home, a palatial estate of incredible pretentiousness. The story, which takes place at night and largely in darkness, opens upon the scene of their walking past a high, grilled gate for what seems a quarter of a mile to the producer's house. After fumbling in the dark, the producer flicks a switch (possibly concealed in a tree) that throws a rose-colored radiance over the façade of a building so imposing that it resembles "the Place de la Concorde side of the Crillon." Entering through an enormous door, Tallman discovers a marble staircase that tumbles "like Niagara" into a grand canyon of a living room.

The producer pours brandy for himself and his guest

while he talks compulsively about his conception for a movie based on medieval legend that involves a scene in which a spy, concealed behind the forty-foot tapestry hanging on his wall, is shot with an arrow. The scene has been bungled, he raves, by his assistant Moonbaum and Moonbaum's marksman. The more he talks, the more garish his movie seems. A motif of stifling heat is introduced, and the deep living room is evoked as a version of hell. Finally, Tallman leaves "the little man" talking to himself and finds his way out of the house into fresh air and the early light of day, able to see now "where he was going." In his use of the baroque Hollywood house that seems as empty and unreal as a movie set, Thurber seems indebted to Nathanael West. But the tale—in its vignette-like form, capturing of the producer's crass speech, and evocation of inner tensions and underlying ugliness—is also reminiscent of the Hollywood stories of Thurber's friend John O'Hara.

Two other stories, "The Greatest Man in the World" (1931) and "You Could Look It Up" (1941), suggest the influence of Ring Lardner. The central figure in "The Greatest Man in the World," like the prizefighter in Lardner's "Champion," is self-centered and vacant. By a quirk of fate, he becomes America's greatest hero when, in 1937, a decade after Lindbergh, he flies nonstop around the world in a secondhand, single-motored Bresthaven Dragon-Fly III monoplane. Jack ("Pal") Smurch is the product of a small Iowa town and a family looked upon askance and feared by local people. At the time of Smurch's flight, his father has been jailed for stealing spotlights and lap robes from tourists' automobiles, and his weak-minded younger brother had just escaped from a reformatory where he had been sent for the theft of money-order blanks from post offices.

Smurch's own earlier years there had been one of the town's uglier memories. He had knifed the principal of his school, and surprised in the act of stealing an altar cloth from a church had bashed the sacristan over the head with a pot of Easter lilies. For each of these offenses he had served a sentence in a reform school. Naturally, when reporters talk to townspeople and to Smurch's mother, a short-order cook in a shack restaurant who tells them that she hopes her son drowns, they realize that they cannot print the true facts of Smurch's life. Instead they describe him as a modest fellow, blond, and popular with girls. A cheap amusement park photo of him is touched up so that the "little vulgarian" looks handsome.

The first half of "The Greatest Man in the World" has the grotesque irreverence of Thurber's spoof "If Grant Had Been Drinking at Appomatox," in which the greatest hero of the Union Army is depicted as a clownish rumpot. The second half becomes pure fantasy. A national crisis develops, and Smurch is sequestered in a nursing home for two weeks ostensibly for exhaustion but actually to keep him away from the press. Finally, when he is conducted to a conference room in New York to be coached on how to comport himself—with a "test" reporter from the *New York Times*, and with the president of the United States and other top officials present—Smurch makes it clear that he will flaunt his true self before the world. As he stands before a window exulting in the sound of his name as it floats up to him from a newsboy hawking papers nine floors below, the President nods grimly to the mayor's secretary, a powerfully built former football player, who seizes Smurch and throws him out the window.

His death, covered up as a tragic accident, is the occasion of a solemn funeral and national mourning. Two minutes of silence are observed throughout the land, supervised in Smurch's hometown by Secret Service men. In the story's splendid ending, a line that had been introduced earlier, in which Smurch's "twisted leer" in the amusement park photo is retouched into a pleasant smile, is brought forward with the effect of a coda. Smurch's mother, in the shack restaurant, bows her head reverently but turns her face away so that the Secret Service men cannot see the "twisted, strangely familiar leer on her lips." "The Greatest Man in the World" combines many elements of Thurber's writing in the 1930s. It is a satire, a parody, a fantasy, and a "dark" fable.

"You Could Look It Up" is similar to "The Greatest Man in the World" in that it relates fantastic incidents as if they were factual. A baseball story with a first-person narrator reminiscent of the worldly-wise deadpan narrators in Ring Lardner's sports tales, it is related in the present but concerned with events occurring thirty years earlier that the narrator keeps reminding the reader are contained in newspaper files and can be looked up. The trainer at that time for a baseball club expected to win the pennant but fallen upon a slump, the narrator speaks in a hard-bitten vernacular so skillfully rendered that it clinches the authenticity of the tale. In a dejected state when the club loses to Columbus, the team's crusty manager, Squawks Magrew, meets a bizarre individual named Pearl du Monville. Du Monville is a midget with a "sneer on his little pushed-in pan" who swings a bamboo cane and smokes a big cigar. Drinking with him after the loss to Columbus, Magrew enjoys his razzing of the team and decides to adopt him as the team mascot.

To the consternation of the narrator and the members of the club, Magrew even signs du Monville as a player—a kind of goad to the team that du Monville could do no worse than they have been doing lately—and in the game against St. Louis sends du Monville in to bat for them. Certain that no pitcher can throw a ball low enough to strike him out, Magrew carefully instructs him to stand at the plate, take four balls, and walk to first base, enabling their man on third base to score a run. Du Monville does as he is told, but when a fourth pitch is thrown level to his chest he swats the ball and scrambles toward first base. He is out at first but, the bases loaded, the other players score runs and Magrew's team wins the game.

Du Monville's appearance on the diamond causes pandemonium in the stands, but the wildest scene occurs at the end when Magrew, enraged by the midget's defiance of his orders, seizes him, whirling him in the air like a discus thrower and hurling him across the field. Du Monville is never seen again but the team has been inspirited and goes on to take the pennant. "You Could Look It Up" is particularly effective in its use of the grotesque, and its smart-talking, cigar-chewing midget is one of the liveliest features of the story. The story may also involve an element of sly parody, however, since Squawks Magrew has a certain likeness to Thurber's editor at the *New Yorker,* Harold Ross. Drinking with the midget, he uses Ross's expressions, crying, "How I pity me," and like Ross he is overworked, gruffly melancholic, and constantly goading those under him to reach new heights of excellence.

Yet other Thurber stories are not satirical at all and some, like "Menaces in May" (1928), his first story published in the *New Yorker,* reveal another side of his sensibility. Evidently autobiographical, "Menaces in May" concerns a man who is never named and who resembles Thurber himself during the time that he was getting started in New York and his first wife Althea Adams had not yet returned from France to join him. It begins moodily with the man in a hotel room at one o'clock in the morning with another man and woman whom he has just met by chance in the city and had known eighteen years before. He had, in fact, been in "puppy" love with the woman, who is now in vaudeville. As he looks at the two together, he remembers that in school he had been studious and shy, no way to have won Julia, and wonders what his life with her would have been like. The situation comes out of Thurber's own experience. Eva Prout, who had been his first boyhood love and whom he idealized for years, had dropped out of school to go into vaudeville and movies; and it is she, really, who is Julia.

The first part of the story is suffused with a sense of regret, of lost romance; but when the man leaves the couple and makes his way in the dim hours to his room in the Village another motif begins to emerge. On the subway an incident occurs between a roughneck sailor and his girl, and the man is tempted to intervene but does nothing. Other sights en route fill him with a sense of fear, and he feels condemned to a lonely isolation. When he reaches his room, he thinks of the imminent return of his wife Lydia. Had he come between the sailor and the girl, he might have been killed, and it had been the thought of Lydia returning to such a thing that had kept him from acting. His inability to act, and the "nameless terror" he feels, now become focused by the woman he married. The somewhat-vague romantic opening is followed by the sharper realism of his fear of Lydia in which Thurber discovers his true subject.

Another early story, "The Evening's at Seven" (1932), is also remarkably evocative. It opens with an unnamed man sitting alone in darkness. It is early evening and he is in his office lost in reflection. Before long he goes out into the street where it is raining, and darkness and rain are thereafter alluded to frequently with motiflike effect. What troubles the man is hinted at when a siren sounds somewhere and its frenzied scream makes him think of "anguish dying with the years." For reasons he claims not to understand, he takes a cab to the apartment of a woman with whom he had once been in love. The scene between them is Fitzgeraldian in its evocation of lost romance. As they talk, he is conscious of the rain outside, of the "soft darkness" of the room, and of "other rooms and other darknesses." Just as he is about to kiss her, however, her sister arrives and the moment is lost.

But it *has* been a romantic occasion and the man, when he arrives at his hotel for dinner at seven-thirty as always, obviously still feels the glow of his evening at "seven." In the dining room of the hotel, the waitress tells him that she believes his wife, the existence of whom has been withheld until this moment, will be down soon. "And the waitress," Thurber remarks in the last lines, "said clam chowder tonight, and consommé: you always take the clam chowder, ain't I right. No, he said, I'll take the consommé." The strain of romance and nostalgia in the tale, and the dominance in it of sentiment, suggest a direction that Thurber's fiction might have taken but did not.

"One Is a Wanderer" (1935), another story of loss, has the form of a sensitive atmospheric sketch. Written while Thurber was living apart from his wife Althea and staying at the Algonquin Hotel, it is as autobiographical as "Menaces in May." The protagonist, a writer named Kirk, lives apart from his wife in a New York hotel room where he leads a desultory existence, throwing his soiled shirts (as Thurber had done) on the floor of his closet and allowing them to pile up for months. On a dark, dank Sunday evening in February, he feels particularly at sea and is lost in the gloom of his thoughts. Not knowing what to do with himself on this Sunday evening, he walks the city's streets for five hours. When he at last returns to the hotel, he asks at the desk if there are any messages for him, but there is nothing. For a time he goes to his office, imagining that he can occupy himself by writing some letters, but he cannot concentrate and returns to the hotel through the slush and the "damp gloom." Seated in a lobby chair still wearing his overcoat, he has several brandies, but no one comes into the lobby that he knows. He thinks of calling on the Graysons, with whom he and his wife Lydia had once shared a vacation, but it would be awkward to see them, since their friends are all couples. "Two is company," he tells himself, "four is a party, three is a crowd. One is a wanderer."

Finally he goes to his room to rest, and after midnight takes a cab to a bar on Fifty-third Street, staying until three o'clock in the morning. On the way back to his hotel in a taxi, he talks to the driver, a man named Willie who has driven him before, and Willie tells him that it is good he is going home because home is the best place there is, after all. Returning to his room, which is hardly a home, he smokes a cigarette and begins to sing "Bye Bye Blackbird," the lyrics of which evoke an escape from woe that Kirk cannot achieve and that has everything to do with Lydia,

who has apparently left him, finding him "unbearable."
Kirk's evening describes a movement in circles, from the
hotel and back again, and then out and back to the room
that is as desolate as Kirk's single life. The story has many
finely muted effects, like the conversation Kirk holds with
the bartender George that is reminiscent of such downbeat
exchanges in Hemingway and Fitzgerald, but the final
effect of the story is that of a cry of pain.

"The Other Room" (1962) published posthumously in
Credos and Curios and one of the last stories Thurber wrote,
is autobiographical only obliquely. It is set in the bar of the
Hotel Continental in Paris and involves a set of Americans
who are staying in the city. When a compatriot of theirs
appears, a man named Bartlett whom they have never met
and is a friend of friends, he confides to them his early
experience of Paris—a story within the story. Bartlett had
been in the American army during World War I and been
wounded at Fère-en-Tardenois, one of the fiercest and
bloodiest engagements of the war. While at the base hospital, stricken with homesickness and disoriented by the
drugs he had been given, he had gone AWOL. In a hazy
mental state, he had found himself in Paris, where a
French girl took him to her small apartment. After going
into the other room to undress she calls to him, and
Bartlett is seized by panic. Young and inexperienced, from
a sheltered background in Cedar Rapids, Iowa, and in love
with a virtuous local girl of seventeen named Martha, he
flees from the apartment in a daze. MPs find him and
bring him back to the base hospital, but later he goes into a
"nose dive" and has experiences with prostitutes in Paris.
Later still, after recovering from his breakdown, he returns
to the US, marries the good Martha, and has ever since
been a faithful, conventional husband.

Bartlett's experience was not exactly Thurber's, since
he had never been in the army or wounded in France. But
he had known Paris as an inexperienced young man from
the Midwest at the same time as Bartlett; and he, too, had
had his sexual initiation there and had suffered a nervous

breakdown. The clash between a sheltered and provincial idealism and the reality of sex results in a never-quite-forgotten trauma for Bartlett, as it had apparently for Thurber. What is striking in Thurber, in many of the stories as well as in the drawings, is the traumatic nature of sexuality. A Midwestern puritan strain in Thurber constantly prevents him from confronting sexuality directly. There is hardly any direct responsiveness to the erotic in his stories, as there is, for example, in D. H. Lawrence, but rather a kind of backing away, a conversion of sexuality into grotesque parody or a deflection of it to a more cerebral concern with inner states of anxiety.

One finds a carefully achieved detachment in Thurber, even in his compassionate stories. "The Departure of Emma Inch" (1935), for example, has a tender texture yet Thurber preserves a distance between himself and the woman the story is about. The tale is narrated in the first person by a man who is apparently meant to be Thurber, since Emma Inch refers to him as "Mr. Thurman," one of the garbled versions of his name that people use in his humor sketches. He and his wife are about to leave New York to spend the summer at Martha's Vineyard and are in need of a cook. The only one they are able to find, recommended by a friend, is a peculiar woman named Emma Inch. She is middle-aged and featureless, and appears with a suitcase and a seventeen-year-old bull terrier named Feely who is all she has in the world. The old dog whines and sniffles, and is pitiful. After engaging Emma Inch, the narrator's wife spends a restless night, feeling vaguely uneasy about the woman and her peculiar dog. The next day they leave with the cook for Martha's Vineyard.

En route, many odd things come out about Emma Inch. They learn, for example, that she has not spent the night before at the hotel room they had arranged for her but with her landlady on the West Side. She has never in her life stayed at hotels, which are foreign to her and frighten her. For another, they learn in the cab taking them to the pier that she has never before been inside a car. Although she is reluctant to take the boat, they manage to get her and her dog aboard, but at the last connection to Martha's Vineyard she tells them that she must go back because Feely, who "talks" to her in low grumblings and snufflings, is ill. Even though she is at the end of Massachusetts, she plans to walk back to the city, a prospect that appalls the narrator but seems to make her happy. Obviously she will be returning to a sanctuary of the familiar, where she and the dog will be "safe." But it will be virtually no life at all. Her name "Inch" intimates her minimalness of identity and of place, but the dog's curious name "Feely" is also revealing, implying as it does an almost-total absence of intelligent thought or cognition. What is particularly disturbing about Emma Inch is her lack of relation to the world around her, so much so that her existence can hardly be imagined by the reader. By her departure, although she has been observed with a close realism, Emma Inch has a dreamlike quality.

Thurber's stories frequently employ a closed form. Even in the sketchy "One Is a Wanderer," the man's return in the dim hours to his room indicates the blank wall he faces in his life, and is a perfectly appropriate and revealing ending. But in "The Departure of Emma Inch," Thurber makes use of an open ending that coaxes the reader to imagine the unimaginable. A similar open-ended technique can be noticed in "The Wood Duck" (1936), a work of an extremely low-key realism in which very little actually happens. The narrator and his wife who live in the Connecticut countryside drive out to a roadside produce stand, and as they approach the building the narrator applies his brakes suddenly to avoid hitting a duck that has been walking about the driveway. It isn't a barnyard fowl, however, but a wild duck from the nearby woods that for some reason has loitered there for two weeks.

As the narrator asks a man who has pulled up in an old sedan about the duck, a car racing by strikes the wild duck, tossing it into the air. It lies on the concrete highway, stunned at first, and then struggles to its feet. At the same time the white setter in the truck of some hunters goes after the bird, pursuing it as it scrabbles lamely toward the woods. The hunters catch up with the dog and restrain him just as he is about to seize the duck, which flutters toward the woods, "going home." Yet later, when the narrator and his wife revisit the stand that day, they find that it has returned. At the end of the tale, the narrator's wife remarks that she is glad the duck has come back, hating to think of it "alone there out in the woods." Ironically, the wood duck is more truly endangered and out of its element in a man-made environment. But perhaps the key word is "alone." At the beginning, as it is seen on the driveway, the duck is "immensely solitary," and its solitude is emphasized by its belonging not quite one place nor yet another, making it a puzzling anomaly. With a power of suggestion, Thurber's open ending forces the reader to reflect on what placelessness means.

In "Teacher's Pet" (1949), the protagonist Kelby is not a solitary, being married and having a comfortable-enough suburban life. Yet all is not well with him. His wife drinks too much, and having just turned fifty he has begun to reflect on the painful sense of limitation and failure that comes to people in middle age. He is even seized by a moment of panic when he finds it difficult to breathe, and deeply repressed experiences break through into his consciousness. The painful memory of his childhood comes over him, for example, when he had been the smartest boy in school but a physical weakling, teased by other, stronger boys as a teacher's pet. The athletic Zeke Leonard had taunted him by calling him "Willber, dear," like his teacher; and twisted his arm behind his back until he sobbed and a crowd of other boys laughed and jeered.

When the Kelbys attend a cocktail party at the house of their neighbors, the Stevensons, Kelby notices irritably that the Stevenson son takes after his athletically built father. History repeating itself, young Bob Stevenson has taunted and harassed another boy named Elbert, who is

"terribly sensitive," the brightest boy in his school but frail
and unable to stand up to the other boys. One day after
the party, in a sulky mood, Kelby comes upon the Stevenson boy mocking Elbert by calling him "Ella." When he
begins attacking Elbert physically, Kelby intervenes and
drives him off. But when Elbert will not stop sniffling and
whimpering, Kelby shouts to him to "shut up." As Elbert
breaks into weeping, Kelby loses all rational control, shak-
ing and cuffing the boy and "sobbing" that he is a "god-
dam little coward." In the story's ironic ending, Mr. Reyn-
olds, who has witnessed the incident, tells Stevenson
what had occurred, and Stevenson remarks musingly that
you "never know about a man." They, of course, miss the
point for Kelby in attacking Elbert has struck out in helpless rage at a surrogate of himself. That his early trauma
has not, after all, been overcome in adulthood is implied in
the resentment he feels toward Stevenson, who makes
little jibes intimating his lack of manliness; and in his wife's
alcoholism, which gives an impression, although touched
upon only lightly, that she has perhaps found him an
inadequate husband.

Two other stories of the 1940s, "The Whip-Poor-Will"
(1941) and "A Friend to Alexander" (1942), involve trauma
that results in violence and come out of Thurber's personal
experience. Both were written shortly after the series of
eye operations that left him blind and in a state of nervous
collapse. In "The Whip-Poor-Will," no explanation is given
for Kinstrey's anguished state of mind. Unable to sleep, he
has somehow developed terrible fixations and begun to
hallucinate. As he lies awake restlessly, he hears the call of
a whippoorwill, the nocturnal bird whose singing by a
house was regarded in old folk wisdom as a harbinger of
death. His drowsing is troubled by dreams in which striking images and symbols appear and evoke his deep inner
disturbance. At times the images have a surrealistic
quality. Kinstrey is beset, for example, by trios of little
bearded men who roll hoops at him. He tries to climb up
onto a gigantic Ferris wheel whose swinging seats are

rumpled beds. A round policeman with wheels for feet rolls toward him shouting, "will power . . . whip-poor-will!" At other times the call of the whippoorwill becomes the sound of the fatal bell on the night of the murder in *Macbeth*. Poe is brought in, too, in a dream in which Kinstrey is attacked by an umbrella that, when clutched, clutches back and becomes a raven crying "nevermore." As Kinstrey wakes from one of these nightmares he leaps from his bed to the window, pounding on the window-pane and running the blind up and down, shouting and cursing. He becomes violent and incoherent.

Others in the house—his wife Madge, Margaret the cook, and Arthur the butler—all enter into Kinstrey's dreams. Madge appears as a little girl in pigtails and a playsuit who points a finger at him in a hospital room that is filled with "poor men in will chairs." One of the sick men is Arthur, who grinningly holds a pair of spectacles before Kinstrey, but at a distance so that he cannot grasp them. He is powerless even to move his arms or legs. Appearing as the umpire at a tennis match, his wife cries "whip him now." Kinstrey's feet are stuck in wet concrete, and the maid Margaret peers at him over the net, holding a skillet for a racquet. Arthur then pushes him down until the concrete covers his head, and his wife Madge laughs. Then in a sudden transition Kinstrey is in his pajamas in the kitchen removing a long, sharp bread knife from a drawer, muttering hoarsely, "Who do you do first?" In another transition, perplexed by what may have brought about such slaughter, the local police and state troopers are at the house grimly investigating the triple murder and suicide. At times Kinstrey's dreams seem perhaps too literary (do nightmare sufferers really dream of *Macbeth*?), but the intensity of his obsession is powerfully felt, and the story may be the more effective by leaving the cause of Kinstrey's despairing madness unspecified.

The unspecified crisis in Kinstrey's life is explained, however, by Thurber's experience of blindness and his terrifying anxiety that his creative life was imperiled. Martha's Vineyard, where Thurber recuperated from his operations, even provides the unnamed setting, the island where Kinstrey and his wife are summering. Thurber once told an interviewer that the story "came somewhere out of a grim fear in the back of my mind,"[1] but this grim fear is not difficult to pin down. The long, sharp knife Kinstrey uses to dispatch the others and himself seemed to Helen Thurber "a symbol for all the cutting Jamie had gone through that year. He thought he was being castrated with all that cutting."[2] Kinstrey's paralysis in the hospital dream, his inability to act, is linked with Arthur's holding out the pair of spectacles while keeping them out of reach. He is deprived of the power of "will" that would restore him to what he was before being overtaken by his terrible dreams, and his frustration finally turns into indiscriminate rage. His rage, however, seems directed principally against his wife. At the beginning he hears a "blind man tapping," while his wife screams, "Help! Police!" as if she knew she were the focus of his anger. Later in his dreams, she is his chief tormentor, and she laughs when he is buried alive in wet concrete. In this story, too, one has the impression of a male-female conflict at the deepest level of the hero's anguish.

Written only a year after "The Whip-Poor-Will," "A Friend to Alexander" also deals with neurotic obsession and recurring bizarre dreams. Henry (known as Harry) Andrews, an architect, begins dreaming every night of Alexander Hamilton. In one dream he is a witness to Aaron Burr's assassination of Hamilton in their famous duel, and in another is sneered at by Burr as a man of no account. Burr even threatens to give him a "taste" of his riding crop. Disturbed when he tells her of his dreams, his wife arranges for them to take a vacation in the country at the home of their friends the Crowleys. On their first day in the country, Crowley takes Harry out with him to shoot at targets, but while shooting becomes alarmed when Harry measures off paces, turns, and fires in his direction. At dawn the next morning, Mrs. Andrews is awakened by the sound of shots being fired beyond the house, and discovers that her husband has been out practicing for a duel "with Burr."

That day the couple leaves for the city, and Harry is examined by a doctor who finds him in perfect health. Yet on an evening soon after, Harry raves again about meeting Burr in a duel, and his wife feels a dark foreboding. The next morning he is found dead in his bed—of a heart attack. Strangely, the three fingers next to the index finger of his hand are stiffly closed on the palm as if gripping a pistol, and his index finger is curved slightly inward as though about to press the trigger. He has, as it were, been shot in the heart. On the surface at least, the story might have been written by Edgar Allan Poe or Ambrose Bierce. But Thurber has provided a Freudian explanation for Harry's behavior that searches into his subconscious conflicts. In a dream early in the tale, Harry looks into Hamilton's face to discover the face of his brother, killed by a drunkard in a cemetery. The moment of recognition is passed over quickly and is not referred to again, but its presence seems intended to suggest the neurotic sources of Harry's obsession. His unbearable guilt over his failure to have protected his brother turns into a desire to die, as Hamilton and his brother had died.

"A Friend to Alexander" is one of Thurber's slighter tales, rather too fantastic to be quite credible, but it is interesting in what it suggests of Thurber's psychology after losing his sight. His sense of guilt was very strikingly evident during his convalescence at Martha's Vineyard when, in a fit of weeping, he told Mark Van Doren that his blindness was a punishment upon him for having written meanly and mockingly of mankind. The idea of self-betrayal and self-punishment are also implied in the inner story of the tale and in its puzzling character configurations. Why, for example, should Harry develop a fixation with Alexander Hamilton in particular? And in recognizing his brother in Hamilton does he not also perhaps recognize himself? Hamilton died young, at forty-seven, the very age of Thurber when he lost his vision. Moreover, Hamilton had been at the height of his powers and of his professional life when he was struck down; and so, with a solid body of work behind him in the 1930s and the recent success on the Broadway stage of *The Male Animal*, had Thurber.

The inner story of "A Friend to Alexander" can be read as a parable of self-condemnation in which Thurber, or a character projection of him, is not only victim but also destroyer. In his fixation with meeting Burr in a duel that seems likely to lead to his death, in reenacting Hamilton's fate, Harry punishes himself for the baser and more unworthy part of himself represented by the drunkard in the cemetery and the brutal and meanly self-assertive Burr. Having an "unworthy" side to his nature and being "guilty" of having mocked humanity in his work, Thurber was possessed by the notion, at least for a time, that he had been responsible for his blindness, that he was being very properly punished. In "A Friend to Alexander," this idea is explored in a fictional situation in which a hero is obsessed by a sense of guilt associated with the destruction of a worthier self, and ultimately wills his own death. Thurber's fictional themes in the crisis of his blindness take diametrically opposing forms. In "The Whip-Poor-Will," Kinstrey projects his despairing aggression outwardly upon others, while in "A Friend to Alexander" Harry Andrews directs it inwardly upon himself.

Written during a great distress, "The Whip-Poor-Will" and "A Friend to Alexander" may be untypical of Thurber's stories to the point of aberration, but the use of dreams they employ is not. Obsession, dreams, and a dream sense are pervasive in his work. A dream sense is constantly evoked in his drawings, his reminiscences of Columbus, his reportage, and it appears in various ways in many of the stories just discussed, giving them a point in common. In "The Lady on 142," the hero dreams his capture by spies and as a dreamer is ultimately humiliated. "The Catbird Seat" has the quality of a dream fable, and so does

"The Greatest Man in the World." The midget Pearl du Monville turns "You Could Look It Up" into a bizarre dream, and the Hollywood house in "The Man Who Hated Moonbaum" has the nature of a waking dream. In "The Other Room," Bartlett is haunted by the dreamlike experience of his discovery of sex and nervous breakdown in Paris. Emma Inch comes out of a dream and goes back into another. The high incidence of dream structures in Thurber's fiction suggests a repudiation of conventional realism for a more "magical" confrontation of his characters' inmost fears and anxieties.

Yet in other stories Thurber writes without recourse to dreams and almost as a naturalist. "The Luck of Jad Peters" (1934), narrated in the first person by a man looking back to the time when he was a boy in Columbus, deals with an older man, the boy's uncle, who is delineated sharply through his dominant trait of braggadocio. The story opens with the narrator's recollections of his aunt Emma Peters, who before her death at eighty-three liked to attend funerals and look at corpses. In her parlor was a souvenir table containing a rough fragment of a rock weighing perhaps twenty pounds and a heavy-framed full-length photograph of her husband Jad, showing him wearing a hat and overcoat and carrying a suitcase. Later, the narrator had learned the story behind the photograph, the first in his collection of souvenirs that, to his own mind, certified him as having been selected by nature as a man bound to be lucky. On the occasion of the photograph he had just left his hotel in New York to board a ship going to Newport. A few minutes after he had checked out, a telegram arrived at the hotel advising that it was imperative he return home, and a boy was dispatched with the telegram to the dock, where the message was received and the ship sailed without him. Eight hours out of the harbor, it sank with the loss of everyone on board.

As the years passed, Peters bored everyone in his community by referring to himself as "lucky Jad Peters" and by his stories of close, providential escapes. In his later years he drank, let his farm run down, and barely scratched out a living. His wife, who had been compelled to listen to his boastful stories repeatedly, barely managed to endure her life with him. Then one day, after talking with a friend on the street, Jad had walked away, only to change his mind suddenly and begin walking back to where his friend was standing. At that moment he was blown against a building and killed by a rock sent flying by dynamiting going on nearby in the riverbed. The humor of the story, told in a loose-sleeved vernacular style, relies in part on a recollection of the opening. The fragment of the fatal rock set before the grandiosely enlarged photograph of Jad Peters is an ironic comment upon him by his spouse whom he had bored and depressed.

But the story also has a certain autobiographical interest. In *The Thurber Album* (1952), published eighteen years after the story, Thurber revealed that his grandfather, William M. Fisher, a remarkably self-important man, had had a large photograph of himself displayed prominently in his living room, together with a telegram advising him urgently to return to Columbus, received just as he was about to board an excursion steamer for Catawba Island that sank with the loss of everyone on board. The genial portrait of William M. Fisher in *The Thurber Album* is undermined devastatingly by "The Luck of Jad Peters," which if not a portrait of Fisher at least implies an antipathy toward him of some intensity. It exposes his self-centered nature and meanness of spirit that had oppressed his wife and members of the Thurber family.

"Doc Marlowe" (1935) is also set in Columbus in a bygone era and is narrated by a man looking back upon his youth. As a boy of eleven, the individual he had admired most was a Doc Marlowe, who sold a snake oil liniment and was a boarder at the rooming house of Mrs. Willoughby, a nurse in the narrator's family. On weekends, he visited at the house and came to know Marlowe, who fascinated him with his stories of having traveled with a medicine show in the wild West. Over the course of years he came to know him better and to learn the truth of his life. He learned that Marlowe, although capable of surprising altruism and generosity, was a charlatan who took advantage of people and cheated at cards. At the end when he is dying, Marlowe gives him a two-headed quarter with which he had won many coin tosses, a legacy that comments on the nature of life, in which the best and the worst, the admirable and the ignoble, are strangely intermingled.

Like "The Luck of Jad Peters," the story comes out of Thurber's own experience. There had actually been a man like Doc Marlowe whom Thurber met at the primitive rooming house of his aunt Margery Albright. How closely he resembled Doc Marlowe in the tale is impossible to know, but as he has been imagined, in any case, Marlowe is a rather unsettling figure. Although representing the wild West to the mind of the boy, he had originated in Brooklyn and had never been in the far West in his life. He had been the proprietor of a concession at Coney Island, a saloonkeeper, and a circus man. In his fifties, as a barker and hawker of a liniment for all ailments, he had traveled with a tent-show troupe that included a Professor Jones who played the banjo, and a Mexican named Chickalilli who threw knives. He comes out of a tradition of cheap American chicanery that Henry James had evoked in "Professor Fargo," and his presence in Columbus dispels many of the boy's earliest illusions of romance in life. The story deals with the necessary adjustment that must be made from the uninformed wonder of childhood to the troubling complexity of adult experience, but what lingers longest in one's mind is the dingy constriction of Marlowe's life, the atmosphere of physical and moral squalor that surrounds him. He makes Columbus seem stifling and ugly. At other points in his career, Thurber reveals an ambivalence toward his native city, which he celebrates as a carnival of eccentricity but at other times intimates as a seedy tragedy from which he can never recover.

Meanness of life or of outlook enters into a number of

Thurber's stories, especially those of the later period. "Everything Is Wild" (1932), a kind of extended vignette in which a man reveals his own selfish and unfeeling nature, could have been written by the early John O'Hara. "The Cane in the Corridor" (1943), which came out of Thurber's anger over Wolcott Gibbs's failure to visit him in the hospital during his eye operations, is bitter and vindictive. "A Friend of the Earth" (1949) concerns a cracker-barrel philosopher so cynical that the reader is more repelled than amused by him; and "Shake Hands with Birdey Doggett" (1953), about a vicious practical joker, goes further than Ring Lardner in making human nature seem apalling.

"The Case of Dimity Ann" (1952), a more complicated and psychological story, is unsettlingly morbid. It concerns a writer-researcher named Ridgeway who stays up all night drinking sullenly. His second wife attempts to humor him, but the revived memory of an episode from his past has begun to disturb him profoundly. While married to his first wife Lydia (the name for Althea Adams that Thurber had used in "Menaces in May" and "One Is a Wanderer"), he had tied up her cat Dimity Ann a "hundred times" with the cord from his dressing gown. Clearly the cat is a surrogate for Lydia, who is implied to have been unfaithful and to have excited an anger in Ridgeway so deep that even many years later he can hardly deal with it. Yet the story, unlike the sensitive and moving earlier ones involving Lydia, precludes any identification with the protagonist. Sheathed in neurosis, Ridgeway remains outside one's sympathy or understanding.

Several of Thurber's other stories that preclude reader identification with a central character are distinctive in deriving from or referring in some way to Henry James. "Something to Say" (1932), the earliest of them, is a grotesque version of James's story "The Coxon Fund," about a writer of brilliant intellectual gifts and with a genius for talk who has actually written very little. When one of his admirers settles a trust fund upon him, freeing him from the necessity of making a living, he ceases to write al-

together. Like James's Frank Saltram, Thurber's Elliot Vereker (whose name derives from that of the protagonist of
another James story "The Figure in the Carpet") is admired
by a circle of friends for having the true creative temperament. A writer-nonconformist, he sits up all night talking
and is notorious for his erratic behavior. His acquaintances
are awed by him as one of the truly original minds of his
generation, a man with "something to say," despite the
fact that his output consists of only twenty or thirty pages,
"most of them bearing the round stain of liquor glasses."
In the end, when they get up a purse that will enable him
to go to Europe, he squanders most of it in a drunken
spree that ends with his squalid death on a rooftop, his
head crushed by a blow from some heavy instrument,
"probably a bottle." Although usually considered a satire,
"Something to Say" is too dark to be really humorous. It is
both similar to "The Coxon Fund" and is not. "The Coxon
Fund" is genuinely satirical, a detached and ironic exploration of the mystery of the creative temperament as it is
revealed in the balked writer Saltram; but "Something to
Say" is concerned exclusively with the condition of the
balked writer as pure hell, with Vereker's incoherence and
guilty self-punishment.

"A Final Note on Chanda Bell" (1949), suggested by
James's story "The Figure in the Carpet," deals with a
female writer, reminiscent in some ways of Gertrude
Stein, whose enigmatic prose attracts a following of individuals from Greenwich Village. Her devotees include a
schoolteacher who has resigned from the human race to
become a bird and a Miss Menta, a nude Chilean transcen-
dentalist. The narrator purports to be Thurber himself, in
the role of a critic who has published an essay in a schol-
arly journal in which he claims to have found the underlying unity in the apparent meaninglessness of her writing.
He quickly becomes part of Chanda Bell's circle, and at her
apartment discovers that her conversation is as bewildering as her prose. She begins sentences in the middle, and
like Joyce in *Finnegan's Wake*, which Thurber had been

having his secretary read to him, is fond of surrogate words that are like "the words in dreams." She uses "rupture" for rapture, "pressure" for pleasure, and mistakes her attorney Charles Vayne for a certain Strephon, "a Jung mad I cussed in the Sprig."

The more the narrator comes to know Chanda Bell, the more it comes over him that he has been mistaken in his essay, that there is no underlying principle of order in her writing at all. Chanda Bell is herself his chief mocker. "You have found the figure, Thurber," she taunts him, "but have you found the carpet?" Before her death, like James, she burns all her personal papers, leaving behind only a cryptic message for him in her desk drawer—three carefully drawn squares, one inside the other, that have the form of a plinth or base for a statue. At the end, with trepidation, Thurber awaits the exposure of his essay before the entire literary world.

Unlike "The Figure in the Carpet," Thurber's story does not fulfill the expectations of satire. Its humor is strained and grotesque. "The Figure in the Carpet" involves not merely a critic's discovery of his self-deception after believing that he had possessed certainty but also a serious moral theme of the sin of egotism, of pride checked and punished, of cold logic shown to be insufficient as a measurement of life. Thurber's tale, on the other hand, reveals no moral sense whatever. A cynosure of the avant-garde, Chanda Bell proves to be spurious and incoherent, but no alternative standards have been implied within the story by which to measure her aberration. It is for this reason that the story is ineffective as satire, and that the reader does not know quite how to respond to it.

In "Something to Say," Elliot Vereker is no genius at all, only a tormented would-be writer with a decided urge toward self-destruction. In "A Final Note on Chanda Bell," Chanda Bell is probably crazy. The narrators who believe in them are at last disillusioned. The calling of art may be elevated and noble, but all that can be discovered by these narrators is ugliness and brutality (in Vereker's case) or mere deception (in Chanda Bell's). It is the narrators, finally, that "Something to Say" and "A Final Note on Chanda Bell" come to focus upon. Betrayed by their guides, they find themselves alone in incoherent worlds without a sustaining vision in which to believe.

In "The Interview," Thurber's final story on a Jamesian theme, incoherence appears again and is once more linked with fraudulence. The tale begins with a young reporter's appearing at the home of the novelist George Lockhorn to find him drinking in the afternoon. Having become ugly with seven highballs, Lockhorn raves strangely, asking the reporter if he has noticed that he is a "maniac" and telling him that he is the "loneliest" man in the United States. His anger is directed partly at his previous wives and partly at himself, as a writer who offers "spiritual hope" when there is none. His latest novel with the very Jamesian title *The Flaw in the Crystal*, which prompts the reporter's visit, has received unfavorable reviews, very likely because it lacks conviction.

But Lockhorn's morose state does not seem due to the unfavorable reviews, as his wife, attempting to smooth over the situation, claims. His bitter inner disturbance and alienation are the truths of his life that in his novels he has attempted to evade. In the earlier stories on Jamesian themes, Thurber portrayed narrators who, seeking access to the sanctuary of art, are betrayed by their guides; but in "The Interview" the guide-betrayer is James himself. Through Lockhorn, Thurber intimates that even in James art is a compensation for a failure of fulfillment in love and personal relationships. From his college years onward, Thurber was fascinated by James, by his psychological fineness and moral elevation. An idealistic strain existed in Thurber himself, an idealism longed for and partly believed in but always proving elusive and out of reach, thwarted by an incoherence in himself and in life. His series of stories on Jamesian themes of artists and writers are a kind of confrontation between Thurber and the admired James, with Thurber rejecting James as a false guide who can provide no escape from ugliness, isolation, and suffering.

"Something to Say," "A Final Note on Chanda Bell," and "The Interview" are not among Thurber's most successful stories, and might even be considered aberrations. Yet they do comment on Thurber's stories as a whole. A series of early stories, such as "Menaces in May" and "One Is a Wanderer," portray men having an autobiographical dimension who cannot handle personal-sexual relationships with women, and by the end, in their tremendous sense of isolation, become cries of pain. In the later Jamesian stories, art proves no redemption from inner suffering and incoherence, and the cry of a painful alienation can be heard in them again. In between these earlier and later stories are tales of a great many different kinds. Yet all have in common a sense of the distance between people, of life as a mystery that yields no answers and offers no security to the individual whose fate it is to be alone, to be among the estranged ones.

5

Portraiture and
Reminiscence:
From *My Life and Hard
Times*
to *The Years with Ross*

Thurber's famous reminiscences of his eccentric family
and early years in Columbus begin with *My Life and Hard
Times* (1933), one of the most strikingly original books
published in America in the 1930s. It is made up of a series
of sketches of a humorous nature in which one is introduced to a Thurberesque anarchy. The sketches purport to
be factual transcriptions of personalities and events of his
youth but have been drawn so "imaginatively" that they
have the effect, in Malcolm Cowley's phrase, of a "dream
book."[1]

The events of the opening sketch, "The Night the Bed
Fell," take place in the middle of the night, and give the
sense of having been dreamed. They are set in motion by a
small deviation from the normal routines of the Thurber
family house. The grandfather (who lives in the past and
believes that the Civil War is still being waged, yet has
moments of perfect lucidity) is briefly absent from the
house, and Thurber's father decides to sleep in the old
man's bed in the attic. His doing so is a whim, there being
no reason for it at all other than as a "chance to think."
Mrs. Thurber fears that the ancient bed is so wobbly that

its heavy headboard may fall on her husband and kill him, but despite dreadful presentiments does not interfere. To clarify what occurred, Thurber first reviews the bedroom arrangements on that particular evening and the various family members involved. Mrs. Thurber slept in her accustomed bedroom, and his brothers "Herman" (who often sings "Marching through Georgia" in his sleep) and "Roy" in theirs. Thurber occupied a bedroom across the corridor from Roy's with his visiting cousin Briggs Beall, who suffers from the fixation that if he falls asleep he will stop breathing, and keeps a glass of spirits of camphor on his bed-stand to save him from suffocating. The army cot on which Thurber sleeps has extensions on either side, and from the edge of one of them, while tossing in his sleep at two o'clock in the morning, he falls onto the floor with a loud crash, setting off a series of nocturnal alarms.

Awakened by the noise, Mrs. Thurber instantly concludes that the bed in the attic has fallen on her husband and calls out in panic. Hearing her, Briggs Beall awakens with a start and believes that he is suffocating. Gulping down the glass of camphor that merely excites his terror further, he gropes his way across the room gasping for breath and smashes the glass of an "open" window. Aroused by Beall's cries, and enveloped in darkness by the cot that has collapsed on top of him, Thurber believes, terrifyingly, that he is entombed in a mine. By then Mrs. Thurber has aroused the other sons from their sleep, but as brother Roy rushes out of his room into the darkness of the corridor he is attacked by the family dog Rex, who mistakes him for an intruder. The clamor increasing, the father awakens in the attic and assuming that the house is on fire cries, "I'm coming." Hearing his words, Mrs. Thurber mistakenly believes that he is calling to his maker on the point of death, and hurries up the stairs to the attic in full cry. Eventually order is restored, the various misunderstandings are sorted out, and the "normal" life of the Thurber family is reestablished.

The humor of "The Night the Bed Fell" (in which the

bed did *not* fall) depends in part on the discrepancy between Thurber's poker-faced and purportedly factual narration and the wildly improbable events described. No one in the Thurber house acts sanely. When the mother hears a loud noise in the night she immediately infers, without pausing to entertain any other explanation, that the bed has fallen on her husband. Hearing her call out, Briggs Beall assumes self-centeredly that her alarms concern him and that he is dying. The members of the family are divided not only by the separate rooms they occupy but also and more importantly by their inability to communicate intelligibly with one another. In one way or another they are afflicted with inner tension or stress that must be coped with separately; when they attempt to make contact with others in their distress they merely spread confusion. Normality is at last restored, but apparently only for the moment since their underlying anxieties remain.

If the events did not occur literally as Thurber claims, the story does reveal the Thurbers as a family unit. Ironically, the source of the confusion can be traced to the father, the sanest member of the household. In withdrawing from the others "to think," he asserts the possibility of establishing order and reason within the family. The mother, however, obeying her unreasoning instincts, will not permit this, and it is she more than anyone who directs the chaos that leads to the father's "fall" from reason, his return to the lower level of the house. Interestingly, too, the father is the most passive figure in the story, just as his wife is the most active. None of the male members of the house, in fact, is capable of affirming a masculine principle of order and control over life. The father is quickly brought down from his attic sanctuary, Briggs Beall is barely sane, and the boys flounder in a household without a strong masculine head.

In "The Night the Ghost Got In," the family is again thrown into outrageous confusion. At one o'clock in the morning Thurber hears noises from the floor below, and going to the head of the stairs looks down into the dim dining room, where he hears the sound of footsteps (floor-boards creaking rhythmically) as of a man pacing, but where no one can be seen. He awakens his brother "Herman" and when they go together to the landing they hear the mysterious footsteps sound on the stairs toward them. In terror Herman flees to his room and Thurber slams the stairway door, pressing his knee against it to keep out the ghostly intruder. When he opens it again the footsteps have ceased, but in the meantime the mother, aroused from sleep and hearing of the footsteps below, concludes that burglars have entered their house. Realizing that since the telephone is downstairs she cannot call the police, she flings open a window, throws a shoe through a neighbor's window and calls out that there are burglars. Believing that the burglars are in *his* house, the neighbor is thrown into a state of terror. When Mrs. Thurber at last makes him understand that the burglars are in *her* house, he calls the police, who arrive immediately in a caravan of cars and motorcycles, followed by a car full of reporters.

When no one responds to their banging, the policemen break down the door of the house and enter waving flashlights. They are stylized policemen, Keystone Cops who belong to farce and speak in a semiliterate vernacular. One of them tells the others that the lady upstairs is "historical," when he means hysterical, and Thurber, who has only a towel wrapped around him, is described as "nekked." The grandfather now enters into the bedlam. Aroused from his sleep he cries out in the attic, which the police then besiege and break into. The old man, convinced that the men in blue are deserters from the Union Army, calls them "cowardly dogs" and attacks them. Seizing a policeman's pistol from its holster, he fires several shots into the air, winging one of the men in the arm. As reporters enter the house, Thurber, snatching an article of clothing hurriedly to cover his nakedness, appears before them wearing his mother's blouse and the confusion is increased. The next morning at breakfast the grandfather, now perfectly lucid, asks what all the clamor had been about, and the events of the previous night seem wholly unreal.

The story's humor thrives on the frenetic disorder of Marx Brothers films, and seems influenced by or is at least comparable to the ludicrous confusion of comic strips. The breaking into the house of the flashlight-waving policemen, their discovery of Thurber draped in a towel on the second floor, the mayhem in the attic—all these things can be visualized graphically in a series of cartoon panels. On a more psychological level, the story comments again on the nature of the family. The father is absent on a trip to Indianapolis, and the male figure nominally in charge is the grandfather, whose grasp on reality is tenuous and delusional. Nor are there other male authority figures who can be taken seriously. The policemen are moronic. Standing at the center of the confusion and relishing her role in it is the Thurber mother who, after breaking one of her neighbor's windows with a shoe, feels so exhilarated that she has to be restrained from throwing the other. Perhaps the most revealing moment of the story occurs when Thurber comes before the reporters to explain himself wearing his mother's blouse. Deprived of a sense of masculine authority, he can identify only with the mother and her anarchic impulses. His psychosexual confusion is a concise epitome of the tensions of the story.

Other pieces in the collection confirm that the Thurbers and their Columbus neighbors are loonies marginally functioning in a pre–World War I world that lacks social cohesion. "The Car We Had to Push" reveals the father as ineffectual—unskillful in driving automobiles and the butt of his son's practical jokes. Their old Reo runs poorly at best and in a spectacular incident is struck and sent flying into the air by a trolley, but the car is merely symptomatic of a more encompassing theme of breakdown. A neighbor called the "Get Ready Man," inspired by the father of one of Thurber's school friends, rides about in an automobile with a megaphone, calling out that the "WORRLD" is coming to an end. In a climactic episode he arises from his seat in the balcony of a local theater where *King Lear* is being performed, and his doomsday cries mingle with the tragic ravings of Lear on the heath and the direful croakings of Edgar and the Fool.

In other pieces the Thurber relatives and servants are evoked with an extreme grotesquerie. Aunt Sarah Shoaf is obsessed by the fear that burglars will get into her house and blow chloroform under her bedroom door through a tube. Another member of the vast Thurber matriarchy believes that electricity is leaking through empty sockets when light switches are left on, and Thurber's mother is fearful that the Victrola will blow up. The procession of servants who live with them, and come and go in the course of time, includes a Dora Gedd, who shoots her lover in the house one night while shouting lines from Shakespeare, and Mrs. Doody, a religious zealot who becomes convinced that Mr. Thurber is the Antichrist. Thurber is surrounded by women, by countless aunts and live-in servants, and comes to share their disordered sense of reality.

In the extraordinary piece "The Day the Dam Broke," Thurber moves beyond the family house to envision a scene of mass hysteria. A serious flood did occur in the West Side of Columbus in 1913, but the East Side, where the Thurbers lived and the panic occurred, was in no danger whatever. In the commercial district of High Street, Thurber would have one believe, someone late for an appointment suddenly begins to run, and then several others start running also. A loud mumble crystallizes into the word "dam," and a cry goes up that the "dam has broke." Two thousand people are abruptly in full flight. Hundreds of citizens hurry past the Thurber house screaming "Go east!," and soon the Thurbers are running for their lives. The grandfather at first believes that Forrest's cavalry is in retreat and rushes into the street exhorting the men to stand off the "Rebel dogs"; yet before long he, too, grasps that the dam has broken and roars, "Go east!" in his powerful voice. Seizing a small child under one arm and a slight, clerkish man under the other, he plunges forward with the mob.

In his evocation of mass hysteria, Thurber uses what might be called a sweeping panoramic lens, moving from one scene of mayhem to another. In one of the most comic scenes Aunt Edith Taylor is playing the piano at a silent movie theater when a man in the audience, hearing the sound of running feet outside, gets up and leaves abruptly, and is followed by several others. A woman cries, "Fire!" and starts a stampede, while Aunt Edith Taylor continues to pound the keys of her piano. In incident after incident authority figures are overthrown. Militiamen ride about in trucks and shout through megaphones that the dam has *not* broken, but are understood to say that the dam has *now* broken, increasing the panic. A little girl arouses a lieutenant colonel of infantry who has been sleeping on his front porch with her cry of "Go east!," and he instantly joins the runners roaring that the dam has broken and summoning hundreds of others from their shops, living rooms, and garages. A venerable, white-bearded doctor having an absurd resemblance to Robert Browning adds to the chorus of fear-stricken cries. Surging masses sweep below the statues of Sherman, Stanton, Grant, and Sheridan who look down at the spectacle with "cold unconcern." Those who speak for established order become disoriented and history blurs into unreality as the incidents escalate into almost surreal fantasy. In a certain respect "The Day the Dam Broke" can be compared to Thurber's series of drawings "The War between Men and Women," composed at approximately the same time. It has its exhilarated abandonment to the irrational, its strange merging of the real and the hallucinatory.

Charles Holmes has remarked that *My Life and Hard Times* illustrates Thurber's conviction that disorder and confusion are "sources of possible liberation." "The major themes of his earlier work," he remarks, "cluster around the conflict between the individual (free, spontaneous, eccentric) and the system (ordered, repressive, con-

ventional). His view of life is romantic, liberal, optimistic."[2] Yet before concluding that Thurber's view can
be summarized as romantic and optimistic, one ought to
consider the later pieces dealing with his experience at the
university. In "University Days" and "Draft Board Nights,"
Thurber moves further out into the world yet finds no
relief from absurdity, only a confirmation of it. He is required to take courses in botany and economics that are
incomprehensible to him, and to participate in the com-
pulsory two years of military drill, for which he has no
aptitude. World War I is then in progress but the under-
graduates train with old Springfield rifles and execute
Civil War tactics. The most maladroit of the trainees,
Thurber is made to repeat military drill year after year, and
is finally called into the office of the superintendent of
training, old General Littlefield. When he appears at his
office, Littlefield does not remember who he is or why he
has sent for him. He swats flies, stares at him absently, and
seems almost comatose.

In "Draft Board Nights," Thurber is ordered almost
every week to report for a medical examination by his draft
board. His vision disqualifies him from conscription, yet
orders to report for a physical keep arriving in the mail. At
perhaps the tenth one he picks up a stethoscope, takes a
place in the line of medical examiners, and is accepted by
the doctors without question as a colleague. After four
months of acting as a medical examiner, he decides to
resume his role as one of those to be examined, but when
he does none of the doctors recognizes him as a former
colleague. His examinations at the draft board end anti-
climactically and absurdly with the blowing of whistles
and ringing of bells throughout the city, announcing the
armistice.

An incident near the end of the book is particularly
revealing. Thurber goes to work as a publicity agent for an
amusement park, the manager of which is a prankster and
probably certifiable as a lunatic. He persuades Thurber to
join him on a roller-coaster, and only when Thurber is in

the gondola with him, catapulting up a sixty-degree arch and looping headlong into space does he learn that the man knows nothing of how to operate the ride. Although the wild ride eventually ends safely, it remains with Thurber in his dreams as terror and trauma that he can never dispel. The roller-coaster incident could not have happened, if it happened at all, when Thurber says it does. He had been a publicity agent for a Columbus amusement park not before the war but after coming back from France and working on the *Columbus Dispatch* in the early 1920s. But symbolically the incident is true. It sums up Thurber's coming of age in Columbus as being wildly disordered. Presumably an autobiographical account of adolescence and early manhood would show the writer's formation, but *My Life and Hard Times* reveals the experience as being merely incoherent. The book is immensely jovial, but its implications of thwarting cannot be overlooked, and are emphasized by Thurber in his preface and concluding note. In the preface he speaks of the humorist's invention as having been set in motion by "the damp hand of melancholy," and in the note points out that there can be "no escape," even for those with the most settled lives, from the raw intrusion of the irrational.

Holmes views the book as a celebration of idiosyncrasy and individuality, but he fails to note its pessimistic implications. Thurber does indeed revel in eccentricity and anarchy that give a sense of release or freedom, but the disorder of his formative years also leaves him maimed and estranged. The symbolic roller-coaster ride results in lasting scars, and the implication of the book generally is that Thurber cannot come of age. The Thurber father does not adequately embody any principle of masculine authority that might guide him, and other male authority figures fail him throughout the work. In the mayhem of "The Night the Ghost Got In," Thurber puts on his mother's blouse, an incident that is more than merely comic, implying a disorientation of personal and sexual identity. He does not go off to war like more virile young

men but is held back in Columbus to experience confusion
and maladjustment. The maiming theme, which has been
linked with a repudiation of the idea of order in life and
with a sense of the individual's isolation, gives Thurber a
certain affinity with Hemingway who, in fact, was an
ardent admirer of *My Life and Hard Times*. Thurber's sense
of absurdity and isolation is so radical, moreover, as to
give the book, despite its having been set back in time to
the earlier part of the century, a relevance to the mid-
Depression when the book was written. It is filled with a
pervasive anxiety and sense of imminent breakdown—the
breakdown of the family, of the larger social fabric, and of
the individual's identity.

In the period shortly after *My Life and Hard Times* was
published, Thurber was drawn back to his Columbus past
in other reminiscent pieces that include "A Portrait of Aunt
Ida" (1934) and "I Went to Sullivant" (1935). "A Portrait of
Aunt Ida" is delightfully droll in its portrayal of another
eccentric female relative. Ida Clemmens is almost preter-
naturally suspicious of catastrophes of national or international importance, and is certain there is something that
officials have concealed in the sinking of the *Titanic*. She
also harbors grave suspicions that the ostensible solution
of famous crimes are merely cover-ups by powerful interests operating out of public sight. Aunt Ida has prophetic
dreams in which tall faceless women in black veils and
gloves pass through a row of cemetery tombstones, and is
unshaken in her confidence of being able to foresee the
future even though her predictions come true only 50
percent of the time. In her last years (she lived to be
ninety-one), she dabbled in astrology, the theory of rein-
carnation, and the New Thought. Believing herself to be
hardheaded in her distrust of what has been officially
explained, she is shown finally to be ridiculously cred-
ulous. One of the finest features of the portrait is that
Thurber never intrudes to make any direct comment upon
her, allowing the reader to discover her curious nature and
estrangement from reality.

"A Portrait of Aunt Ida" has a wry geniality, but "I Went to Sullivant" is more tonally complex, both more exuberant in its humor and more disturbing. It begins with Thurber's noticing privileged boys boarding a bus for a private school, which causes him to reflect on the "tough" public school he attended in Columbus. At the Sullivant School fourth graders, held back year after year, were sometimes eighteen, and one pupil in the fifth grade was twenty-two and had a mustache. Their baseball team's road season, according to Thurber, was called off when their first baseman crowned the umpire with a bat during an altercation over a called strike, and a fight broke out that spread through the business section of the town and lasted for hours. As the sketch progresses, it becomes ever more preposterous. One of the largest and most formidable of the fourth graders, for example, is a black boy named Floyd who wears a pair of long gloves the year round. He becomes the protector of Thurber, a studious boy who knew "how many continents there were and whether or not the sun was inhabited."

Floyd's most serious rival was another black boy named Dick Peterson, who held a mandolin, his most prized possession, in one hand while fighting boys of his size with the other. Fights seem to have been the chief staple of life at Sullivant. They rage "for no reason at all" at street corners, in winter with snowballs and iceballs and in other seasons with fists, brickbats, and clubs. Dick Peterson is always in the vanguard, his mandolin in one hand, the other hand flailing, and he is captain of Sullivant's undefeated baseball team. In a final sentence, however, Thurber remarks abruptly that in the sixth grade Dick Peterson was killed in a barroom brawl. As with many of Thurber's reminiscences, it is hard to know how much of "I Went to Sullivant" is factual and how much imaginary, an ambiguousness that reinforces the dreamlike sense of the account.

It is dreamlike surely that fourth graders should be grown men, and that their experience at Sullivant should consist largely of irrational violence. The members of the baseball team are gigantic for their grade to the point of freakishness, and grotesqueness is evoked in various ways in the piece. It is weird, for example, that Floyd should wear long, furry, elbow-length gloves even in warm weather, and that Dick Peterson's "education" at Sullivant should culminate in his barroom death. Thurber says very little of himself, leaving one merely to imagine what a scarring experience his years at Sullivant must have been like. One notes, however, that no one in the sketch has any sense of coherent identity. The mandolin Dick Peterson carries incongruously in one hand might suggest sensitivity, or romance and love, yet he is immersed in brutality that is senseless and takes his life. Floyd is without identity, too; no one at the school is even sure if Floyd is his first or last name. What coherent sense of self could Thurber possibly have acquired from such an early experience that is at once so comic and so horrible?

Thurber did not attempt another book-length treatment of his Ohio background until the early 1950s, when he published *The Thurber Album* (1952), a collection of mellow profiles of his ancestors, family, and early associations in Columbus. With a single exception, the pieces first appeared in the *New Yorker*, and they have the witty, sharply drawn quality characteristic of *New Yorker* reportage. The first, "Time Exposure," introduces the reader to several forebears in what Thurber seems bent upon establishing as the most eccentric family in America. Judge Stacy Taylor, on his mother's side, was a sturdy pioneer who became a man of substance and prominence in his area, but two of his third wife's relatives are wildly peculiar. Dr. Beall, a homeopath, wore the same spike-tailed coat, striped trousers, and black bow tie from youth until old age; and when removing his plug hat his thick white hair would always stand up on end. He smoked cigars in bed, frequently setting himself on fire. His sister, Mary Van York, slept with a pet snake, and during her lifetime of ninety-three years smoked a rough estimate of two hundred thousand pipefuls of Star plug tobacco.

In "Adam's Anvil," Thurber recounts the life of his maternal great-grandfather Jacob Fisher, another pioneer in Ohio, and a man noted for his prodigious strength. It was not unusual for him, for instance, to pick up horses in his blacksmith shop to move them from place to place. A man of ardently held if not always logical views, he thrashed men who supported the policies of Andrew Jackson and then nursed them, forgivingly, back to health. Another chapter, "Man with a Rose," is devoted to one of Jacob's sons, Thurber's maternal grandfather William M. Fisher, who owned a thriving business establishment in downtown Columbus. Consummately odd, he went about with a red rose clamped between his teeth that he had capped in gold, and when he traveled always announced himself importantly as "William M. Fisher, of Columbus, Ohio." William Fisher's wife Katherine, known as "Aunt Kate," is the subject of another chapter, "Conversation Piece." The family philanthropist, she was constantly solicitous of her large flock of relatives, a number of whom were singularly odd. Aunt Fanny, for example, was plagued by recurring dreams in which she gave birth to Indian, Mexican, Chinese, and African twins.

Her oddity pales, however, beside that of Aunt Margery Albright in "Daguerreotype of a Lady." Short, round, and set close to the ground like a cabbage, Margery Albright had suffered an injury in her youth that left her partly crippled. One leg remained permanently twisted, so that she could not stand fully upright, and she swayed from side to side when she walked. In climbing the stairs of her primitive house, she had to grasp the banister with one hand and with the other pull her twisted leg up beside her good one. She took in boarders, some of whom (like "Doc Marlowe") were raffish, and nursed people to health with homemade herbal remedies. These early profiles, such as the one of Margery Albright, are realistically observed yet have a strange quality of distortion in their larger-than-life-size notation of idiosyncrasy. They have been written with a witty perfection of phrasing and love of the tall tale reminiscent of Mark Twain, to whom Thurber was constantly compared by critics.

Thurber's sketch of his father, in "Gentleman from Indiana," is relatively free of oddity. A dreamer who relished the Hoosier verses of James Whitcomb Riley, Charles Thurber had entered at an early age on a career at the organizational level of politics, but was out of place in the smoke-filled rooms where the realities of precinct politics were worked out. Believing in a selfless devotion to the ideal of good government, he was continually hopeful and continually disillusioned. Charles Thurber ran for office on two occasions, without being elected, and spent his working life in respectable but relatively modest posts as an administrative assistant to office holders. In his private life he was addicted to solving puzzles and entered thousands of contests, estimating the number of beans in an enormous jar, making up slogans, finding the hidden figures in drawings. Although Thurber does not quite say so, his father's puzzle-solving obsession seems an escape from a life in which he was not notably effectual.

"Mame" Thurber, in "Lavender with a Difference," gives the impression of being more energetic as well as more peculiar than her husband. She had originally wanted to go onto the stage, and in her married life reveled in high-spirited pranks and practical jokes. After filling the cellar with dogs of all descriptions, for example, she persuaded her aunt Mary Van York, who hated dogs, to open the cellar door. In the tumult that followed, the cries of the broom-wielding Aunt Mary and the barking of the multitude of dogs barely drowned out Mrs. Thurber's laughter. On another occasion "Mame" Thurber arrived in a wheelchair at a spiritual healing meeting, arising from it at a dramatic moment to declare that she was "cured." Her pranks continued, unabated, into old age.

Like the portrait of Margery Albright, however,

Thurber's sketch of his mother tends to be sentimentalized. He does not probe deeply into her character, and one has no way of knowing how she may have impressed a less-prejudiced observer. As snapshots from an album, the pieces are also unreliable. The portrait of William Fisher, for example, conceals the tensions that existed between him and the Thurbers. Thurber does not mention that his family actually lived at the Fisher mansion (where Fisher treated young Thurber cruelly) until they were apparently asked to leave. The good-natured sketch ends on Fisher's seventy-seventh birthday with the arrival of a photographer to take a group picture, William Fisher at the center, surrounded by his smiling offspring. The photograph is as deceptive as Thurber's portrait. His creation of the past generally gives the impression of a reality carefully shaded to bring out only those aspects of it that suit his purpose.

When Thurber turns to his associations in the city in the second half, the book begins to thin out and even to disintegrate. The profiles of several of his professors at Ohio State—Joseph Russell Taylor (who instilled in him a love of Henry James), William Graves (a bachelor with a naive devotion to his old fraternity), and Joseph Villiers Denney (dean of the college of liberal arts and a defender of academic freedom)—are written at too great a distance from their subjects. Thurber catches only certain surfaces of their lives, and one wonders how well he knew them or how affected he had been by them. The admiring profiles of Billy Ireland, cartoonist for the *Columbus Dispatch*, and Robert O. Ryder, editor and "paragrapher" for the *Ohio State Journal*, seem forced. The writing in this section seems aimless, and one keeps asking what is the point of all this?

The failure of the *Album* to come together can be explained partly by Thurber's ill health and despondent mood at the time. His thyroid condition had become acute, and his nerves were so frayed that he was barely able to write at all. Some years later he explained that "the

Album was a kind of escape—going back to the Middle West of the last century and the beginning of this, when there wasn't this [Cold War] fear and hysteria. I wanted to write the story of some solid American characters, more or less, as an example of how Americans started out and what they should go back to—to sanity and soundness."[3] But the "sounder" world of earlier-day Columbus seems merely self-deceiving, an escape from an unbearable present.

Other reminiscent pieces, written at various times, are concerned with France, where Thurber had lived just after World War I and at other times in the 1920s and 1930s. "The First Time I Saw Paris" (1957) is a splendid recollection of Paris at the moment of the Allied victory when a "kind of compulsive elation" overtook the city that "psychiatrists strive to cure." The freshness of its sense of scene is especially impressive in view of the fact that the sketch was written very late in Thurber's life. But of all the French reminiscences, perhaps the most haunting is "Remembrance of Things Past" (1936), about Thurber's stay at a farm in Normandy owned by a certain Madame Goriault. Madame Goriault is a magnificent French Thurber grotesque—a woman "possessed of an unforgettable toothiness," whose smile, under her "considerable mustache," is quick "and savage and frightening."

Under the impression that all Americans are rich, she believes ("was it not so?") that Thurber must carry a thousand dollars in his pockets for tobacco and odds and ends. "It was not too fantastic," Thurber remarks, to imagine her stealing into his room at night with a kitchen knife and a basket to pluck from him his thousand dollars and his life. Her English vocabulary is limited to a few key phrases, and in a lunatic way she takes great delight in repeating the phrases together—"I love you," "kiss me," "thousand dollars," "no," "yes." Her mercenary nature, and that of her daughter, who takes after her and will one day make some man "a miserable wife," are focused so sharply as to be almost frightening. Realistic as the piece is, it yet has the effect of a vividly remembered hypnotic dream.

The Years with Ross (1959), written at the end of Thurber's career, is partly an escape into the past, but it has more edge than the Album and obviously engaged Thurber more deeply. The death of Harold Ross in 1951 had marked a turning point in Thurber's relationship with the New Yorker, for although he continued to be published in the magazine he was no longer as dominant a presence in it as he had been and felt slighted by its new editors. In the book, he is able to reclaim the great days of his New Yorker prominence, a time when, working under Ross, he and White and Gibbs had set the tone of the magazine. In the Album, Thurber had been an annalist of the lives of others, but in The Years with Ross he is both observer and participant. Always highly competitive in his attitude toward others, Thurber enters into a partly adversarial relationship with Ross in which, although having to answer to him he enjoys the advantage of being able to see all through and around him. The result is a reminiscence highly charged with encounter and confrontation.

Thurber had begun writing about Ross, and exploring his possibilities as a "character," long before he began the memoir. A version of Ross, as Thurber acknowledges in the book, had appeared in his fairy tale The White Deer (1945) in the figure of King Clode, a gruff and harassed monarch who uses Ross's expressions. Even earlier, in 1943, Thurber began work on a play about Ross and the New Yorker that he struggled with, on and off, although without success, for the rest of his life. In the late 1950s he showed the manuscript of several hundred pages to Elliott Nugent, who discussed its various problems with him.[4] But they apparently could not be resolved, and the play was never completed. It enabled him, however, to begin to shape his conception of Ross as a "dramatic" character. Thurber observes at the beginning that Ross was "never conscious of his dramatic gestures, or his natural gift of theatrical speech. At times he seemed to be on stage, and you half expected the curtain to fall on such an agonized tagline as 'God, how I pity me!' " In passages of the memoir Ross disappears for a time, making one long for his reappearance as one might a favorite character in a play, and many of the incidents recounted have the nature of little dramatic "scenes."

Thurber was not alone in sensing Ross's potentialities for the stage. Wolcott Gibbs drew on him for the editor Dodd in his play *Season in the Sun*, which was presented on Broadway in the autumn of 1950. If there is any doubt that Dodd is meant to suggest Ross, it is dispelled by Gibbs's stage directions when Dodd first makes his appearance at Fire Island to beguile, bully, and coerce his defecting staff writer back to work for the magazine:

Dodd should really be played by Harold Ross of the *New Yorker*, but failing that, by an actor who could play Caliban or Mr. Hyde almost without assistance of makeup. He is a dark, untidy man almost continuously involved in maniacal gestures—sweeping his hand wildly through his upstanding hair, rattling what must be a gargantuan bunch of keys in his pants pocket, throwing his arms about to indicate his perpetual state of derision, amazement, and disgust with a world that seems to him wholly populated by astounding incompetents. The effect can really only be achieved by imitating the real Ross.[5]

Thurber was persuaded to do a series of pieces on Ross by the editors of the *Atlantic Monthly* in May 1957. The first appeared in the magazine's November 1957 issue, with additional installments published in each succeeding issue through August 1958. Although the *New Yorker* was less than enthusiastic about the project, it provided full cooperation, even supplying an office and secretary, and giving Thurber access to Ross's correspondence of thirty thousand letters. The pieces were begun in America and completed in England, where Thurber fleshed out the installments into book form.[6] The format of the book varies very little from its serialization. Rather than moving in chronological order from Ross's birth to his death, it creates his life through a series of graphic biographical essays that strive, as Thurber remarks in his foreword, for a unity of effect.

Thurber's format is not as unusual as it might seem, since other memoirs, installments of which first appeared serially in the *New Yorker*, employed the same method. S. N. Berhman's *Duveen* (1952), which Thurber refers to in the book and was the last manuscript on which Ross worked before his death, takes this form. A splendid work, *Duveen* gains tremendously in immediacy by entering at once into Joseph Duveen's career as the most successful and flamboyant of modern art dealers. Subsequent chapters focus upon his dealings with his millionaire clients (like the Morgans, Huntingtons, and Fricks) that bring out his self-confidence, craftiness, and powers of persuasion; and the final section relates his greatest triumphs achieved on the eve of his death. Like *The Years with Ross, Duveen* is anecdotal and brings its subject to life through the keen observation and wit of *New Yorker* reportage.

One of the most impressive features of *The Years with Ross* is that Thurber has captured Ross so hauntingly as a man and as a presence at the *New Yorker*. Whether anxiously avoiding others as he ascends an elevator alone to his office in the morning or bursting into staff writers' offices in a highly agitated state, he exerts an extraordinary hold over the minds of those who work for him. He is both "exhilarating and exasperating," a man of great inner restlessness and many-faceted moods. Obsessed by his work, Ross is married to the *New Yorker* and driven by a vision of it that he himself does not fully understand. Thurber describes him as walking along the street hunched slightly forward as if pressing against an invisible force, and the moment captures the dogged will with which he held the reins of the magazine, giving it its character and direction.

But Ross is striking, too, in his vulnerability, in the

surprising gaps that existed in his knowledge of the world and of literature. His lack of familiarity with literature, indeed, is one of the most startling features of the memoir. He appears in the doorway of the checking department, for example, to ask if Moby Dick is the man or the whale, and he has never heard of William Blake. An especially amusing moment occurs in the chapter in which Ross entertains H. L. Mencken at his Park Avenue apartment. When Mencken mentions Willa Cather, Ross attempts haltingly to place her, and asks if she had written *The Private Life of Helen of Troy*. Although unable to see Mencken's face, Thurber feels the puzzled quality of his silence and explains that Ross reads only what goes into the magazine, and has not read a novel since *The Riders of the Purple Sage*. Ross is marvelous in the way he defies any expectation or supposition of what the editor of the *New Yorker* might be like.

Self-contradiction in Ross appears throughout the book and is at the heart of Thurber's portrait of him. It is a deeply puzzling contradiction, for example, that Ross, who is like a bull in a china shop, should have been possessed by a vision of urbanity. The man who created the *New Yorker* was not even from New York but from the outback of Colorado. A reporter for western newspapers at a precocious age, Ross edited *Stars and Stripes* during World War I, and was later on the staff of the *American Legion Weekly*. This background, chiefly as the editor of publications for servicemen, was an unlikely training ground for his management of a magazine whose first issue proclaimed that it was not written "for the little old lady in Dubuque."

Although belonging to the Algonquin Roundtable, Ross was its least-worldly member. Largely uninformed of culture, he was constantly wary of being taken in by it as an editor. Where Ross was most at home was with a world of facts and details, verified several times over in what would become one of the most tenacious checking departments in American journalism. Ross's extraordinary attention to detail, however, placed unusual demands on his writers that resulted in a magazine style distinctive for its grace and clarity. Ross goaded his writers ceaselessly in the direction of excellence and ultimately, and ironically in view of his meager familiarity with literature, left an indelible imprint on modern American letters.

Self-contradiction is particularly evident in those sections where Thurber discusses Ross's male-oriented biases and male chauvinism. He often protested that he was surrounded at the office by "women and children," yet frequently seems helpless himself, especially before the threat of sexuality, which he would like to banish from the office. When he learns that human beings all have both male and female hormones in their systems, he becomes depressed comically by the thought of having female hormones in his body. His prudery at times is startling, as when he tells Thurber that a pair they know are "s-l-e-e-p-i-n-g" together. "He was the only man I have ever known," Thurber remarks, "who spelled euphemisms in front of adults."

The greatest blows to Ross's masculine ego, however, are dealt when his mother arrives from the far West on periodic visits. She regards and treats her middle-aged, thrice-married son as a growing young man who needs his rest, and reproaches him if he stays out later than eleven o'clock at night. Ross is so intimidated by the thrifty old lady that he conceals from her the cost of hotel rooms and dinners at New York restaurants, allowing her to believe that lunch at the Algonquin costs only fifty cents and dinner less than a dollar. Mrs. Ross is unimpressed that her son is editor of the *New Yorker,* which is not read back home, and hopes that he may better himself some day by working for the *Saturday Evening Post;* and she is so out of touch with modern life that when the telephone rings, associating the ringing with door bells, she hurries to a mirror and fluffs her hair before picking up the receiver. Yet Ross cowers before her judgments, and in one of the most comic moments of the narrative asks Thurber to find him a doily that looks as if it had been knitted by a man, having told his mother that his late appearances were due to his attending a men's sewing class that met late at night because its members worked during the day.

If Ross's portrait had been written by Edmund Wilson, he would undoubtedly have paid more attention to Ross's origins and, like Taine, have attempted to account for him through "race, milieu, and moment." In *Here at the New Yorker* (1975), Brendan Gill comments on Ross, whom he evidently disliked, from such a perspective. He observes that Ross's denigration of women and members of minority groups derived from the primitive bigotries of his Irish origins:

In matters of sex, Ross was a notably ignorant man, as well as a prude. (One of his wives confessed that she had never seen him naked; he came to bed in a nightgown.) He had been born in Aspen, Colorado, in 1892, at the flood-tide of Victorian puritanism, to a Protestant schoolteacher from Kansas and a Protestant immigrant from the north of Ireland, and the views of life with which they furnished his young mind were based on the suppositions of a far earlier time. Talking with Ross in the thirties or forties of this century, one had to remember that if the topic was sex, or black people, or Jews, or Catholics, his attitudes and much of his information had been the ugly commonplaces of almost a hundred years before. He was a throwback and not always an appealing one.[7]

Thurber's portrait of Ross, however, works entirely against any rationale that might explain him. He points out Ross's mania for system and order, and refers to an executive editor's belief that it was acquired in the army, with its bureaucratic maze of channels and memos, but concludes that it is hard to pin Ross down "with any label." Thurber's Ross is an enigma, a man of bewildering variability. In an irascible mood, his anger is dispelled suddenly by a Thurber jest. Firmly set in his opinions, he constantly changed his mind, adopting the very proposals that he had at first adamantly opposed. Niggardly in his payments to his writers, he was capable of surprising generosity, and spent many hours of his time attempting to advance their careers.

In an amusing passage, Thurber writes of having done an impersonation of Ross before a group of Ross's friends at Dorothy Parker's apartment. Ross calls him into his office shortly afterwards and demands to see the impersonation, while protesting that he cannot see what there is to impersonate. But even as he says this his face undergoes its startlingly rapid changes of expression and his hands fly nervously in the air. Ross is always captured as being at the mercy of his nerves, of an intense inner agitation that contributed to a serious case of ulcers and kept the offices of the *New Yorker* in uproar. He doted on creating a perfect system for keeping track of manuscripts and verifying facts that never worked to his satisfaction. When the least thing went wrong, he would cry, "The system's fallen down!" A good deal of the memoir is devoted to Ross's obsession with finding a perfect executive editor. For years executive editors came and went as Ross was at first extravagantly convinced that he had found the ideal man he was seeking, only to become disillusioned and renew his search. Ironically, in Thurber's view, his ideal executive editor had been under his own eyes all the while in Ralph Ingersoll, whom he lost needlessly to *Fortune*.

One of the chief ironies of the portrait is that Ross should have thought of himself as being virtually the only person at the *New Yorker* possessing common sense. In fact, Ross's lapses from sense were frequent and he was at times surprisingly gullible. He was a compulsive gambler who was unlucky at cards, and once lost twenty thousand dollars to Raoul Fleischman, the magazine's wealthy financial backer; and was so careless in his personal finances that he kept loose checks in his pants pocket and made them out as the need arose without keeping a record of them. In a chapter entitled "The Secret Life of Harold Winney," Thurber recounts how Ross's private secretary embezzled over seventy thousand dollars of his personal funds. With his cold voice, pale fingers, and way of moving about the corridors and offices "like a shadow," Winney was distinctly odd, yet Ross turned over to him complete control, with no safeguards whatever, of his bank accounts and securities, and in doing so put temptation in his way. Winney was an excellent forger, and since Ross had authorized him to act in his place his withdrawals at the banks were never questioned. Winney's secret life (which included heavy losses at the racetrack and expensive gifts to boyfriends) was as bizarre as Ross's confidence that he possessed exactly the right qualities of oversee his finances.

Thurber's feline observations of Ross contribute to a very meditated conception of him as a baffling personality, a man whose contradictions appear on almost every page. An energetic man, Ross suffered from a chronic sense of melancholy. The architect of the magazine's exacting prose style, he was unable to master the style himself. Obsessed by accuracy of detail, his own memos were frequently misspelled. One of the chapters is devoted to Ross's longtime friendship with Alexander Woollcott, with whom he worked on *Stars and Stripes* and later shared a communal apartment in New York. The section is rich in anecdotes about the collision of their very different temperaments and personalities, but what strikes one most is that this friendship of Ross's should have been incongruous.

The portrait of Ross is enlivened by the presence of Thurber as his adversarial friend, always conscious of his foibles. In some respects Thurber tends to exaggerate the role he played at the magazine (he had never been its managing editor as he mentions at one point), and he often places himself in a superior position to Ross as the more levelheaded of the two, even taking him aside to explain some elementary matter to him. A number of those close to Ross at the *New Yorker* were offended by Thurber's memoir when it appeared. William Shawn, Ross's successor at the magazine, did not acknowledge the copy of the book Thurber sent him, and the Whites became distant in their friendship with Thurber. The Whites, particularly, felt that the portrait invaded Ross's privacy, demeaned him, and made him seem clownish. Yet others at the magazine, including Wolcott Gibbs, who read the book in manuscript just before his death, found Thurber's portrait an effective evocation of the "real" Ross.

The memoir can be faulted in some respects. One feels especially that to have guided the *New Yorker* as skillfully as he did for twenty-six years Ross must have been a more inward and uniquely gifted man than Thurber has made him out to be. Yet his conception of Ross, even with what it leaves out, is a likeness that grips one's mind and lingers in one's imagination. Edmund Wilson remarked of *The Years with Ross* that both "as a literary portrait and a history of journalism, it will certainly become a classic,"[8] an assessment that seems just.

Yet a case can be made that *The Years with Ross* is less a biography in a strict sense than a work of the comic imagination. It highlights and emphasizes what it wishes to in order to create a Thurberesque vision of reason in conflict with the irrational. Thurber reveals one absurd contradiction in Ross and then another, until the reader is awed by such a profusion of the irrational in a man claiming to speak for common sense. In *Let Your Mind Alone!* and other early works, Thurber stressed the futility of achieving a rational adjustment to life or understanding of oneself; and at the end of his career, in *The Years with Ross*, he refocuses this theme through the *New Yorker*'s founding editor.

Obsessed by an ideal of his magazine, Ross is described by Thurber as "Sir Harold" in quest of the "Holy Grail"; yet he is constantly thwarted by the unreasonable, not only from without but also from within himself. As Ross's self-contradictions proliferate, the work takes on a quality of Thurberesque fantasy. Thurber alludes to Lewis Carroll's White Rabbit, and refers to Ross's frequent meetings to consider tearing down the office walls to attain the perfect running of the magazine as "Through the Looking

Glass conferences." As the editor of the *New Yorker*, Ross is astonishing, and he serves to underscore the bizarre nature of the actual that is pervasive in Thurber's other writing.

Although Ross appears in part as a kind of father figure to Thurber, they were about the same age—Ross thirty-four when Thurber came to work for the magazine and Thurber thirty-two. Curiously, a number of rather striking similarities existed between them. Thurber refers to Ross's nervous hands that were constantly in motion, but many of those who knew him have also remarked on Thurber's hands that were always flighty and restless. Thurber observes that Ross's was a case of "a truly severe Momism," but the role played by Ida Ross in his life is similar to that of "Mame" Thurber in his. In each case, as Thurber acknowledges, "it was the mother and not the father that dominated the scene." Both men, who were not originally from New York, were insecure in their relation to sexuality and to women. Ross complains that in woman-dominated America men cannot mature, remaining children all their lives, and he is evoked as such a case himself, as a Thurber child-man. The portrait becomes finally a Thurberization of Ross as a great eccentric, a figure belonging in Thurber's gallery of eccentrics. But in the many likenesses that come out between Ross and himself, Thurber gives the impression of commenting on himself as a baffled idealist *through* Ross.

As a comic performance with an underlying sense of fantasy, *The Years with Ross* has more in common with Thurber's other work than it might at first seem. His drawings, for example, depict a familiar middle-class world at the moment when commonsense and reality has begun to dissolve. His men with walnut heads and dots for eyes are comically distorted versions of actual citizens, but the distortion reveals them more fully, touching the heart of their condition, than a strictly literal representation of them could do. In the stories, Thurber's men are readily recognizable as white-collar functionaries, yet have a caricature quality in their extreme helplessness and isolation; are comically and "terribly" diminished by being set against a universe to which they cannot apply for solutions to their dilemmas. Thurber's reminiscent sketches and books have in common with the stories a use of distortion and unsettling caricature.

The Thurber family members in *My Life and Hard Times* are like cartoon characters, having been deprived of any control over their lives. Thurber has made no attempt to draw them realistically, since realism cannot bring out as fully the truth of their conditions. They are, instead, through a mocking exaggeration and removal of familiar systems of order, revealed in their inchoate inner states of anxiety. Through a fragmentation of coherence, Thurber creates the impression that identity itself is unknowable, that individuals must live with an inner chaos. The dreamlike aspect of *My Life and Hard Times* stresses the contradictions of the self, with incongruity replacing a daytime world of logic.

In *The Thurber Album*, the various ancestors and family members are drawn more realistically, yet the portrait subjects in the first and stronger half at least are also heightened in effect and made deliberately grotesque. In their idiosyncrasy, they are too large for the frame of a strict realism, belonging fully neither to normal reality nor to pure fantasy. In drawing these ancestors as he has done, Thurber also implies their legacy to him. Rather than providing an orderly tradition, they reveal intense psychological states and conditions involving fixations, phobias, and irrational anxieties. Thurber is different in this respect from Henry Adams who found a sense of order in the past that, even if this earlier order has begun to disintegrate, still provides him with a basic reference with which to define his identity. For Thurber, the past is anarchic and irrational, furnishing merely the ingredients of his dreamlike inner life.

The grotesqueness of the figures in "I Went to Sullivant" and "Remembrance of Things Past" is not due

merely to Thurber's love of oddity. They reflect upon
Thurber's own anxieties. In "I Went to Sullivant," the black
boy, Dick Peterson, asserts a masculinity that leaves young
Thurber alarmed and confused, and is linked with violence, irrationality, and death. In "Remembrance of Things
Past," Madame Goriault is imagined stealing into his room
at night with a sharp knife ostensibly to rob him, but one
would also think to castrate him. Madame Goriault's
daughter is a younger version of herself, and will one day
make some man "a miserable wife." One can only imagine
what the experience of marriage with her would be like.
For Thurber it would surely be filled with threat and fear.
Although about others, these reminiscences of Thurber's
become a way of saying something about himself.

   The Years with Ross is concerned centrally with Harold
Ross, yet Thurber has drawn him in such a way as to make
him mirror conflicts in himself. Ross's domination by his
mother, sexual fear, and ambivalence toward women all
have their counterpart in Thurber, who was approximately
Ross's age and had come out of a similarly repressed
background. Ross's obsession with his magazine and
Thurber's obsession with his art link them together as
high-strung men who do not confront life directly so much
as attempt to deal with it through an idealism that makes
them vulnerable. The emphasis of *The Years with Ross*, like
that of the other reminiscences, is upon the tensions of the
inner self as it struggles to know itself. In these portraits
and recollections, whether brief vignettes or of book
length, Thurber's allegiance is not to facts, which would
interest a biographer, but to the incongruities of dreamlike
experience that demand the attention of the poet.

6

Humor Pieces, Parodies, and Reportage

Thurber's humor pieces for the *New Yorker* begin rather hesitantly. Typical of them, although not written at the very beginning, are his humor essays, later collected in *Let Your Mind Alone!* (1937), that satirize the American success myth. In these sketches, Thurber attacks the assumptions of the many best-sellers of the day, ranging from Walter B. Pitkin's *The Secret of Happiness*[1] to David Seabury's books on "masterful adjustment," which promise the individual enlightenment and control over his destiny. Thurber's articles all follow the same pattern: the search for order is countered by the disorderly in life and in people. But the sketches consist of such foolery (in one, a man becomes embittered and leaves the city as the result of a prankster's interference in his life) that his case against the success myth is left largely unproved.

It is unproved but it underlies much of the later writing, which often questions the possibility of the individual's attaining either happiness or self-realization. In many cases, but especially at the beginning, Thurber is indebted to Benchley in the comic persona he adopts. A Benchleyesque persona, for example, can be noted in his sketch "The Gentleman Is Cold" (1935), in which Thurber is markedly unsure of himself, even in such matters as getting into his overcoat. His overcoat does not fit well and has recently lost its buttons so that when he walks in the wind, clutching his hat, it billows all around him. Because of the overcoat, he is repeatedly made a fool of in public. In the lobby of his hotel, when a doorman attempts to assist him with his coat, he falls back into the man's arms; and at a restaurant, when a waiter helps him into his coat, his arm becomes entangled ridiculously in the lining of the ripped left sleeve. Thurber is ineffectual in the piece, however, not only with coats. Looking into a mirror, he cannot recognize himself, seeing what appears to be a "slightly ill professor of botany," a man who is "lost." Like other men in his sketches, he has no firm identity and is unsure of his masculinity.

In several of the early pieces, Thurber resembles his fictional character Mr. Monroe. He goes into a sporting store, in "Suli Suli" (1936), to buy a javelin, but when the salesman looks at him skeptically becomes flustered and hastily concocts a story about wanting a *pair* of javelins to mount over his fireplace. Told by the salesman that they have no javelins in stock, Thurber retreats feeling unnerved and humiliated. In "Gun and Game Calls" (1936), he enters another establishment to enquire about the repair of his derringer—a small, rusty weapon that no longer works. But when the "muscular, keen-eyed" salesman, assuming that he wishes to buy a gun, asks him questions about firearms, Thurber becomes nervous, having no real knowledge of guns, and "creeps" away defeated. He seems defeated sexually, too, since the javelin and pistol that cause him such anxiety are striking phallic images.

In other sketches, Thurber is stripped of artistic as well as personal importance. "The Hiding Generation" (1936) recounts his supposed attempt to emulate Malcolm Cowley's *Exile's Return* by writing a book about his worldly experience and inner conflicts, only to recognize that nothing of any moment has ever happened to him and that he has nothing to say. "How to Write an Autobiography" (1937) is similarly anticlimactic. It begins with Thurber's noticing that the letters of left-wing writers, discussing the development of their intellectual lives, read as if carbon copies of them had been kept for publication. Unable to summon his faculties, Thurber is concerned instead with his feet. Passing out on a bed at a Village party, he awakens and leaves, wearing the shoes belonging to his host. Two sizes too small for him, they pinch his feet horribly, and for days he worries that his feet have swollen unaccountably.

In two pieces that imply a comparison of himself with Henry James, "The Letters of James Thurber" (1939) and "The Notebooks of James Thurber" (1949), he comes to recognize that the effect of his letters has been "nil" and that his notebooks contain only trivia. One of the most amusing of the early sketches is "My Memories of D. H. Lawrence" (1936), in which Thurber is denied distinction in his life even at second hand. Approaching "D. H. Lawrence" at a railway station in Italy, he discovers that the man is actually a George R. Hopkins, an admirer of Coolidge and owner of a paper factory in Fitchburg, Massachusetts. Later in New York, "Lawrence" calls him on the telephone, but he turns out to be a prankster friend and Thurber is again mocked in his effort to find importance in his life—or some link with Lawrentian passion. The humor of these pieces draws on the self-deflation and self-parody of Benchley, but more distantly they evolve from the influential cultural type in nineteenth-century literature of the superfluous man.

In other pieces, however, Thurber does acknowledge having an inner life that is at times quite vivid. It is not an orderly intellectual life but a disorderly imaginative one, heightened by his disabilities. "The kingdom of the partly blind," he writes in "The Admiral on the Wheel" (1936), "is a little like Oz . . . anything you can think of, and a lot you would never think of, can happen there." An electric welder, as Thurber sees him dimly, is a "radiant fool" setting off a skyrocket, and any number of other everyday sights draw him into an inner world of fantasy.

"Aisle Seats in the Mind" (1935) begins with Thurber's recalling Mary Pickford's criticism of salaciousness in films, the need (as she rather quaintly put it) to act as a "guardian" rather than an "usher" at the portal of one's thought. Thurber's reaction is that he is *all* usher to his thoughts, many of which are quite weird. When his black maid Margaret, for example, tells him that she is having trouble with the "doom-shaped" part of the refrigerator, he is no longer quite sure that he is living in the "real" world. The maid reappears in "The Gentleman in 916" (1941) when she writes to him that she had tried to see him at his house in December but was told by the "timekeeper" that he was in Florida. The thought of a "timekeeper" at his house, he relates, made his hair turn white overnight. "What Do You Mean It *Was* Brillig?" (1939) introduces another maid, Della, who has such a peculiar way of speaking (wreaths, for instance, become "reeves") that only "Lewis Carroll could have understood her completely." Her speech short-circuits the rational, compelling Thurber to live at the edge of fantasy.

In his reportage pieces written in France in the late 1930s, Thurber delights particularly in the sense of things seen askew. In "An Afternoon in Paris" (1937), he enjoys the contradictions between expectations of ambassadorial office and its realities. Contrary to popular belief, he notes, the American ambassador in France during World War I, except for the first few months, was not Myron Herrick but a William G. Sharp of Elyria, Ohio. Sharp's dispatches to the State Department were notoriously pedestrian and one, which reported that a shell had exploded in a street a few blocks from the chancellery and killed a white horse, became a joke of the foreign service. "La Grande Ville de Plaisir" (1937) deals with Nice as a setting of bizarre happenings and improbable people. While working there as a reporter for the international edition of the *Chicago Tribune*, Thurber had been present at the paper's office when a tall, sinister young Hindu appeared, claiming that he had been hired as a proofreader and demanding to begin work. When the editor told him that he had never hired him, the menacing Hindu declared that the editor was an impostor, the notorious dope fiend "lame-leg Charlie," and strode from the room, promising to return.

In the French sketches, Thurber finds his distinctive voice and one is no longer conscious of Benchley in the background. One of these, "A Ride with Olympy" (1938) is an illustration of the "madness" of Thurber's comic imagination. Staying with his wife at the Villa Tamisier at Cap d'Antibes, Thurber has a caretaker named Maria, a large, even-tempered woman whose first husband died at thirty-eight "of grief over poor investments," and whose present one is a Russian named Olympy Sementzoff. Olympy, who has the "wistful" air of the ancien régime, does not speak English and even his French is shaky. Although a poor driver and unfamiliar with Thurber's foreign-made car, he volunteers to drive him down a steep mountain road to town. They start off on what becomes a wild ride, Thurber shouting that they are going too fast, and Olympy unable to understand him. They graze an English couple about to cross the highway who stare back in astonishment, and speed on down the mountain pass, spinning around hairpin turns. Olympy does not know how to apply the brakes, but finally, after sideswiping a pole, the car comes to a halt, saving what is left of Thurber's sanity. The humor of the anarchic ride depends in part on the revelation of the helplessness of the two men, each ineffectual yet neither able to communicate with the other.

In "La Fleur Des Guides Francais" (1938), Thurber savors the incongruity and oddness of the *Guide Gastronomique International,* whose coverage of the United States places Chicago "100 miles south of Milwaukee" and misnames and mislocates chief restaurants in New York. The Hotel Blackstone, for example, is said to stand at the corner of Fiftieth Street and Fifty-eighth Street. But the disordered sense of reality in the *Guide Gastronomique International* is mild compared to that of the French dime novels about Buffalo Bill and Wild Bill Hickok described by Thurber in "Wild Bird Hickok and His Friends" (1937). In one of these novels, while hunting Seminoles in Florida, Buffalo Bill falls into a tiger trap set for him by Indians, exclaiming, "Mercy me!" He is rescued in the nick of time by his friend Wild Bill, sometimes however called Wild Bird, who, upon finding him in this predicament, cries, "My word!" In another novel, two strangers turn up in a small Western town arousing suspicion and the local sheriff buckles on his gun belt, remarking "*Alors, je vais demander ses cartes d'identité!*" At such moments the familiar American Western takes on an air of hallucination.

A farcical disordering of reality is a feature, too, of Thurber's early parodies. In "If Grant Had Been Drinking at Appomatox" (1930), for example, Thurber turns history on its head. The sketch begins on the morning of a beautiful day in April 1865, as General Ulysses S. Grant lies drunkenly asleep in his hammock, confidential notes from spies scuttling here and there in the breeze from an open window. When horses approach and Grant is awakened by an aid, he mutters "hoof steps" with a "curious chuckle." General Lee appears, his eyes taking in the disorder of the room disdainfully, and Grant mistakes him for the bearded poet Robert Browning. In the last line, his wits still addled by drink, Grant surrenders his sword to the astonished Lee. The final "frozen" moment does not detail the reactions of the others present but compels the reader to imagine them rather in the manner of the final panel of a comic strip.

"A Visit from Saint Nicholas,"[2] which appeared in the Christmas 1927 issue of the *New Yorker*, is a comic rendering of " 'Twas the Night before Christmas" in the form of a dramatic scene narrated by a husband in the laconic style and staccato sentences of Ernest Hemingway. It begins: "It was the night before Christmas. The house was very quiet. No creatures were stirring in the house. There weren't even any mice stirring." Before long Saint Nicholas appears on the rooftop and comes down through the chimney with a bundle of presents. His arrival is witnessed by the husband-narrator, who then quickly becomes embroiled in a domestic dispute in which he and his wife speak in the manner of Hemingway characters:

"What was it?" asked mamma. "Saint Nicholas?" She smiled.

"Yeah," I said.

She sighed and turned in the bed.

"I saw him," I said.

"Sure."

"I did see him."

"Sure you saw him."

"Recollections of Henry James" (1933),[3] a brilliant piece never collected in book form, is considerably more complex than the parody of Hemingway. It is written in part in long, involved sentences that mock the style of the late James, and has been imagined as a dramatic scene. Noting that almost every autobiography he has read lately has devoted a chapter to reminiscences or impressions of James, Thurber is prompted to write his own memories of the great man—without actually having met him. His recollections have the form of what might well have been: a literary gathering in a house in Edwardian England in which James, in his elaborately indirect style, relates the plot of the popular mystery play *The Bat*. The literati are all assembled for the occasion—Stephen Crane, Edmund Gosse, Hugh Walpole, Arnold Bennett, Ford Madox Ford, and Ezra Pound; but also present, incongruously, are such figures as Gene Tunney and "Doug and Mary Fairbanks."

James's relating of the plot of *The Bat* turns it into an excruciatingly subtle work with sensitive characters who question their own motivation until the plot and even the characters themselves begin to seem unreal. Joseph Conrad, cast as James's adoring disciple, is constantly awed by the Master's subtlety, exclaiming, "By God, there was never anything like this!" Complicating the parody, and played off in counterpoint to the main plot, is a second speaker, Joseph H. Choate, the American lawyer and Ambassador to the Court of St. James. He sits in a chair adjacent to James, and speaks at the same time James does. Choate's worldly anecdotes, however, are quite different from James's ruminations.

Choate recalls the time when he had been stranded without money in New Orleans and unable to think of any way to get back North. A black man named Sam tells him that he could steal a rowboat and be in Canada by "mawnin'," but Choate persuades Sam, falling ridiculously into Sam's dialect, to try the adventure himself. "Look heah, man," he tells him, "you-all proceed discreetly to de ribber jist she gittin duhk, and having selected a rowboat, get in an' row no'th; by mawnin' you-all absolutely certain to be in Canada." At dawn, Choate finds Sam by the dock still rowing but without having moved an inch, since the boat has not been untied from its mooring. When Choate calls to him, Sam cries: "Who knows me up heah?" Choate's comic story comments upon James himself, whose narrative involves only a delusion of forward motion. James and Choate complete their narratives at approximately the same time, and the gathering breaks up with Conrad, entranced by James's performance, exclaiming, "My God, there will never be anything like this again." Intricately constructed and outrageous, "Recollections of Henry James" is one of the finest of Thurber's early parodies.

Other parodies include "The Man Who Was Wetly" (1931), which spoofs the colonial tales of Kipling, but Thurber is at his best in "One More April" (1934), a parody of Galsworthy that reaches dizzying heights of absurdity. "One More April" begins on a transatlantic liner where three English people, strangers to one another, meet in the main dining saloon and play a game of piquet. With starchy English reserve they sit seven feet from the table so that, even with arms extended at full length, they are unable to lay their cards upon the table. In the course of conversation, in which they discuss English people who are related in an extremely complicated way, it comes out that the woman and younger man at the table are actually husband and wife and that the old man, who is between ninety-five and a hundred, is their cousin. The piece ends with the old man's sudden recognition that he has forgotten to put on his pants and that he is not Adrian Mont at all, as he had explained, but Adrian's brother Mark. His recognition comes at the culmination of an amnesia induced by Galsworthy's peculiar style in *The Forsyte Saga* that Thurber both mimics and parodies grotesquely.

A sense of the absurd is implicit, too, in Thurber's parodies of the mindless naturalism of James M. Cain in "Hell Only Breaks Loose Once" (1934) and of Erskine Caldwell in "Bateman Comes Home" (1936). The parody of Caldwell was a particular favorite of Thurber's, and had been rehearsed by him in recitations before friends before being committed to paper. Wolcott Gibbs, indeed, once observed that "people who have witnessed [Thurber's] interpretation of Jeeter Lester can have no doubt that they have seen great acting."[4] Written in the manner of *Tobacco Road*, "Bateman Comes Home" is a carnival of fantastic poor whites of the deep South—abnormal, mentally retarded, and morbid in their rural isolation.

The patriarch, Nate Birge, is shown at the beginning chewing a splinter of wood and watching the moon come up lazily out of the old cemetery, "in which nine of his daughters were lying, only two of whom were dead." He has gangrene in one foot, and still dreams of the day when his son Bateman, who went away in 1904, will return with a thousand dollars for his pappy. "Thuh hell with thut," cries his wife Elviry, grown understandably disillusioned. Instead of Bateman, Nate's sister Sairy, burdened with two heavy suitcases, appears with her young man, Ramsay, who smokes a cigarette and runs a pocket comb through his hair. No respecter of women, Ramsay tells Sairy to "shut yore trap before I slap it shut," and knocks old Elviry unconscious by striking her over the head with her skillet. Then Faith, one of Nate's daughters who is crazy and has just set fire to an auditorium, appears. Finally, Ben Turnip, a half-witted neighbor boy with double pneumonia, arrives and tells Nate that he is Bateman and has brought him a thousand dollars. "Glory gahd to Hallerlugie!" Nate exclaims wildly as the parody breaks off with Thurber's explanation that if continued a bit this material would make a novel.

The use of parody also enters into a group of reportage pieces about the once—often briefly—famous that Thurber wrote for the *New Yorker* in the 1930s under the general heading of "Where Are They Now?"[5] These often-overlooked pieces, written under the pseudonym Jared L. Manley, appeared in the magazine between 1936 and 1938, and consist of twenty-five separate profiles, only three of which have been collected in book form. "Invitation to Dinner" deals with Andrew Summers Rowan who carried the famous message to Garcia on the eve of the Spanish-American War. The exploit became the subject of an editorial in 1899 by an Elbert Hubbard, editor of a little monthly magazine in East Aurora, New York; and before long companies all over the country were requesting copies to inspire their employees to greater devotion to their work. By 1913, forty million copies had been ordered, and the exploit—Rowan summoned by President McKinley to the White House and his delivering a crucial message in an oilskin pouch to Garcia in the jungles of Cuba—had become part of American folklore.

As Thurber intimates, however, Rowan was an unlikely hero. A lieutenant upon his graduation from West Point, he was still a lieutenant at the age of forty. His single accomplishment was the publication of a rather "stiff and stodgy" book of maps and illustrations called *The Island of Cuba*, the material for which had been taken from other books. On the basis of this geography, Rowan was called to Washington twelve days before war was declared on Spain and dispatched to Cuba to meet with the insurgent Calixto Garcia y Inigues in the interior of the island. Rowan had never actually been to Cuba, but with the aid of guides was able to carry out his mission and to return safely to the mainland. But, as Thurber remarks, his completion of his mission was overshadowed "by the literary style and the burning business message of the sage of East Aurora." In fact, there had been no oilskin pouch containing a written message; there had been no message at all, only a verbal inquiry as to Garcia's needs (not surprisingly, Garcia said that he could use more rifles). President McKinley had never dispatched Rowan personally, and undoubtedly had never heard of him.

There were no further notable deeds in the career of Charles Summers Rowan. In 1908, at fifty-two, he took an early retirement from the army and lived quietly in San Francisco for years. In the 1920s, however, he was called out of obscurity to make inspirational speeches before Boys' Clubs and American Legion posts, and two Hollywood films that included an apocryphal romance between Rowan and a Cuban girl were made of his exploit. Washington honored him with the Distinguished Service Cross. The finest ironies, however, involve Garcia, who proved absolutely valueless to the American army. It would have been better for them, in fact, if he had not existed. Incensed by an American general's demand that he discipline his unruly followers, he allowed two thousand Spaniards to march through his lines to join the defenders of Santiago, and otherwise sat out the war. At the end of the war, Calixto Garcia y Inigues was included with Cuban generals invited to Washington to present their views on reconstruction to President McKinley, but died in his bed in Washington before meeting the president. He was buried with the military honors becoming a hero in Arlington National Cemetery. The undercutting of the heroic in this profile is reminiscent of Thurber's drawings of approximately the same time, "Famous Poems Illustrated," in which such figures as Lochinvar and the sad-eyed youth carrying the banner "Excelsior" to his death in the Alps are envisioned as being comically prosaic.

Many of the "Where Are They Now?" profiles are framed ironically by the contrast between early fame and anticlimactic aftermath. "Finnigin" treats the career of Stricklin Gillilan, a small-town editor and columnist who wrote up an anecdote about two Irishmen, "Finnigin to Flannigan," containing the phrase "off agin, on agin, gone agin Finnigin," that made him famous. For the rest of his life, on various lecture circuits, he recited the Irish anecdote several thousand times at least, yet never again wrote anything memorable. "The Banana Boys" deals with two young song writers, Irving Conn and Frank Silver, who composed a novelty song, "Yes, We Have No Bananas," that became an enormous popular success. In middle age, the two were still performing the number in a band but had failed to write anything else that was even moderately successful. The reader has the sense in these pieces of lives that have become diminished grotesquely.

Certain of the pieces, such as "Most Popular Personage," about Gertrude Ederle, are ironic to the point of cruelty. In 1926 Ederle became the first woman to swim the English Channel, and was welcomed back to New York with the wildest reception ever given in honor of anyone. A year later, however, she was driven into oblivion by the transatlantic flight of Lindbergh. For a time she did a tank act in vaudeville, but had to quit because of a nervous breakdown accompanied by deafness, and in 1933 was left an invalid by a fall. Thurber closes with a view of Ederle living, unmarried, with her family in the Bronx, a loving cup on a pedestal in a corner of the living room, presented to her at the time of her tumultuous reception in New York, "the year before Lindbergh," proclaiming her the "Most Popular Personage of Her Time."

But even in the gentler pieces, one has an impression of lives lived backward, from large to small. Reformers lose their audiences and live in ever narrower, shabbier, and more marginal rooms; child prodigies do not live up to their expectations, becoming neurotic misfits. The best of the profiles reveal Thurber's impressive gift for concise, idiosyncratic portraiture. "Izzy and Moe" relates the lives in tandem of Izzy Einstein and Moe Smith, the most famous prohibition enforcement officers in New York in the 1920s. Bulky men (Moe weighed 250 pounds) who dressed almost identically, they closed fifty to a hundred speak-easies a week, making all the papers and becoming so well known that they retired in 1925. The romance of their prohibition days did not follow them in their later lives. At the time the profile was written, both are salesmen for the same insurance company and belong to its "400 Club," as high-pressured go-getters who write $400,000 worth of business a year. Each has sold policies to at least half a dozen men whom they once arrested.

Moe, who lives in Flatbush, keeps a picture of himself as a pugilist in his wallet "as a kind of momentum," and goes to the races at Saratoga, where he often runs into Izzy. Izzy Einstein lives on the lower East Side with his wife and four sons, two of whom have the law firm of Einstein & Einstein; the two others are studying law and will join the firm, which will then be Einstein, Einstein, Einstein & Einstein. The youngest is named Albert, after the great physicist whom Izzy once met. When he "ast" him what line of work he was in and was told that he was a "discoverer," Izzy replied that he was a discoverer, too, "only I discover in basements." This use of "high" contrast at the end is the culmination of deflation throughout, without direct statement, of these two onetime notables. As prohibition enforcement officers they had merely been myrmidons, and their later careers are standardized to the point of caricature. That their careers and personal lives even in their altered circumstances have run in tandem serves to emphasize a lack of identity in them. They adjust easily to their commercial environment, becoming cartoonlike figures of unthinking middle-class existence.

The yoking of crime with middle-class grotesquerie is especially effective in "41313 NY," dealing with the Rosenthal murder case of 1912.[6] While at the café of the Hotel Metropole on Forty-second Street near Broadway, the gambler Herman Rosenthal was informed by a waiter that someone wanted to see him outside. When he went out to the street, four men shot him to death and sped off in a car with the license plate "41313 NY." A passerby caught the license number and went to the police station to report it, but was himself thrown in jail. A reporter for the *World*, however, which only two days before had printed an article hinting that Rosenthal was about to go before the grand jury to implicate Police Lieutenant Charles Becker in gambling and corruption, learned of the jailing and roused the district attorney from his sleep. The district attorney, a Charles S. Whitman, went immediately to the station to demand the witness's release and the identity of the owner of the car. The owner was located and revealed to Whitman that the vehicle had been hired on the night in question by a gambler known as "Baldy" Jack Rose. Rose was, in fact, a bagman for police lieutenant Becker.

Two days after the killing, Jack Rose appeared at the police headquarters with a story that he had rented the car to visit a relative uptown. "Baldy" Jack Rose lived up to his nickname. His physiognomy, Thurber remarks, "was not unlike that of Peter Lorre, the movie actor; even his eyebrows and eyelashes were gone, the result of typhoid in infancy." Rose was put in the Tombs with two gambler associates, Bridgie Webber and Harry Vallon, and before long they gave confessions identifying the killers as Lefty Louie, Gyp the Blood, Whitey Lewis, and Dago Frank. The four were convicted and executed, but the case against Becker was harder to prove. Eventually, a corroborative witness was produced who testified to a meeting uptown between Becker and Rose, Webber, and Vallon at which Becker commanded them to get rid of Rosenthal, and Becker was convicted and went to the electric chair.

At the time the article was written, district attorney Whitman had become governor of New York, but Thurber is more interested in the destinies of the three gamblers who turned state's evidence, particularly its star witness "Baldy" Jack Rose. Webber, who died the year before, had lived as a man without a past in New Jersey, the vice president and secretary of a paper-box company in Passaic. The other two, still living, are business associates. Harry Vallon, a "small, gray, dignified man," works for

"Baldy" Jack Rose, who operates a chain of suburban road-side restaurants. Shortly after the sensational trial, Rose announced that he had reformed and went on platforms during World War I lecturing soldiers on the evils of gambling and other vices. With the backing of legitimate business friends, he started his own motion-picture company, the Humanology Picture Corporation—the phrase "humanology," according to Rose, meaning "the sense of being human." The movie venture ended in 1917, but not before Rose had made, among others, six pictures based on the poems of his favorite poet, Ella Wheeler Wilcox!

Now sixty, Rose always wears a cap to cover his baldness, and jogs around the neighborhood before driving to one of his restaurants in an old-model Chevrolet. He takes particular satisfaction in a new machine in his restaurants that shapes, grills, and serves hamburgers automatically. "It takes the mystery," he remarks in the last line, "out of hamburgers." The movement of the piece is from an exotic world of urban lawlessness to a thoroughly known and standardized one of middle-class conformity, from an "open" city to a "closed" suburb. In either case, "Baldy" Jack Rose is evoked as someone strangely without dimension as a human being. His "humanology" motion pictures are in their way as unreal as his earlier association with Lefty Louie and Gyp the Blood. Although Rose's reformation saves him from the brutality of gangsterism, it results in a banality so complete as to deny him any trace of individual identity.

"A Sort of Genius," perhaps the finest and most haunting of the profiles, also involves a sensational crime. In 1922 the Reverend Edward W. Hall, rector of the Protestant Episcopal Church of St. John the Baptist in New Brunswick, New Jersey, and Mrs. Eleanor Mills, wife of the sexton of the church and Hall's lover, were found murdered in a deserted spot in the country. Discovered leaning against one of the clergyman's shoes, as if it had been carefully placed there, was one of his calling cards. Mrs. Hall and her two brothers, Henry and Willie Stevens, were suspected of the murder but a grand jury failed to bring an indictment. Then in 1926 new evidence came to light and they were brought to trial. A key witness for the state was a Mrs. Jane Gibson, called by the press "the pig woman," who said that while traveling at night on her mule she had seen a woman and two men at the murder scene. She identified them as Mrs. Hall and her brothers.

Attention focused particularly upon Willie Carpender Stevens, who was believed to be mentally retarded and lived on the income of a trust fund set up for him by his well-to-do parents. He stuttered, was an epileptic, and cut a decidedly odd figure. His appearance at the trial is described vividly by Thurber:

He had a large head and a face that would be hard to forget. His head was covered with a thatch of thick, bushy hair, and his heavy black eyebrows seemed always to be arched, giving him an expression of perpetual surprise. This expression was strikingly accentuated by large, prominent eyes which, seen through the thick lenses of the spectacles he always wore, seemed to bulge unnaturally. He had a heavy, drooping, walrus mustache, and his complexion was dark. His glare was sudden and fierce; his smile, which came just as quickly, lighted up his whole face and gave him the wide beaming look of an enormously pleased child.[7]

Childlike he was in many ways. He spent most of every day at the firehouse, playing cards with the firemen and running errands for them. Yet a doctor testified that Willie was "a sort of genius," who read books over the heads of average people. In his jail cell while awaiting trial, he passed the time reading books on metallurgy. A hundred million people waited eagerly to see what would happen when Willie took the witness stand. Under prolonged questioning, however, his account of his innocence could not be shaken and he was acquitted. As the years passed, Willie continued to live in the Gothic shadow of the murder case. Sixty-four when the article was written, he still resides in New Brunswick, where he reads books on mineralogy and engineering, and apart from children whom he sometimes befriends has few associates other than firemen. He seems another of Thurber's trapped people—trapped by his past, his peculiar physical appearance, and his evident maladjustment. He is an anomalous figure out of Thurber's "dream book" who cannot come of age or find his place in the world.

The "Where Are They Now?" profiles have in common with the humor pieces and parodies a sense of life that delights in things seen from baroque angles. The profile subjects come to life and are revealed particularly through an inner dynamic of their struggle to know themselves, to come to terms with reality that is finally baffling and bewildering. All have in some way a disordered sense of reality, achieving apparent size only for a moment and then having their sense of reality taken from them. The chief impression of the profiles is one of powerlessness. The public or external world operates unreasonably and without any apparent rational purpose. The once mighty or celebrated become displaced, their lives strangely misshapen, and in the end they all seem curiously alone.

The fate of finding oneself alone is an essential condition in Thurber, and to an exceptional degree his work is private. In a review of Granville Hicks's mammoth anthology, *Proletarian Writers in the United States*, in the March 25, 1936 issue of *The New Republic*, Thurber rejected the politically partisan approach to fiction of Marxist writers, whom he compared unfavorably to such *New Yorker* writers as Robert Coates, whose work possessed humor, objectivity, and detachment. But he is, in effect, defending himself. Thurber has no ideological commitments of any kind that affected his writing deeply. His play *The Male Animal* (1940) does defend academic freedom against the incursions of the political right, but the liberalism of the play is vague and consists of little more than the desire to be left alone. Moreover, the political theme seems tacked onto the play. What is felt most deeply in the work is the isolation and helplessness of Tommy Turner, the English professor with a little boy's name, when he has to confront the outer world of sexuality and masculine power.

The end of the early phase, which is also the major phase, of Thurber's humor pieces can be readily dated by the onset of his blindness in the early 1940s. His sketches of the next twenty years, until his death in 1961, expand upon—with some important differences and with declining creative energy—the forms he had explored previously. His later parodies include "The White Rabbit Caper" (1949), a spoof of the radio broadcasts of Dashiell Hammett's detective character Sam Spade that involves the use of a group of comic figures from the animal kingdom. These characters include detective Fred Fox, his client old Mrs. Rabbit who has come to him in search of her great-great-great-great-great-great granddaughter Daphne, Inspector Mastiff, and Oliver Owl. But the triumph of the parody is Thurber's creation of Franz Frog.

Franz Frog is encountered at his Lily Pond dive that is decorated wholly in the color green, and illuminated "softly but restlessly" by thousands of fireflies imprisoned in the hollow crystal pendants of enormous chandeliers. Franz dresses entirely in green and wears emerald rings, and as he speaks his eyes bulge and his throat swells ominously. When detective Fox comes to see him, Franz rumbles, "Whong you wong, Fonxxx?" in a cavernous voice. Staring up at the ceiling, his mammoth mouth gapes open, and as the fireflies in the chandelier overhead become frightened their light suddenly goes out. The parody employs the hard-boiled vernacular of naturalism, yet Franz Frog is a figure of the purest Thurberesque fantasy.

The later pieces also include additional parodies of Henry James, one of Thurber's lifelong fascinations. Thurber owned the thirty-five volume Macmillan edition of James's works, and his recall of the various stories and novels was surprisingly exact and minute. "He could remember characters," Clifton Fadiman noted, "that I think even professionals in the James field had forgotten."[8] In his chapter "James Thurber's 'Four Pieces,'" in *The Battle and the Books* (1964),[9] Edward Stone has searched through Thurber's writing to trace his numerous allusions to James and specific pieces related to him that in addition to the four "generally recognized" include at least five or six others. James appears, he points out, not only in the early writing but also in later parodies, in his essay "The Wings of Henry James" (1958), and was discussed by Thurber in a radio broadcast with Mark Van Doren in the 1950s.[10] But while Stone illustrates that James was part of Thurber's literary consciousness, he does not establish the exact nature of Thurber's relationship to him.

In his essay "James Thurber: A Critical Study," Otto Friedrich has addressed this question, and made rather large claims for James as an "all-pervading" influence. Thurber's early views tend, he remarks:

to be uncertain and negative, but there remained in the back of his mind a positive image of what the American writer could be. . . . James as a literary figure is the implied object of most of Thurber's later critical writing and it is implicit in most of Thurber's best fiction. As Thurber's critical writing broadens out to cover all of 'the literary life,' James becomes increasingly the central figure.[11]

But there is really no central figure who can be used to explain Thurber, and it is difficult to make out how James's influence can be "all-pervading" when much of Thurber's writing, which is extremely diverse, is not Jamesian at all. Thurber's fictional characters, for example, are quite unlike James's inasmuch as they often have no cognitive interiors. Their subjective experience is frequently guided merely by daydreams and fantasies. At times, but only at times, Thurber does revert to James in his imagination as a great American writer of the past with whom he feels a certain kinship, and upon whom he projects the vulnerabilities of his own very private and, as it were, "feminine" sensibility. This vulnerability is implied in his parody "The Beast in the Dingle" (1948), a spoof of "The Beast in the Jungle" that, in its sweep of allusions, also brings in such other James works as "The Turn of the Screw," "The Figure in the Carpet," and "The Jolly Corner." But although Thurber mimics the mannerisms of the late James delightfully, the parody lacks a strongly focused dramatic interest. A more successful and more dramatically focused parody is "A Call on Mrs. Forrester" (1948).

"A Call on Mrs. Forrester" parodies not only James but also Willa Cather, adapting situations from *The Ambassadors* and *A Lost Lady*, and focusing upon a diffident narrator's response to their heroines. It begins with the return of a man of fifty to Dakota, where he had been platonically in love at an impressionable age with Marion Forrester, once the cynosure of the town and now a fallen idol. As he stands on a bridge on his way to her house, he imagines all the telltale signs of the decay of her character, rather frightening himself in the process. A comic version of James's Lambert Strether, he wants to retain his idealistic illusions that become jeopardized in the drama enacted in his imagination. In his musings he calls on Marion Forrester, confronts her moral deterioration, and confesses his love for Madame de Vionnet. She taunts him, however, that Madame de Vionnet, beneath lovely appearances, is no different than she—threatening the last and most cherished of his illusions. In the end, standing on the bridge in the rain, he decides *not* to go to the Forrester house.

The parody is finely written with many elegant touches, and it is as if the carefully wrought styles of James and Cather bring out a loving care for language and nuance in Thurber. At the same time, he projects his own sensibility onto the two writers. Strether's scrupled hesitations become enlarged in Thurber's narrator to the point of making him a comic study of male passivity (he never actually *does* anything except to stand in the rain and then withdraw) and sexual insecurity. The object of Thurber's polished satire throughout much of the piece, the narrator becomes at the end the butt of his broad humor. When he turns to leave Marion Forrester in his reverie, he opens the door of the hallway closet instead of the front door, and an enormous pile of junk and clutter falls on him; and untangling himself from this debris, he finds himself holding a "comic parasol," an image having the connotation of his being unmanned.

Ultimately, although a kind of kinship with James is implied, "A Call on Mrs. Forrester" becomes self-parody. As a young man Thurber hopelessly idealized women, and in *Is Sex Necessary?* had burlesqued this tendency in men as if to free himself of illusions he had still not overcome. "A Call on Mrs. Forrester" revives this problem in Thurber's late middle age, touching a still-vital nerve that gives the piece its life. The passage from an evanescent idealism to sober reality in Cather's *A Lost Lady* provides the movement of Thurber's parody, in which the narrator must first accept his illusion about Marion Forrester and then, more disturbingly, about Madame de Vionnet, which has shielded him from having to confront his deficiencies as a man.

Other humor pieces of the period are written in a variety of different modes. "Joyeux Noël, Mr. Durning" (1949) and "File and Forget" (1949) are exercises in the comic naïf, pieces consisting of an exchange of letters that reveals Thurber marooned in bureaucratic confusion and reduced to comic helplessness. "*What* Cocktail Party?" (1950), on the other hand, is quite sophisticated. In this piece Thurber attends a cocktail party at which the guests discuss T. S. Eliot's recent play *The Cocktail Party* and have extremely esoteric theories about what Eliot's cocktail party actually means. Fearing the loss of his sanity, Thurber prepares to leave only to be engaged in conversation by the butler, who has yet another theory about the play. At the end he decides to walk back to his apartment rather than risk a conversation with the cab driver waiting for him in the street. "My Friend Domesticus"

(1944) and "See No Weevil" (1952) seize mirthfully upon minutiae. "My Friend Domesticus" deals with the peculiar customs of the hearth cricket, bringing the small creature marvelously to life; and "See No Weevil" reveals comically that the "Thurberia Weevil," unlike the boll weevil, does not destroy plants and is "harmless." The best of the later reportage pieces, "There's Something Out There" (1957), about the Loch Ness monster sightings, is strictly objective yet constantly witty.

But allowing for exceptions here and there, a decided falling off can be noticed in Thurber's humor pieces in the 1940s and 1950s. His book collections continued to appear regularly, but many of them collect material he had published earlier in the *New Yorker. My World—and Welcome to It* (1943) gathers writing chiefly from the 1930s, and *The Thurber Carnival* (1945), an anthology of selections from Thurber's earlier books contains only a few new pieces, all of them inconsequential. *The Beast in Me and Other Animals* (1948) includes new parodies and reportage, but also "Talk of the Town" articles from as far back as the late 1920s, with the highlight of the volume Thurber's remarkable animal drawings—"A New Natural History" and "A Gallery of Real Creatures"—from the beginning of the decade.

New humor pieces are contained in *Thurber Country* (1953), and still others appear in his last books *Alarms and Diversions* (1957), *Lanterns and Lances* (1961), and the posthumous *Credos and Curios* (1962). But the last books particularly are weak and give the impression of the breakdown of Thurber's powers as a humorist. The majority of the pieces in *Lanterns and Lances* did not even appear previously in the *New Yorker,* which had begun to reject his articles. Even some of those they did publish, Bernstein told me in conversation, were taken "out of charity."[12]

A number of the later sketches center upon cocktail parties at which Thurber jousts with featherheaded hostesses or holds elaborate conversations with other guests that turn out to be about nothing. There is something of S. J. Perelman in "The Ordeal of Mr. Matthews" (1947)—in the fantastic narrative manner, quick word play, and incongruous juxtaposing of characters who are unable to communicate with one another. While Thurber laments the decline of the foppish wit practiced by Wilkes and Disraeli, a Mr. Matthews, whom he has just met, mutters that "Ed's certainly brought the business up from nowhere." After much meandering talk and an alarming number of highballs, Thurber is led away by his wife, her "firm, familiar grip on his arm." "The Waters of the Moon" (1947), dealing with another cocktail party, involves a hoax perpetrated by Thurber upon a Mr. Peifer, editor of a literary review, but the humor of the hoax (about the career of a nonexistent writer) seems joyless. "The Lady from the Land" (1961) is a party piece of no apparent point in which Thurber consumes a large number of drinks while feeling estranged from everyone around him. Its sense of things, of life and people, is woozy.

Thurber seems estranged in other pieces by the nature of his fixations. Under the influence of Peter De Vries, he became obsessed by word games, which he incorporated into his humor sketches. In "Here Come the Tigers" (1947), he is roused from sleep by two friends who challenge him to construct words from the letters of other words, and lies awake until dawn before discovering that gaiter, goiter, and aigret can be made from the word "tiger." Unable to sleep in "Do You Want to Make Something out of It?" (1951), he constructs antipathetic "C-M" combinations (Capulet and Montague, Candida and Marchbanks, and so on), and in "The Watchers of the Night" (1959) devises palindromes, words and phrases that are spelled the same forward and backward. These word-game pieces, the humor of which is disturbingly slight, draw Thurber into such a private, interior world that he seems to close out an outer one.

Too many of the late humor pieces are concerned with complaints about modern life. In some, Thurber deplores the decline of proper English usage. "The Psychosemanticist Will See You Now, Mr. Thurber" (1955) laments the deadening effect on the language of jargon; and "Friends, Romans, Countrymen, Lend Me Your Earmuffs" (1955), "Come Across with the Facts" (1960), and "The Spreading *You* Know" (1960) harp on the same theme. In other sketches Thurber deplores the decline of humor in the 1950s, the work of "morbid" playwrights such as Tennessee Williams, sexual explicitness in novels, and practically every feature of the life of the time. He asks why there are no longer any wholesome family comedies like *Life with Father*, and in "Return of the Native" (1950) recalls Columbus in the 1890s with absurd sentimentality as though in protest of a present in which he can no longer find any point of relation.

Thurber's complaints give the impression that he would like to have the world more settled and obedient to reason. Yet it had been the disorderliness of life that had engaged him in the more exuberant earlier work. The humor sketches, reportage, and parodies of that time had celebrated deviations from reason as the very moments that magically reveal man in his struggle to find a context that would make sense of his existence. Existential sufferers, Thurber's people had been clown figures on a heightened, dramatic stage. One had looked on in amazement as the individuals in the "Where Are They Now?" profiles turned into grotesques who grope for a sense of identity; as the parody characters belied a sense of an underlying order; and as Thurber himself, in a variety of fantastic situations, became the fool of life.

Yet even in this difficult later period of blindness and illness, Thurber's humor did not wholly desert him, as *The Years with Ross* reveals. Particularly in the new forms he explored, the fables and fairy tales, Thurber scored notable successes that not only add to his achievement but in some ways crown it. Both forms belong to a child's world, suggesting a deepening isolation and subjectivity. Yet they have a remarkable intensity and bring out the poet in Thurber as well as the consummate humorist. They are also contemplative as well as dramatic, and in them good and evil meet in a new arena of fantasy.

7

~~~~~~

The Fables and Fairy Tales

Thurber's earliest fables began to appear serially in the *New Yorker* in 1939, and were published to critical acclaim in *Fables for Our Time and Famous Poems Illustrated* in 1940. With only two exceptions, the twenty-seven fables in the book, which end with comic and pungent morals, are concerned with creatures from the animal kingdom who are able, through a suspension of disbelief, to converse with one another. They come out of an ancient tradition of fable writing going back in Greek literature to Aesop and in seventeenth-century France to La Fontaine, but while the ancient fables illustrate received or traditional wisdom, Thurber's give the sense that no dependable codes exist to guide human conduct. In sensibility and style they are distinctly modern.

Nothing in the American literature of Thurber's time or in the immediate background quite explains them. George Ade, who wrote fables in slang in the late 1890s and the earlier part of the twentieth century, has an affinity with Thurber as a fable writer in the harsh irreverence of his humor; but his fables deal with human beings rather than animals and lack Thurber's polish and artistry. Don Marquis's *Archy and Mehitabel* (1927) and its sequels, dealing with the experiences of a cockroach and an alley cat, bring creatures vividly to life and make them dour commentators on the human condition. But Marquis's free-verse columns are not shaped as fables, and their sensibility is different than Thurber's. Among Thurber's contemporaries who wrote in the animal-fable form, two who come to mind are Marianne Moore, whose monumental translation of La Fontaine's fables appeared in 1954; and William March, whose fables, which began to appear in the late 1940s, were particularly admired by Thurber.[1] But March could not have been an influence since his fables appeared after Thurber's first collection, and Marianne Moore was a translator, if a rather free one, of La Fontaine rather than a deviser of fables "for our time."

The fables derive their energy in part from Thurber's command of vernacular speech. As a fly is about to alight on flypaper, a bee advises him abruptly, "Hold it, stupid." Two turkeys, a young one named Joe and an old one named Doc, square off with lively epithets, the young one threatening to bat his opponent's teeth "into his crop," and the old one swearing that he will "have his gizzard." A two-timing stork is greeted by his wife who calls him a "phony obstetrician" and crowns him with a chimney brick. A seal who goes off to join a circus returns wearing smart city clothes and a pair of seventeen-dollar shoes. "He gave [the other seals]," Thurber writes, "the Big Town stuff right away: the latest slang, liquor in a golden flask."

Deception and failure, one of the major themes of the fables, is illustrated in a number of different ways. In "The Little Girl and the Wolf," a retelling of "Little Red Riding Hood," a little girl carrying a basket of food to her grandmother comes upon a wolf in a dark forest. After she reveals that she is bound for her grandmother's house, the wolf disappears and the little girl before long arrives at the house to find "somebody" in bed in a nightcap and nightgown. She quickly perceives that it is the wolf, who no more resembles her grandmother than the MGM lion "looks like Calvin Coolidge," pulls an automatic out of her basket, and shoots the wolf dead. The moral, that it is no longer as easy as it used to be to fool little girls, turns traditional wisdom on its head.

In "The Tiger Who Understood People," the best-laid plans go awry. A tiger who has escaped from a zoo and made his way back to the jungle, persuades a leopard to stage a mock fight with him that other animals will bring a freshly killed wild boar to see. The scheme is thwarted, however, when the other animals fail to appear. By midnight the tiger and the leopard are so enraged that they fall upon each other, injuring one another so badly that when two wild boars appear they are able to attack and kill the tiger and leopard easily. The tiger's ingenious plan ends in his own undoing.

In other fables creatures are undone by their credulity. In "The Owl Who Was God," a group of animals come to the conclusion that the owl is the most awesome of creatures because it can see in the dark and responds in hoots, like "two" and "who," that seem to answer their queries, and they form an admiring procession behind the owl as it crosses a highway. Unable to see in the daylight, however, the owl proves a poor guide. A truck speeding down the highway runs them down, killing many of them, including the owl "who was God." In "The Sheep in Wolf's Clothing," two sheep put on wolf's clothing and appear as spies at a fete day in Wolfland. When they discover that the wolves gambol and frisk just as sheep do, they hurry back to write up reports of their discovery for a newspaper syndicate and the *Sheep's Home Companion* that there are no differences between sheep and wolves. After reading the accounts the sheep draw in their sentinels and let down their barriers, and one night soon after, "howling and slavering," the wolves descend on the sheep and kill them in droves.

One after another, Thurber's animals are deceived by their own guile or lack of it, by their being too prudential or too careless, so that the moral of one of the fables, that there is "no safety in numbers, or in anything else," might apply to them all. The animals cannot evade the peril of life, and in an impressive number of cases they not only fail but also die. The circumstances under which the fables were written seem significant, since Thurber began to write them just after the death of his father, Charles Thurber, and at a time when he knew that he would soon lose his vision. The death and undoing that is pervasive in the fables, the sense they give of the fragile nature of existence, have a source in Thurber's own immediate experience.

Two of the fables are unlike the others in having human beings rather than animals as their subjects. "The Unicorn in the Garden," discussed previously, springs from the inmost depths of Thurber's imagination and is the most powerful of the fables. But "The Green Isle in the Sea" is also impressive. One "sweet morning" in 1939 a little old gentle man throws open the windows of his bedroom to let in the "living" sun, and is slashed at by a venomous black widow spider. He then goes downstairs to have a splendid breakfast, but as he is about to sit down his grandson pulls the chair out from under him, and he falls to the floor nearly breaking his hip. Out in the street he limps toward a little park with many trees that is to him like a green isle in the sea. On the way he is tripped up by a "grim" little girl who rolls her hoop at him, and in the next block is mugged by a man who takes his money and a gold ring given him by his mother when he was a child. At last reaching the little park that is to him "a fountain and a shrine," he finds that half its trees have been killed by a blight and the other half by an infestation of bugs. Their leaves are gone, Thurber writes in the startling last line, "so that the hundreds of planes which appeared suddenly overhead had an excellent view of the little old gentle man through their bombing-sights."

"The Green Isle in the Sea" is reminiscent in some ways of the memorable early scenes in Nathanael West's *Miss Lonelyhearts*, in which Miss Lonelyhearts goes to the little sanctuary park in New York City seeking spiritual renewal to find only blight. But the image of the planes overhead evokes a very specific moment in time, is a reminder of the war that is being waged in Europe and will soon engulf the world. The world at war comes as the climax of the irrationality experienced by the little old man as he starts his day and is subjected to one aggression upon his humanity after another. The final image of the fable is almost surreal, and nothing else like it appears in the other pieces, but "The Green Isle in the Sea" is not out of place in the book, which gives throughout a sense of the perilousness of life, of innocence jeopardized.

Thurber's second book of fables, *Further Fables for Our Time* (1956), contains a larger number of pieces, forty-seven in all, most of which appeared originally in the *New Yorker*. *Further Fables* contains nothing as powerful as "The Unicorn in the Garden" or "The Green Isle in the Sea," and perhaps a third of the fables do not show Thurber at his best. Yet the majority are on a par with those in the first volume, and they illustrate what has happened to Thurber in sixteen years time. They reveal more attention to word play, for example, and have something of the verbal virtuosity of the fairy tales. A rudimentary human female emerges from the sea and begins "flobbering" toward the shore. The conversation of a pair of hippos consists of "wuffled" statements and "gurbled" replies. An aged bat, receiving disturbing news, "chittered, quickered, and zickered." A meddlesome female rabbit enters a room "buttocky, buttocky." The ocean bottom reveals only "soggy glup and great gobs of mucky gump."

A number of the fables focus upon domestic situations involving animal couples whose conflicts are also human ones. In "The Bragdowdy and the Busybody," a female hare neighbor chides a male guinea pig for his lack of industry, telling him that he ought to be in the laboratory having injections to see if a serum is deadly or not. She interferes in the couple's life to such an extent that before long Mrs. Pig joins all manner of uplifting women's clubs, and in the end the hare's husband and the male guinea pig run off together to Tahiti to find some peace. In "The Grizzly and the Gadgets," a grizzly bear is driven to distraction by his wife's obsession with household gadgets, goes berserk, tearing the house apart, and runs off with a female bear named Honey. In "The Chipmunk and His Mate," a chipmunk is vexed by his wife's inability to sleep at night as she worries about the management of the house. When she dies, after falling asleep at the wheel of the family car, he marries her sister, who turns out to be another unsleeping worrier. At the end, the chipmunk finds a "sleepy-time gal" and goes off with her to Maracaibo to sleep happily ever after.

"The Sea and the Shore," perhaps the best of the domestic fables, concerns a primordial male and female who are beginning to emerge from the sea. Although still fairly shapeless, the female is possessed by an instinct for taffeta and jewelry that impels her toward shore. To the hesitant male, she cries that she will only need to lose a "little amorphousness" around the waist that should not take more than "a million years." Eons later, urged on by a flicker of desire, the male begins struggling slowly up the sand toward the female, calling, "Hey, Mag, wait for baby!" Vintage Thurber, "The Sea and the Shore" is analogous to certain of the drawings, such as "The Race of Life," in which the female is in advance of the male and in touch with instinct and biology as the woefully vague male is not.

Several of the fables comment on the political or spiritual climate of the 1950s. "The Peaceful Mongoose," for example, involves a McCarthy-like witch-hunt of a peace-loving mongoose by other mongooses. The mongooses spread a rumor that he is procobra, even whisper that he is a "mongoosexual," and finally banish him from their community. But by far the greatest number of fables dwell on the theme of the vanity of life. "The Truth about Toads" begins merrily at the Fauna Club, where the various animals boast of their importance to the world—until the bartender, a raven, decides to put up a sign reading that if you open most hearts you will "see graven on them Vanity." When a toad enters and boasts of his preeminence among animals in possessing a precious jewel in his head, the raven slugs his frappé and the toad passes out. A woodpecker then drills his head with his beak, but no gem of any kind is discovered. In the stinging moral, Thurber remarks that if you open most heads you will find nothing shining, "not even a mind."

A remarkable number of animals are punished sharply for their vanity. In one fable, a butterfly flutters her wings before a phoebe, exclaiming, "This is heaven," and in a sudden transition the fledglings in the phoebe's nest cry, "This is heaven" as they enjoy the butterfly for desert. In "The Lady of the Legs," a frog is complimented on her legs by a French restaurateur, who tells her that she will be served like a queen in his restaurant under his personal supervision. Without grasping the double entendre, the frog swoons in a transport of joy, and the restaurateur deftly removes her succulent legs that, under his personal supervision as he had promised, are served Provençal, with a bottle of Montrachet, to a celebrated bon vivant.

One of the most firmly punished of the animals, in "The Cat in the Lifeboat," is a cat named William who has a great opinion of himself and has been pampered by his wealthy mistress. She makes William, in fact, her sole heir in her will and takes him with her on an ocean voyage. At sea, however, the passengers have to abandon ship and William is tossed from a lifeboat into the ocean by a crew hand. He manages to swim to an island inhabited by great cats, and there because he is still in shock and can no longer remember his name, is dubbed Nobody from Nowhere. Before long he loses his life in a barroom brawl when a panther asks his name and William gives what seems to the panther an uncivil reply, saying that he is Nobody from Nowhere. The moral of the grotesque fable, that man's life is a little journey from "swaddle to shroud," could apply to many of the other fables, which stress the transitory nature of life, the passing of all things.

It seems relevant that the fables were written while Thurber's mother, the proud "Mame" Thurber, lay dying in a Columbus hospital. For a month, while she remained in a coma, the family kept a deathwatch, and it was under these circumstances that the fables began to come to

Thurber. They are varied, and include charming variations of Aesop's story of the fox and crow who contend guilefully for a piece of cheese, but the tenor of many of them is dark and misanthropic. In the bold "The Bat Who Got the Hell Out," a bat who believes that human beings possess greater importance than bats because when they die they go to heaven forsakes his companions in a cave to find a place in the rafters of a church. After hearing the sermon of an evangelist, however, in which the idea of heaven is made to seem meretricious, he returns to the darkness of his cave, no longer envying man or even continuing to think of him. In "The Human Being and the Dinosaur," man boasts that he is to be the monarch of the future while the dinosaur is doomed to extinction, and the dinosaur replies that "there are worse things than being extinct, and one of them is you." Such fables make one think of Mark Twain's bitter pronouncements on the "damned human race."

The volume opens with "The Sea and the Shore," in which the human male and female emerge gropingly from the sea, and concludes with "The Shore and the Sea," in which lemmings throw themselves with unthinking panic into the sea while an aged lemming scholar sighs and prepares for the next cycle of lemming existence that will contain exactly the same folly. The two fables comprise the futile history of man. The fables are fascinating in their animal fantasy that would delight a child, but they have, too, the pessimistic intelligence of the moralist. In the fineness of their handling, they are among the notable things of Thurber's later period, and E. B. White was not wrong when he wrote to Thurber, just after *Further Fables for Our Time* was published, that "you are the only living fable writer."[2]

Compared to his fables, Thurber's fairy tales are strikingly romantic and, on the surface at least, optimistic. The circumstances surrounding the writing of the first of them, *Many Moons* (1943), were grim. While at Martha's Vineyard recuperating from his eye operations and confronted by his blindness, in a state of high nervousness and drinking heavily, Thurber wrote *Many Moons* rapidly, then suffered a nervous collapse. Fearful of losing his sanity and needing to be surrounded by people, he went to stay with his friend "Jap" Gude and his family. But after leaving Martha's Vineyard he had no memory of having written *Many Moons*, the manuscript of which was discovered two years later by the caretaker at the Gudes' house. Published in 1943, it met with such critical and popular success that Thurber was prompted to write additional fairy tales, publishing five in all spanning a period of fourteen years.

Many Moons is a fairy-tale comedy that begins as a parody of Poe's romantic poem "Lenore," about the heartbreaking death of an idealized young woman. Thurber's fairy tale is set in a "kingdom by the sea," its heroine little Princess Lenore, a child who has fallen ill from "a surfeit" of raspberry tarts. She tells her father, the king, that if she has the moon she will be well again, and the king immediately summons his Lord High Chamberlain, quite seriously demanding of him that he produce the moon for his daughter. Confronted by such a stupendous demand, the Lord High Chamberlain wipes his forehead nervously with a silk handkerchief, blows his nose into it loudly, and produces a parchment scroll from his pocket containing a list of the wondrous things he has obtained for the king. But he cannot, he concedes, procure the moon. The Royal Wizard is then summoned, and he too produces a scroll listing the amazing things he has found for the king. But he, also, admits that he cannot obtain the moon. The Royal Mathematician is then called in, and although an esteemed adviser who has discovered the square of the "hippopotamus" and how much "Is" you need to make an "Are," he confesses that he cannot get the moon for the king.

Finally the court jester is called to console the king by playing a sad melody on his lute. When the king explains the source of his unhappiness, the jester suggests that he talk to the princess herself to find out from her how far away she thinks the moon is. It is, she tells him, just a little smaller than her thumbnail and no higher in the sky than the topmost branches of the tree in which it sometimes gets caught. And it is made of gold. The jester goes to the royal goldsmith and has a moon made for the princess, and when he presents her with it she feels so well that she leaves her bed to go out to play in the garden the next morning. The king's worries, however, are not over since by nightfall the actual moon will appear in the sky and the princess will know that she does not possess the true moon. When the king applies to his chief advisers for solutions, they all fail him once more, but the jester again has an idea. When he talks to the little princess, he finds that she is not troubled by the presence of the moon in the sky because she believes that moons are renewable, like the horns of unicorns that when lost grow back again. The fairy tale ends happily as the moon in the sky seems to wink at the jester.

Despite the stressful circumstances under which it was written, *Many Moons* is absolutely poised and assured, possessing a serene and pervasive irony. Poe's "Lenore" is woeful in a romantic and handkerchief-wringing way, but *Many Moons* smilingly declines to be tragic, resolving its great-yet-small crisis with a sense of wonder appropriate to the little princess's years. Much of the comedy of the fairy tale derives from Thurber's portrayal of adults. The king, presumably the mightiest man in the kingdom, is comically powerless, and so too are his most venerable senior advisers. Indeed, when the Lord High Chamberlain reads from his scroll, he stumbles onto some items from his wife's shopping list that make him seem foolish. Similarly, when the Royal Wizard begins to read from his scroll, he discovers that he has the wrong scroll— from someone returning his philosopher's stone as spurious. He quickly finds the correct scroll, but in the meantime his authority has been destroyed. Moreover, none of the three principal consultants knows how far away the moon is or what it is made of. In responding to the problem by logic and reason they are foiled, and it takes the jester to resolve the dilemma by entering the mind of the Princess Lenore herself. She alone knows that the moon is imagination.

The Great Quillow (1944), written a year after Many Moons was published, seems inspired by Many Moons and extends its themes. Instead of a royal court beset by a dilemma, one has a little town placed in jeopardy by the appearance of a marauding giant. In place of the court jester, one has the town's toy maker who, against all odds, saves the day. The giant Hunder has been evocatively named. "Hunder" rhymes with "thunder" and "plunder," and the "Hun" of the first syllable is also a reminder of the German aggression in Europe occurring when the fairy tale was published. But the toy maker's name, too, is suggestive, its quill and pillow associations giving the idea of the poet and dreamer.

The early part of The Great Quillow contains some of Thurber's finest fairy-tale comedy. The townspeople are small businessmen with burgher manners and mentalities, and they condescend to Quillow as the sturdy tradesmen had laughed scoffingly at artists in the tales of Hawthorne. Quillow, indeed, is more than a little reminiscent of Hawthorne's artist of the beautiful for he, too, is a miniaturist who devises small, ingenious works of art having little practical value. The little clown he creates who juggles three marbles associates him with wonder; his trumpeter who plays seven notes of a song on a tiny horn links him with music and festival; and his paperweight in which roses burst into bloom in falling snow connects him with creativity and spiritual renewal. His creations, like the twelve diminutive men in scarlet who emerge from the dial of the town clock on the stroke of every hour to play a melody on little silver bells with little silver hammers, are aesthetic adornments to the life of the community. But they earn him little respect from its burgher leaders.

When he appears in their midst, they call him "the Great Quillow" with mirthful derision. Furthermore, they play a little game, creeping up behind him and pretending to wind up a key in his back as if he were a mechanical figure of his own devising. In a genially accommodating spirit, when the imaginary key in his back is turned, Quillow walks about stiff-legged, with jerky movements of his arms, joining in the fun and increasing the laughter. Quillow attends civic meetings at the city hall, but stands in the shadow of such worthies as the blacksmith, the shoemaker, the tailor, and the baker. When the giant Hunder descends upon them, making demands for their sheep, a leather jerkin to fit a giant, a constant supply of giant-sized pies, and a giant-sized house, they are thrown into despairing confusion. None of the authority figures, the sturdy shopkeeper-tradesmen, can resolve their crisis or dispel Hunder from their town. To do this it takes the toy maker Quillow.

While entertaining Hunder with stories, Quillow tricks him into believing that he is coming down with a terrible ailment. Under his supervision, the townspeople speak to the giant in "woddly woddly" gibberish until he believes that he is losing his mind. When they paint the chimneys of their houses black and appear before him as blue men, Hunder is convinced that he has reached a terminal stage of illness and, advised by Quillow, rushes into the sea to purge himself. Floundering farther and farther out into the sea, he sinks at last beneath the waves.

In *Many Moons*, the court jester, a figure of lowly social station but of exceeding wit, resolves a court crisis by finding a child's solution to a child's problem. The crisis he handles is comic, and he is a hero only on a modest scale. But in *The Great Quillow*, the toy maker becomes a genuine hero, rescuing the town from the threat of the giant. The vindication of the artist, however, is ambiguous since his triumph is uncomfortably like that of Walter Mitty in one of his dreams. The finest parts of *The Great Quillow*, in fact, are the early satirical ones in which Quillow is made to play the fool before the chortling tradesmen, and where his impractical miniaturist interests convey the idea of impotence. The inner parable of *The Great Quillow* concerns World War II and the human spirit that, against the greatest odds, will vanquish brute force. But on this level, too, Quillow is ambiguous, for how can a man as marginal and elegant as Quillow stand for the power of the human imagination?

It might be useful to pass over the middle fairy tales for a moment to look at the final one, *The Wonderful O* (1957). Written in the late 1950s, *The Wonderful O* is a thinly disguised attack on McCarthyism and the witch-hunts of the Cold War era. It begins as a parody of *Treasure Island* when a sinister seafaring man appears at midnight at the door of an inn. He has a green parrot on his shoulder, wears his hair in a pigtail, and speaks in a voice as deep as a "gong in a tomb." The seaman, Littlejack, confers at the inn with a man who is dressed in black and whose name is Black. Black and Littlejack talk of a secret map and of their need for a ship. When one is found they set sail for a certain island on a mission of plunder. In the course of the work characters from *Treasure Island* (like Ben Gunn and George Merry) are alluded to, and Thurber creates the atmosphere of dark and sinister adventure.

What comes out early is that Black has a morbid obsession with the letter *o*, which he associates with the death of his mother from a ship's porthole. Since that traumatic event he has attempted to hold life, in all of its freedom and variety, under constriction. When Black and Littlejack reach the island, inhabited by a peaceful group of townspeople, Black not only directs the pillage of the island in search of buried treasure but also demands that the letter *o* be stricken from their language. There may no longer be lovers since the word contains an *o*, or musical instruments or flowers having an *o* in their names. Books on subjects such as history, philosophy, and philology, that have an *o* in them, are ordered destroyed; and professors, scholars, instructors, and tutors are banished. The townspeople live in fear under the censorship and persecution of Black, who is very much a fairy-tale villain and speaks like

one. When Littlejack's parrot squawks at him, Black cries
that he will "squck his thrug till all he can whupple is
geep."

In the end the tables are turned on Black and Littlejack. The townspeople meet secretly in the woods to de-
vise a means to free themselves from Black's tyranny.
Among them is a maiden named Andrea, who remembers
a book on the shelf of her father, an old scholar, that tells of
an enchantment laid upon the island many years before
when evil men had appeared in search of treasure. As the
ancient book had foretold, an enchanted castle appears
again luminously, and when Black and his crew plunder it
in search of treasure but fail to find it by a certain hour,
they are set upon by avenging spirits, including Mother
Goose astride a broom, who represent the free play of
imagination throughout all human time. In a sequence
filled with the sense of nightmare, Black and his men,
driven back to their ship, are terrorized by storms and sink
beneath the waves. The fairy tale ends with the townspeople celebrating the letter *o*, which rather than meaning
nothing comes to stand for such values as hope, love, and
valor that make life meaningful.

The Wonderful O contains some delightful things, but it
tends to be too didactic. Thurber's moral is laid on so
heavily that the reader feels he is being given a sermon.
The latter part, with its deus-ex-machina rescue, is cum-
bersome and rather too fanciful. Even the lovers, Andreus
and Andrea, are thinly created. They are supposed to be
allied with natural impulse, imagination, and love, as opposed to Black's rigid and life-fearing monomania, but life
does not pulse in them. Perhaps most seriously of all, the
fairy tale is strained by Thurber's obsession with language.
He introduces scores of words with the letter *o* in them,
both in the early part when Black and his confederates
regiment the lives of the townspeople and in the latter
section dealing with the avenging phantoms. This reveals
Thurber's philological keenness but in the end becomes
excessive.

Of the five fairy tales, the middle ones, *The White Deer* and *The Thirteen Clocks*, are the most mature and complex. *The Thirteen Clocks* (1950), the latter of the two, was written in Bermuda during four months and, according to Thurber, passed through twenty-two different drafts. In its essentials, *The Thirteen Clocks* is the most conventional of Thurber's fairy tales, being set chiefly at a haunted castle and having an evil villain and a pair of romantic young lovers who are united at the end. In *Many Moons, The Great Quillow,* and *The Wonderful O,* Thurber defends imagination against worldly wisdom or brute force, but in *The Thirteen Clocks* he deals overtly with romantic love.

The tale's gloomy and spooked Coffin Castle is inhabited by a "cold, aggressive" duke, his various henchmen, and his "niece" the princess Saralinda, whom he plans to marry. Its thirteen clocks no longer run since the duke, like Macbeth, has "murdered" time. He cannot live in the vital world of ongoing time, but must exist in a lonely isolation from others. Everything about the duke is cold, not only his heart but also his hands that he keeps covered with gloves both when sleeping and awake. He limps cackling through the "cold corridors of the castle," as he devises new schemes to thwart those who come to win the hand of Saralinda. One day a young prince appears in the town by the castle, posing as a minstrel named Xingu, and is warned by townspeople that the duke hates people having names beginning with X, and will slit him from his "guggle" to his "zatch."

He is befriended, however, by the Golux (light), a creature having the power of invisibility, and soon after appears at the castle to apply for the hand of Saralinda. The duke's response is to clap his gloved hands together for his henchmen, who throw him into the castle dungeon to be fed on water without bread and bread without water. Yet the next morning, the duke decides that it will be a finer punishment to assign him an impossible task as his bid for the hand of Saralinda, the failure of which will mean the forfeiture of his life. He tells him that he must find a thousand jewels in nine and ninety hours and return with them to the castle when its thirteen clocks are all striking five.

As the prince leaves the castle fearing that he cannot find the thousand jewels in time, he is met again by the Golux, who tells him of a certain Hagga, a woman who weeps jewels. Accompanied by the Golux, he journeys to find Hagga through a distant land that includes a "ticking thicket of bickering crickets" and glades where "bonged the gongs of a throng of frogs." But when he at last reaches Hagga's hill, he learns that even the saddest stories will no longer make Hagga weep. The resourceful Golux, however, decides to make her laugh until she weeps jewels that strew the floor before her. The prince and the Golux gather up the jewels and hurry back to the castle, for the time is short: the jewels Hagga weeps from laughter, unlike those she weeps from sorrow, last only a fortnight and then turn to tears.

In the final section, as happens in *Macbeth*, a series of seemingly impossible contingencies all come true. On her first appearance Saralinda is associated with warmth, and in part comically the cold duke holds up the palms of his gloves before her as if she were a fire at which to warm his hands. Near the end she holds her hands before the frozen thirteen clocks and sets them going and striking five as the prince arrives. Time is restored to the world, the burden of a dark enchantment is thrown off, and the cold duke is destroyed by his dark overlord the Todal, "a blob of glup" who glups him up. As fairy tales classically do, *The Thirteen Clocks* ends with the happy union of the prince and princess.

The Thirteen Clocks is a work of immense charm and humor, and it is apparently optimistic about romantic love to a marked degree. Yet one ought to be wary of taking the tale at face value. At the end, for example, Thurber undercuts his theme of a romantic fulfillment. As the prince and princess are about to leave for the blessed isles of Ever After, the Golux tells them to remember laughter, which they will need even in Ever After. The princess Saralinda also seems to see, as people on "clear and windless" days often "think" they see, the distant shining shore of the blessed isles—lines that cast the romantic ending further in doubt. There is, moreover, a distinctly dark implication in the tale's epilogue when Thurber reminds the reader that the jewels of Hagga's laughter that last only a fortnight are unlike the jewels of sorrow that last forever.

The tonal complexity of *The Thirteen Clocks* can be noticed, too, in Thurber's treatment of the duke, since it involves not only humor but also an element of poignancy. If he inflicts suffering upon others, he also suffers himself. His desire for the warm and living Saralinda testifies to his yearning for release from his lonely isolation. Like Macbeth, he has lost his faith, and in the coldness and darkness to which he is committed is a reminder of a tragic dimension in the fairy tale as well as a romantic one. Curiously, one of Thurber's fables, "The Turtle Who Conquered Time," included in the *Further Fables*, seems relevant to the duke. In the fable, a squirrel dispels the happy illusion that the letters "44 B. C." written on the shell of a turtle indicates that the creature is of an awesome age, since the inscription is clearly a childish prank. "The truth," the squirrel tells the other animals, "is not merry and bright. The truth is cold and dark."

The prince and princess are perfect in every way, but the duke has been maimed. He walks with a limp because one leg is shorter than the other, but that is not all. He wears a patch over one eye, having lost the eye at the age of twelve, and his other eye is apparently weak since he uses a monocle in order to see. The eye the duke has lost in childhood and his subsequent envelopment in darkness suggest that he is an aspect of Thurber himself. It is as if he has played off one part of himself against another—a romantic versus a pessimistic self, and this gives to the fairy tale a very controlled ambiguity.

In considering *The White Deer* (1945), it would be well to keep the ambiguity of *The Thirteen Clocks* in mind.[3] The longest and most ambitious of the fairy tales, a work that passed through twenty-five different drafts, *The White Deer* is set in a medieval world of magic and enchantment. Its texture is denser than that of any of the other fairy tales and its language, as Edmund Wilson observed in his review of the work in the *New Yorker,* is "the essence of poetry."[4] Many of the lines in the tale can be scanned as free verse, and Thurber has made use of a rich variety of verbal effects that contribute to the sense of a spell or dream. Its cast of characters is large, and it has been conceived dramatically, each of its chapters having the effect of an act in a play.

The White Deer begins in an elder time in a kingdom beyond which lies an enchanted forest or "wondrous wood." In the enchanted forest between the Moonstone Mines and the Centaurs Mountain, rationality and the laws of logic are suspended and all becomes contradiction and paradox. The forest can be recognized, Thurber claims, by a fragrance that one can never forget and never remember, and here toadstools grow that are heavy as hammers but when released into the air float lightly over the treetops trailing "black and purple stars." *Alice in Wonderland* rabbits tip their heads as men tip their hats, removing them with their paws and putting them back again.

In the woods beyond the castle (although rarely in the enchanted forest), King Clode and his sons pursue their favorite pastime of hunting, sometimes depleting the woods of game, and in such fallow periods they remain at the castle to await a new generation of deer and wild boar to pursue. King Clode's sons are three—Thag, Gallow, and Jorn, the youngest of the princes and a poet-musician. Thag and Gallow live only for the hunt but Jorn, although an able horseman and hunter, is opposed to killing, preferring to set his verses to the music of the lyre. As the third son with a noble calling, he is like the woodchopper's third son of folklore who is called to high adventure; and Jorn is, in fact, the fairy tale's Prince Charming.

The court retinue includes such figures as Quondo, a

dwarf, and the castle wizard whose magic consists of such minor wonders as sleight of hand and juggling, since he is not privy to the magic of the wood wizards. At the center of the court is King Clode (whose name suggests "clod"), a basically good-hearted but often disgruntled and oafish man who roars and paces about pulling his mustaches. Inspired by Harold Ross, the comic king uses a number of Ross's expressions, crying, "Done and done" and "Nobody ever tells me anything." When a comet falls to earth, King Clode, who often feels harassed, exclaims quite seriously, "They aim these things at me." Even in their attitudes, Ross and King Clode are similar. Ross was obsessed by his magazine and distrustful of women, and King Clode is a misogynist who is single-mindedly interested in hunting. In a letter written just after the book was published, White wrote to Thurber praising his "beautiful Deer" and expressing particular admiration of King Clode. "The King, I think," he remarked, "is a magnificently funny character, and ought to last forever—which is more than you can say of Ross."[5]

As they prepare for the hunting to begin, King Clode tells a story-within-the-story of how, as one of three sons, he had hunted in the enchanted forest and brought a deer to bay that was suddenly transformed into a tall, dark young princess—a maiden who had been changed into a deer years before by a wicked old woman jealous of her beauty. The hunting party had then escorted the princess to her father's kingdom in the North where, in accordance with the custom of that land, the princess exercised the privilege of claiming one of her rescuers as her husband. King Clode and his brothers, Cloon and Garf, were each set tasks. Cloon was bested in combat with a great falcon and Garf was never heard from again, but King Clode succeeded in his exploit, wresting a great diamond from what proved to be an artificial monster made of clay and sandalwood. He and the princess were then married, and before her death (which King Clode does not seem much

to lament, being ill at ease with feminine grace and deli-
cacy), she bore him three sons.

The hunt on which they embark the next day takes
them into the paradoxical enchanted forest where a million fireflies change suddenly to snowflakes and the solid
world of factuality vanishes. Here they encounter a wood
wizard in a blue robe and red peaked cap who tells King
Clode that he had met him twenty-six years before, and
offers to show him the forest's "barking trees," "musical
mud," and "wingless birds." Further, he causes a fleet
white deer to materialize before them that they then pursue through a surrealist landscape, bringing it at last to
bay by the side of Centaurs Mountain. As Thag and Gallow are about to loose their arrows, however, the white
deer is transformed into a tall, dark maiden. The young
men kneel before her while King Clode (who wants no
lovely maidens, only a good hunt) glowers and tugs at his
mustaches.

The chapter ends with their returning with the princess to the castle through a fantastic world of ruby ridges,
silver swamps, and fiery fens. A galloping, page-long sentence, evoking their journey magically past the turquoise
tarn, across the musical mud, and by the flocks of wingless
birds brings this section to a close dramatically. The chapter is dramatic in essence since Thurber has introduced all
the major characters and provided full exposition of their
situation concisely. One sees the conflict between the
brothers, between the youngest son and his father, between the castle and the enchanted forest, and is eager to
learn what will happen next.

In the following chapter set at the castle, the princess
cannot remember her name or anything about her earlier
life, having only a deer's recollection of forest branches
and green leaves. The royal recorder attempts to prod her
memory by going through the alphabet reciting the names
of kings who might be her father, but to no effect. Search-
ing through the castle's library of ancient lore, however, he
finds a book with an account of a deer befriended by a

wood wizard who bestowed on the creature the power when brought to bay of changing into a lovely young maiden. But her transformation is only conditional. Should love fail her thrice she must resume her former shape forever. Before long it is arranged that King Clode's three sons shall perform perilous labors in the name of love for the princess that is successful will break the spell upon her. The chapter ends with King Clode roaring his misgivings.

The next three chapters are devoted respectively to the tests in the enchanted forest of the princes Thag, Gallow, and Jorn. All accomplish their tasks and return to the castle at the same time to claim the princess. When they apply for her hand, however, she tells them that if ancient lore is correct she is "in truth" a deer, and Thag and Gallow withdraw their marriage proposals. Only prince Jorn offers his love, telling her that what she is now she "will be forever." With his love pledge she blooms into even greater and more wondrous beauty, and a young prince appears (transformed from the dwarf Quondo) who explains that he is Tel, brother of the princess Rosanore of the Northland; and he tells the story of her enchantment by a jealous woman named Nagrom Yaf (Morgan Le Fay spelled backwards) as a vengeance on their house. The enchantment could be broken only if a king and his three sons brought the deer to bay, but even then if she did not know and could not speak her name; and only if, despite all doubt of her to the contrary, one of the king's sons should declare his love. Only then could she again be princess Rosanore. The work ends in festivity, as Jorn dances with Rosanore and a verse is recited celebrating "the rose, the fountain, and the dove." The party then prepares to ride off in full panoply to the Northland, the gruff King Clode, won over now, exclaiming, "I blow my horn in waste land, so to speak."

The White Deer is Thurber's most glowing tribute to the ideal but it is not unmindful of the nature of the actual world. It is strongly intimated, for example, in the perilous labors that Thag and Gallow perform. Prince Thag is assigned the task of hunting alone and killing the great Blue Boar of Thedon Grove in the Forest of Jeopardy and of bringing back its golden tusks. Thag rides off into a mysterious forest where he confronts a roundish, balding man in the crotch of a tree who gives the idea of the moon. The speech of Thag and the moon man is comically distorted by the sticky, sweetish liquid dropping from the trees, making true communication between them impossible. This derangement of sense is Thag's introduction to the shining Valley of Euphoria lying just beyond.

In the Valley of Euphoria, Thag meets three men who giggle and chortle while holding masks in their hands exactly like their solemn faces. They wear the masks, they explain, only on yesterdays and tomorrows, and so "know no sorrows." The self-deceived men bid him tarry with them, but Thag continues onward to a green valley where he hears the sound of frolic and frivolity and where, as he flashes past on his charger, a man cries "Carpe Diem." On and on Thag rides, through a "mist of moss" and a "storm of glass" and a "musical stream" whose sweet soft waters beguile him so that he is barely able to save himself from drowning. The forest is swept by fire and torrential rains, but Thag gallops forward on his steed "singing."

Arriving at last in Thedon Grove he finds the great Blue Boar fast asleep. The creature awakens too late and has only time to roar, "Scarroooof!" before Thag kills him with his lance and takes his golden tusks. His task, after all, turns out to be easy, and he then races back through the menacing woods where flocks of "buzbuz birds" fly at him, opening and closing their scissorlike beaks. Thag's adventure and safe return is both heroic and, in the confrontation with the sleeping monster, anticlimactic. He has survived the perils of Euphoria, but he is not necessarily a deep man, deep of heart and faith.

Prince Gallow's perilous labor, to overcome the Seven-Headed Dragon of Dragore that guards the Sacred Sword of Loralow and bring the sword back to the castle, is still more revealing. Entering a peaceful wood, he discovers signs hanging from trees that read Seek Grailo, Even Better Than the True Grail, 7 League Boots Now 6.98, and We Put You on an Urn, Men Put You on a Pedestal. The signs belong to a commercial culture where values are debased and cheapened. As Gallow scans the signs, one of which announces a free visit to the Seven-Headed Dragon of Dragore, a man wearing a silver cap and a garment made of brass salutes him. The man in metal, who might have stepped out of the Oz books of L. Frank Baum, is a kind of salesman. He tells Gallow that in the Forest of Willbe all men are brothers, and offers to sell him three parchments for three emeralds that will be his passes through the woods. He is to give the red parchment to a man in white, the blue parchment to a man in red, and the white parchment to a man in blue. The colors are significantly those of the American flag, and they suggest that the Forest of Willbe is America itself.

When Gallow comes upon the man in white, who turns out to be a con man, the man tells him that the parchment he has given him is not in order but that he will be able to make it right for three emeralds. After giving the man in white the emeralds, he rides on until reaching a man in blue who tells him that no one can read the parchment he has given him without the use of a mirror. The inscription on the parchment explains that the present exists but without a past or a future; but in the reverse image of the mirror the present becomes the future. In the Forest of Willbe, in other words, the individual's present is really a projection of what the future will be—leaving him without a sense of identity, only a dream life. The man in white sells Gallow the mirror for three emeralds, and later Gallow meets the man in red, another con man who at the price of more emeralds purports to make him invisible, although he does not, and directs him to the Dragon of Dragore through the Moaning Grove of Artanis.

Artanis ("Sinatra" spelled backwards) is filled with the sound of the moaning of lonely maidens for a lover. The air is heavy with the scent of roses, and the sky above is bright with the light of a million moons. Closing his eyes and ears to this, Gallow gallops on to a white light just beyond which is a kind of fair where tables are spread with baubles and gimcracks and people dance about making a whirring and buzzing sound as if they were mechanical beings. A man in black and blue cries, "Here you are, brother! Try your luck," as he hands Gallow seven balls for twelve emeralds. In a striped tent before them is the Seven-Headed Dragon of Dragore, which turns out to be a mechanical contraption, "the greatest mechanical wonder of the age." If Gallow can toss the seven balls into the open mouths of the seven moving heads, he will win the Sacred Sword of Loralow.

The carnival game, however, is rigged. For a price the pitchman will keep the heads stationary so that Gallow can toss the balls in the heads easily. Gallow agrees to give him the golden saddle on his horse, tosses the balls into the gaping mouths of the seven heads, and claims the sacred sword. Yet as he leaves the tent, a "small tired man" opens a chest, takes out one of a hundred identical swords, places it in the paws of the mechanical monster, yawns, and shuffles away. If Thag's journey in the Valley of Euphoria describes a world of immediate pleasure that is merely empty escapism, Gallow's depicts one in which no pleasure in any deep sense is possible because nothing is sacred. The Forest of Willbe is roamed by con men who prey on the unwary, and it is characterized by spiritual deadness, by the mechanical and sterile. The America Thurber evokes in the Forest of Willbe, with its advertising slogans, illusion of the present as the future that deprives individuals of identity, and mechanical wonders is as bleak and as little able to lead to a realization of the ideal as the America evoked by Nathanael West.

Yet in the chapter devoted to Jorn's exploit, Thurber seems to say that an ideal of love is realizable. The princess, who is in love with him and wishes him to succeed, sets him the easiest task. His encounter with the Mok-Mok is not a perilous task at all, since the Mok-Mok is artificial, and made of clay and sandalwood, and when he comes upon it he finds that it has collapsed. Its head has broken off from its body, on which (in Thurber's illustration, among the last with the aid of the Zeiss loop that he was able to do) are inscribed with such in-joke initials as EBW (E. B. White), MVD (Mark Van Doren), and HWR (Harold W. Ross). A witch, however, creates a formidable test for Jorn, and he succeeds in it, vanquishing a Black Knight in the name of love. When he returns to the castle, he breaks the spell upon princess Rosanore, and the prince and princess ride off into a bountiful future.

But how seriously can this ending be taken? Among the characters in the work who challenge it is Tocko, the royal clock maker. Before becoming the royal clock maker, he had been the royal astronomer—until he began to lose his vision and to give out alarming reports that "everything was going out." As the royal clock maker, Tocko carves such disquieting legends on sundials as "It is darker than you think" and "After this brief light, the unending dark." He has the pale, misty eyes of a blind man, and one has the sense that he is an aspect of Thurber. Tocko's sundial inscriptions and the wasteland evoked in the exploits of Thag and Gallow are reminders that the real world does not lend itself readily, if at all, to fairy-tale happy endings.

Another problem in the romantic scheme of the work is the princess. In a letter to White about *The 13 Clocks*, Thurber wrote that the princess Saralinda "will bear elaborate description, but being the paper doll she is, any actions or speeches of hers indicating that she can live up to her description would destroy her. Like Cinderella and her prince, Saralinda and hers are Kewpies under their clothes."[6] Princess Rosanore, too, is really a Kewpie. What is perhaps most interesting about her is King Clode's anxiety that she is "in truth" a deer. He had been unable to accept his own wife, a transformed deer, for that reason. What is implied in his anxiety is that however ideal woman may seem to be, she belongs in fact to the imperfect natural world and is involved in its destructive energies. A light-dark imagery is employed throughout the tale, particularly in the white deer-dark princess idea, and this contrast calls attention to a longing for the ideal that is challenged by the gross and impure world of matter.

Princes Thag and Gallow are unattractively named, Thag suggesting "thug" and Gallow a hangman's platform. Standing for purely physical endeavors or might, they cannot resolve the dilemma embodied in the princess of the real and the ideal. But Jorn, whose name suggests "born" and "yearn" associated with the creative life, is a poet-dreamer who refrains from violence and in an act of faith is able to bridge two opposing worlds, or so Thurber urges the reader to believe. But can one really believe in Jorn's success? Isn't it, after all, the Kewpie, the chaste idea of woman, that he wins? Rosanore may be a "dark" princess, but there is notably no sexual dimension to her, and she is quite unlike the aggressive females in Thurber's writing and drawings whose self-assertion implies a threatening sexuality. In *The White Deer*, invoking "the rose, the fountain, and the dove," Thurber proposes a cessation in the war between the sexes. Yet this can only happen in a fairy tale, through the use of a princess who has every grace and no sexuality (Rosanore turns out *not* to have been a deer in the first place after all), and the effect of all this is to render Thurber's resolution of conflict highly ambiguous.

How momentary the communication between people is at the end of *The White Deer* is indicated by a dark and apocalyptic fable written by Thurber at the end of his life. "The Last Clock: A Fable for the Time, Such as It Is, of Man" (1959) is set in a country "the other side of tomorrow" in which an ogre has fallen into the habit of eating clocks. He has already eaten most of the clocks of the castle when his wife, an ogress, brings in a doctor to look at him. The doctor, however, says that he cannot treat the ogre because his consumption of clocks is outside of his "area."

An aged inspirationalist is then called in, but his inspirationalism has become a "jumble of mumble," and before falling asleep on a sofa observes that the final experience will be "mummum."

As the days go on, the ogre eats all the clocks in the town, sprinkling them with watches as if they were salt and pepper, until there are no more clocks left. Without clocks, the life of the town grinds to a halt. People oversleep, factories close, shopkeepers shut up their businesses, schools do not open—and an emergency meeting of the town council is called. Specialists who are brought in explain that the problem is outside their expertise, and the case then goes before the supreme magistrate of the supreme council. But the supreme council meeting also proves to be useless. Hearing a clock ticking in the council room, the magistrate orders that this "last clock" be placed in a museum, where it is allowed to run down.

The life of the town continues to deteriorate. Nothing works or runs, people cannot communicate meaningfully with one another, and eventually the sands of a nearby desert gradually move in and bury the timeless town. Eons later, in an ending that looks forward to Kurt Vonnegut, a party of explorers from another planet, descendants of people from Earth who had reached Venus a thousand years before and intermarried with Venusians, probe through the ruins of the old inspirationalist's library. They find a document in his shaky hand containing the word "mummum" and an old clock that they do not understand but take back with them as a relic of the "Time of Man on Earth." The transcendence proposed in *The White Deer* has by the time of "The Last Clock" turned into a nightmare of senselessness.

The fantasy of the fables and fairy tales is hardly new in Thurber's work. Stories like "The Catbird Seat" are also enchantments or socialized fairy tales in which Thurber's little men are often like children trapped in menacing adult words. Thurber's drawings of such men in combat with viragoes give the sense of bewitchment, too, and are charged with the sense of pure innocence and pure aggression. That Thurber should have discovered the fable and fairy-tale forms in the 1940s and 1950s seems in hindsight almost to have been inevitable, since they were anticipated in the earlier work. But his discovery of these forms was not of course predictable at all, and that he took possession of them with such authority is one of the surprising features of the later period. They illustrate that even in a difficult time Thurber was capable of growth as an artist, not so much in exploring wholly new themes as in finding new ways in which to refocus his earlier ones.

The fairy tales particularly plunge the reader into antirational experience at a far remove from ordinary life. In their removal from the actual world into an inner or subjective one, they also reflect on Thurber's blindness. If the physical world is no longer as visually present to him, he has compensated by creating a mythical one with the most cunning verbal invention and ingenious effects. In writing to Thurber about *The White Deer,* White remarked that his fairy tale represented "the strange case of a writer's switch from eye work to ear work. I can't believe that anybody could make such a switch and live."[7] In no other work of Thurber's is such intricate verbal artistry sustained at such length. Both witty and lyrical, *The White Deer* is one of Thurber's major works.

Essentially the fairy tales are lyrical-satiric meditations on the theme of freedom and restriction, of powerlessness and heroism. The notion of heroism that had been implicit in Thurber's earlier writing chiefly in its being balked is brought forward and reexamined. It receives its most extended consideration in *The White Deer,* a work having a certain affinity with Henry James. In James, one finds a confrontation between spiritually "good" or uncorrupted characters and others who are powerful in a worldly sense, and the contest between them is often unequal. But sometimes James's innocent characters actually prevail. In *The White Deer* and the other fairy tales, those who have preserved their innocence and remained uncorrupted by worldly values are finally rewarded and recognized for their true worth.

The fairy tales are reminiscent of James perhaps most of all in Thurber's use of the artist as a hero of culture. In *Many Moons*, it is the court jester (the artist as humorist) who resolves the tragicomic dilemma that the most learned men of the court cannot; in *The Great Quillow*, the toy maker (the artist as miniaturist) saves the day after all the shopkeepers and tradesmen have failed; in *The White Deer*, the poet-prince rather than his huntsmen brothers gains the hand of Rosanore. In his parodies, Thurber identifies with James in a negative and self-deprecating way as a man of delicate imagination and vast sexual insecurity. But in the fairy tales, he proposes the artist as hero, and in doing so assumes a new and positive kind of identification with James. It is as if the ordeal of blindness had summoned in Thurber the strength to continue as an artist and to declare the heroism of the calling that James had enunciated in his own career.

Too much, however, can be made of Thurber's affirmations in the fairy tales that, as has been brought out, are qualified by many kinds of ambiguity and give the sense that Thurber was not as wholly convinced that idealism may prevail as he seems to assert. The fairy tales bring Thurber to the limit of such affirmation as he had been able to make, but they do not quite dispel an impression that the individual is alone in an inscrutable and baffling world. Locked into an essential privacy, his sensitive artists achieve dreamworld vindication, but always in the background is the wasteland that threatens them and has tremendous power and where, as Walter Mitty says, "things close in."

8

~~~~~~~~~~~~~~~~~~~~~~~~~~~~~~~~~~~~~~~

Conclusion: Thurber in Context

In literary histories—such as Walter Blair's *Horse Sense in American Humor: From Benjamin Franklin to Ogden Nash* (1942; rev. 1962), Walter Blair and Hamlin Hill's *American Humor From Poor Richard to Doonesberry* (1978), and Norris Yates's *The American Humorist: Conscience of the Twentieth Century* (1964)—a distinctive tradition in American humor has been traced in which Yankee shrewdness becomes westernized to reflect the expansive energies of the frontier, and then urbanized in the twentieth century to reveal the helplessness of the average man in an age of technology.[1] "Instead of roistering Davy Crocketts and Mike Finks," Robert Morsberger remarks, the protagonists of modern American humor "are repressed, squeamish, and hypersensitive. Such figures recur frequently in James Thurber's work."[2] No disagreement exists that Thurber illustrates perfectly this transition occurring in modern American humor.

Yet if Thurber helped to alter the tradition, he writes with a consciousness of what it had been. In *My Life and Hard Times*, for example, he establishes a modern humor in which the individual is at sea while drawing from a frontier tradition. It would be difficult to read the extravagantly droll episodes in the book, told with poker-faced solemnity, without being reminded of Mark Twain. The strongly farcical tall tale belonging to exuberant frontier story telling is used by Thurber to create bewilderment and confusion. Rather than being revealed as sturdy and self-sufficient, the individual is exposed as a clown. The devices of western humor are used against it, as exuberant clowning turns into desperation.

My Life and Hard Times illustrates Thurber's contradictions, since it is striking both in its joviality and its underlying alienation, in its "down home" Midwestern voice and its urbanity. The narrative voice is familiar, almost folksy, yet suggests great detachment and is elusive. Thurber's attitude toward his characters is affectionate, yet he is always distant from them, never revealing himself at all fully in the specifics of his inner conflicts. The episodes of the book are shaped as dream structures that close out a well-defined outer world to emphasize a fantasia of consciousness in which an attempt to find an integration between the self and the world is frustrated hysterically. When Thurber's characters attempt to act they are immediately engulfed in farce. The grandfather, as the eldest member of the family, should possess wisdom and dignity but instead is the greatest lunatic, withdrawing into a Civil War dreamworld as a means of surviving.

The sense of disorientation in the work is achieved partly through incremental episodes, with one incident of misunderstanding escalating into another. At the same time the characters mirror each other in their inability to act purposively and effectively. By "The Day the Dam Broke," the mirror characters become hundreds who rush through the streets unable to distinguish reality from fantasy. When the "real" world is broached at the end with World War I, Thurber cannot enter it. If the exuberant farce of frontier humor confirms the individual's ability to control his destiny, in Thurber it leads to the extinction of the possibility of his assuming an active role in life or even of knowing who he is.

Thurber's affinity with the exuberant frontier tradition is paradoxical in view of the important role he played at the *New Yorker,* which even at the beginning adopted the attitude of big-city urbanity. Schooled by White, he learned to write the "Talk of the Town" columns that virtually represented the magazine to the world, and his reportage has the wittiness and polish of *New Yorker* writing at its best. Yet one has the sense of Thurber's not quite fully "belonging" at the magazine, not at least in the sense that the Whites had belonged. Bred in the Midwest, he never became a metropolitan sophisticate. A man of what Peter De Vries has called "an almost eerie sensitivity,"[3] an eccentric with deep and curious fixations and peculiar ways of looking at things, Thurber did not quite belong anywhere.

Thurber's closest association at the *New Yorker* was with White whom, with a single exception, according to Helen Thurber, he loved "more than any other man in his life."[4] The affection was reciprocated. As Scott Elledge, White's biographer, points out, White wrote in his journal in 1927 that "one of the persons I like best in the world is Thurber."[5] Thurber acknowledged White's influence on his writing at various times, but less well known is that Thurber also influenced White. Elledge has pointed out to me in conversation that many of White's early, uncollected casuals might almost be mistaken for Thurber's work.[6] Their early collaboration in writing *Is Sex Necessary?* is striking in the easy confluence of their styles—to such a degree that readers might well be unable to detect which of them had written which of the chapters.

In his biography, Elledge has noted similarities in their backgrounds. They were born in the same period, White five years younger than Thurber, and came from Anglo-Saxon Protestant families. They had been editors of their university newspapers and had written the scripts for campus musicals. After college, they worked for newspapers, admiring the great American paragraphers but disliking their assignments as reporters. Both were skeptics who possessed a natural sense of humor, admired Benchley and Don Marquis, and loved parody and other forms of satire. Both were attracted to the shorter forms of writing and were stylists. "In other ways," Elledge observes, "they were different. Whereas White was a quiet, reserved, and private person, modest about his talents and careful to say no more than he meant, Thurber was voluble, gregarious, and sometimes extravagant."[7]

But they were also different in certain of their ostensible similarities. White derived from an upper middle-class family in Mount Vernon, New York, that, unlike Thurber's, was unusually close and without friction between the parents. Although White's father suffered financial reverses in the depression, he had provided his family with the sense of their belonging solidly to a certain class and place. President of a company that manufactured pianos, he had a large, elaborate frame house built for his family in a neighborhood of substantial and expensive houses. In 1917, White followed his two older brothers to Cornell University where, despite his shyness, he was popular and successful. He was not only editor in chief of the university newspaper but also president of his fraternity. His writing attracted the attention of the faculty, and when he graduated he was invited to teach in the English Department.

Thurber, by contrast, came from a family having a chronically insecure sense of its social position. A cloud of failure hung over the father, and neuroticism within the family was intense. A friend recalls that Thurber's brothers were "practically recluses" and were "even more eccentric than Jim."[8] The Thurbers were sheltered by the mother's well-to-do parents, but only grudgingly and for a while, and moved frequently. Thurber did not attend an Ivy League university like White but the local state university, where he commuted from his family house and was a loner and misfit. Although after meeting Elliott Nugent he did enjoy a measure of success on the campus, he never finished his degree, leaving to experience inner confusion and nervous breakdown. If White's background lent him an essential stability, Thurber's left him scarred and at war with himself and the world.

At the beginning of their friendship, White was Thurber's mentor and conscience, but during the course of the 1930s their relationship underwent a change. Thurber became more famous than White, reaching a larger, indeed an international audience. Although admired for his "Notes and Comment" column in the *New Yorker* and highly regarded by other professionals, White considered himself a failure. It seemed to him that he possessed a gift for merely "trivial" writing and had published nothing that would last. He was afflicted by a variety of neurotic ailments, and suffered from depression and hypochondria.

White was late in finding himself, but find himself he did. In 1938 he bought a farm in Maine, where he remained until 1943, when he returned to New York, but in 1954 went back to live in Maine permanently. White's withdrawal to Maine became the making of him, for it was there that he did much of his finest work. In the early 1940s, Thurber was stricken with blindness and the years that followed were harrowing and difficult. During this time, however, White's reputation expanded dramatically. His essay collections—*One Man's Meat* (1942), *The Second Tree from the Corner* (1954), and *The Points of My Compass* (1962)—belong to this later time, as do his children's books *Stuart Little* (1945) and *Charlotte's Web* (1952) that are among the most popular of their kind in the world and made him financially independent. In his later life, White was heaped with public honors, not only honorary degrees from Dartmouth, Yale, and other universities, but also the Presidential Medal of Freedom (1963) and the National Medal for Literature (1979). If Thurber was the more renowned humorist, White regained parity with him as a *New Yorker* writer of national stature.

The friendship of Thurber and White that had begun so splendidly in the late 1920s continued throughout their lives, but it became more distant and at times was strained. When Thurber moved to Connecticut and White to Maine, they saw much less of each other; but even at those times when they were together in New York the personal differences between them became increasingly evident. White was a very modest and private man, while

Thurber was assertive to the point of becoming obstreperous in social situations. White has remarked that "there was never a kinder, nicer friend" than Thurber, but that after his third drink he "became a madman."[9] He noted that Thurber's hostility was often directed toward women, and at one gathering the nearest woman to attack was his wife Katharine, an incident that was never forgotten. After that, the Whites often avoided Thurber at night. White expressed his admiration of Thurber on many occasions, but he also remarked that Thurber "was the most self-centered man I've even known."[10]

At the end of the 1950s, as has been mentioned previously, Thurber and White had a falling out over *The Years with Ross*, partly over the issue of Ross's right to privacy. The Whites had loved Ross and were pained to see him made fun of before the world. Thurber's portrait and White's wounded reaction to it point to important differences between them. For years Thurber had drawn caricature portraits of his ancestors and family members, who dramatized superbly his sense of the familiar and closely known as being almost inconceivably strange, and in the book had done the same with Ross. He had no sense of what Elledge, in our conversation, called "the sanctity of privacy and love" that were so important to White. The humor of each was accordingly quite different, White's sly but never cruel, Thurber's coming from a less-contained, more anguished and deeper creative drive.

As the personal relations of Thurber and White changed over the years, so did the direction of their careers. Thurber explored the inner dynamics of personality, with an emphasis upon isolation and inner suffering. His work is haunted by a sense of the incongruous that is a corollary to inner psychic dislocation. Thurber's comic sense and his pessimism both come from this disjunction, from the unbridgeable gap between the self and the world. White, on the other hand, searched for a sense of identity through an integration of the solitary self with his surroundings—with nature, family, and others.

On his farm in Maine, White immersed himself in the normal, the healthy, and the ordinary; and these things become the subject of much of his writing. "He writes a good deal," Edward Sampson observes, "about his farming, and related activities in Maine; chickens, sheep, fertilizer, the weather—these matters provide material for sometimes routine comments, and sometimes masterpieces of incisive and often beautiful evocations of pastoral simplicity and honesty."[11] Thurber himself, in his sketch "E. B. W." (1938), had particularly noted this aspect of White:

He spends most of his time delousing turkeys, gathering bantam eggs, building mice-proof closets, and ripping out old fireplaces and putting in new ones. There is in him not a little of the spirit of Thoreau, who believed "that the world crowds round the individual, leaving him no vista, and shuts out the beauty of the earth; and that the wholesome wants of man are few." Now and then, between sunup and milking time, Andy White manages to do a casual or a poem for *The New Yorker*, or write a book. Many of the things he writes seem to me as lovely as a tree—say a maple after the first frost, or the cherry hung with snow.[12]

White writes of nature at times with a sense of oneness between the individual and the natural world. Yet he is not a mystical romantic. He is always conscious of the concrete, and one cannot think of him apart from his family and neighbors. His mind dwells on the small, even the minute, making them the starting point of his reflections on life that are expressed with an elegant informality and authenticity. In creating this remarkable style,[13] White also created himself, establishing an identity that is both modest and large. This ingratiating and pondering style reflects White's deep concerns with freedom, privacy, and personal integrity while retaining a sense of relation to others. White found a sense of identity in a setting of pastoral quiet in which the demands of ego are stilled, but Thurber took as his subject the irreconcilability of man and his world. In Thurber the conflicts of ego cannot be willed away but rather are an obsessive preoccupation.

White's children's books and Thurber's fables and fairy tales illustrate their differences. In *Stuart Little* and *Charlotte's Web*, one finds an enormous pleasure in the small and modest. Although mouse-small and a vehicle of humor, Stuart Little becomes admirable in his independence and search for intellectual integrity. As he drives along in his miniature car at the end, one feels that he may just possibly find some semblance of the ideal he seeks. If not extremely optimistic, an optimism is at least not disallowed. The same is true of *Charlotte's Web*, in which White writes with a consciousness of the cruelty of nature to farm animals, yet allows for the possibility of communication between creatures, of benignity in life as well as destruction.

Thurber's fables and fairy tales, on the other hand, remind the reader of the individual's isolation, of the great gap between ideals longed for and the powerlessness of the self to bring them into being. Generally speaking, nature in the fables is either inscrutable or malignant. The fable creatures are not wise enough to order their destinies, and many lack consciousness, knowing only vanity. Death strikes quickly and unpredictably. In various ways Thurber's fairy tales evoke the opposition between imagination and power. His artist figures are allowed to triumph, yet in a way their triumph is a kind of dream escape from their powerlessness and isolation. If there is a cautious optimism in White's reading of the human situation, there seems hardly any, in an unqualified sense, in Thurber.

What one finds frequently in Thurber is an unequal contest between innocence and aggression. The contest can be seen dramatically in Thurber's most powerful fables "The Unicorn in the Garden" and "The Green Isle in the Sea." Both are concerned with sanctuaries of gentleness and innocence that are violated by the external world. In "The Unicorn in the Garden," the violator is a woman of cold and unreasoning self-assertion; in "The Green Isle in the Sea," aggression takes the form of malignancy in nature and human nature that culminates in the ferocious and unreasoning energies of war. No middle ground exists in which the individual might come to terms with himself, and therefore the possibility of self-integration or a successful achievement of identity is foreclosed.

In the "Where Are They Now?" profiles, the public landscapes Thurber evokes are invariably mocking. Individuals who seem for a moment to possess a degree of control over their lives quickly sink beneath the public landscapes in which they had momentarily figured, becoming stripped of any coherent sense of self. Presumably, Thurber's people might find a sense of wholeness in their private lives rather than their public roles, but the reverse if true. His couples illustrate Chekhov's remark that if you cannot take loneliness you should not marry. Their domestic lives lead to ever-greater confinement and neurotic suffering.

In his conventional marriage, Mr. Bidwell in "The Private Life of Mr. Bidwell" suffers ever-increasing isolation, is gripped mysteriously by powerful and irrational fixations. At the beginning he holds his breath for as long as possible as if he wished to stop breathing all together. At the end he is a solitary figure along a country road who attempts to see how many steps he can take without opening his eyes, withdrawing into quasi blindness as if to close out the world. His psychic withdrawal suggests not only self-punishment but even a death wish. In "The Remarkable Case of Mr. Bruhl," Mr. Bruhl, a conventional family man, also experiences mysterious anguish, developing a fixation with a notorious gangster. When he is shot in place of the other man in a gangland killing, it is actually a moment of triumph over his lifelong existence as a nonentity. Ironically, however, his attempt to escape leads only to death.

Family life in Thurber, rather than being an avenue to self-realization, is the setting of constant thwarting. The

family home in *My Life and Hard Times* is a gathering place
of freaks and strangers. The various members of the
Thurber family do not come together in a mutuality of
understanding but remain solipsistically separate. Some of
them suffer from strange fixations and phobias, but all live
at the edge of their strained nerves, and their attempts to
communicate with others prove unmanageable. The wild
episodes bring a boisterous release into anarchy, but it is
anarchy rather than stability that defines the family's life.
In *The Thurber Album*, Thurber represents his family and
ancestors more realistically, yet the eccentric ancestors
hardly constitute a tradition of stability, and the portraits
of the father and mother come uncomfortably close to
Thurber's "little" man and his aggressor wife. Vivid and
skillful as some of the portraits (especially the early ones)
are, they give little sense of oneness within the family or of
the family's belonging cohesively within their community.
The Thurber ancestors and family members remain distinctly separate and apart from one another in a queer
isolation.

An essential background figure in Thurber's work is
Freud. Norris Yates has remarked that "an orthodox
Freudian would see Thurber's Little Man as tormented by
the conflict between the unconscious 'beast' of sex and the
repression of it by the superego, which is shaped and
dominated by this man's environment. The repressed animal finds its outlet in anxieties, fixations, and obsessions."[14] *My Life and Hard Times* illustrates this Freudian
conception, since the house seethes with repression and
frustration, and its eruptions into unrestrained anarchy
have almost the nature of orgasm. Earlier, in *Is Sex Necessary?*, although it spoofs Freud and sex therapists, Thurber
follows Freud closely in noting, as in the case of George
Smith, how personality becomes neurotic through a repression of sexual drives.

Freud's notion of the unconscious is evoked frequently
in Thurber's work, not only in the drawings, with their
marvelous strangeness, but also in the stories. Dreams

appear often in them, and in "The Whip-Poor-Will" the protagonist's feverish dreams provide the psychic symbols of his distress. "Mr. Preble Gets Rid of His Wife" is set in the cellar of the protagonist's house, evoking the unconscious from which his dreams of aggression emerge; and Mr. Bruhl assumes his alter-ego identity with the hardened criminal while he is sleeping, and emerges from his bedroom brandishing a phallic pistol. Although Thurber disclaimed a belief in Freud and his theories, Freud's conspicuous influence on Thurber is as apparent as it is appropriate, since the subject of much of his fiction is psychosexual disturbance and frustration of personality.

Charles Holmes has emphasized that in his allegiance to freedom, spontaneity, and abandon, Thurber belongs to a romantic tradition. Thurber is romantic in some respects, particularly as an antirationalist, but he cannot really be compared to nineteenth-century romantic writers like Wordsworth, who saw God in nature and found transcendence in the freshness of impulse and natural feeling. Nature for Thurber is hardly benevolent. Often it seems cruelly mechanistic, the source of destructive or irrational drives, such as the power seeking of the strong over the weak. Sex itself is a primary biological drive, and its effect on Thurber's characters is devastating. Abandonment to anarchic impulse brings only momentary euphoria and is linked with maiming. One has the sense of a very deep sense of guilt in Thurber that is allied with his frequently pessimistic outlook. His characters are often self-punishing caricatures, little men who are stripped naked and exposed as unworthy.

Thurber possessed a strain of idealism in his nature, but it never becomes quite coherent. From adolescence onward he tended to idealize women, but this thwarted impulse quickly turns to rage and an inordinate resentment of women. A hostility to women is constantly implied in his work, particularly in the brooding sense of threat posed by wives to his husbands. One has the sense that Thurber longed to believe in an ideality in life, but that it always proved elusive and beyond his grasp. In "The Last Flower," he defends idealism when he pictures natural impulse and love as being deeper and more enduring than the destructive forces of civilization. But the parable breaks down under scrutiny since "love," represented by the burgeoning of the frail flower and the mating of the naked man and woman, is inseparable from biology and its snares that lead to the war of the sexes. If love is sentimental and ambiguous in the parable, the natural drives that lead to war and destruction seem unquestionably real. Although the last flower survives to bloom again, its survival will merely be accompanied by another round of cataclysm and annihilation.

When Thurber attempts to affirm positive values in life, he is apt to become self-contradictory and unconvincing. In *The Thurber Album*, he proposes an earlier-day Columbus as a model of a healthier age in American life, one that the nation ought to try to return to. Yet the eccentric family ancestors seem disturbingly neurotic, and the inhabitants of Columbus in the 1890s and the earlier 1900s give an uncomfortable sense of meanness and isolation from one another. In composing the album, Thurber conveniently forgets that he had been maimed forever by his growing up there. Rather than convincing the reader that earlier-day Columbus had represented a golden age in American life, the book seems an escape from a present that Thurber can hardly bear.

Thurber was fascinated throughout his life by Henry James, who possessed an aesthetic autonomy and moral idealism he would like to have shared but in the end cannot. *The White Deer,* one of the finest works of the later period, shows Thurber in his struggle to believe in an idealism of love and beauty beyond violation. But the inner plotting of the fairy tale exposes the enormous gap between the tale's ostensible realization of love and perfection and the wasteland of the actual world, with the result that the romantic ending is made to seem a beautiful lie. A sanctuary of the ideal is sometimes contemplated longingly and yearned for, but the underlying reality of Thurber's vision is isolation and dispossession.

The relatively few critical studies of Thurber have been unduly vague about his relation to other American writing. He comes importantly out of the literature of the 1920s and has particularly strong ties with T. S. Eliot, whose Prufrock anticipates his little men whose timidity, squeamishness, and inability to enter life invite mockery. Eliot's *The Waste Land*, moreover, enunciates the nature of the world in which these men must live, a world of spiritual sterility and emptiness that they cannot alter and that fills them with dread.

Thurber can also be compared to F. Scott Fitzgerald and Ernest Hemingway, particularly in the sense they all share of a private self that stands apart from the outer world and is threatened by it. His favorite novel by a contemporary American writer was *The Great Gatsby*, a work he knew by heart.[15] In 1934, just before the publication of *Tender Is the Night*, Thurber met Fitzgerald in New York at Tony's bistro, and they spent many hours together talking until dawn, as Thurber relates in his sketch "Scott in Thorns" (1951). In "Scott in Thorns," Thurber notes their similarities (their having both come from the Midwest and been born only a year apart, for example), and praises Fitzgerald for his craftsmanship and artistic soundness. But he remarks, too, that Fitzgerald was trapped in a romantic tradition, implying a difference between Fitzgerald and himself. Thurber's stories contain a few echoes of Fitzgerald, and a touch of his special nostalgia can be noticed in "The Evening's at Seven"; but while sharing a certain pessimism with Fitzgerald, Thurber dispensed with his romantic atmosphere and doomed, larger-than-life-size heroes. Thurber's own writing is stripped down to bare essentials, and in the diminutive scale of their conception his protagonists are really anti-heroes. Fitzgerald describes the breakup of ideals, but

Thurber begins where Fitzgerald left off, after romantic illusion has already been destroyed.

Despite their obvious differences, Thurber is much closer to Hemingway. Like Hemingway's, his stories deal-ing with the relationships of men and women contain the taut inner tensions of a struggle for domination, and some imply a specific awareness of Hemingway. Their fiction, moreover, has a related sense of the external world as empty and threatening to individuals who find them-selves alone and helpless. Hemingway's story "A Clean, Well-Lighted Place" evokes the individual's isolation through a terrible yet nameless fear of life that threatens him, and this kind of fear, never fully specified but spring-ing from an innermost depth of consciousness can be noted again in certain of Thurber's stories. One sees it in "A Box to Hide In," a story having the abbreviation and evocativeness of Hemingway's work.

In a curious way, Hemingway and Thurber are both hyperconscious of manhood, and a good deal of the inse-curity and fear in their stories are relevant to it. Heming-way's heroes are men with virile interests who go off to war, enjoy hunting and fishing, and have a passion for bullfighting; while Thurber's men are weaklings. Heming-way stands at one end of the masculine spectrum while Thurber occupies the other, but they share a sense of isolation. Hemingway's men withdraw tensely into certain "codes" that enable them to cope with fears that might otherwise make them go to pieces. Thurber's withdraw into dreamworlds in which they can be assertive and effec-tive. In neither case can they enter into human rela-tionships, particularly relationships with women, with trust and confidence.

But if in some important respects Thurber comes out of the 1920s, he also belongs to the 1930s, when he first achieved fame and when much of his best work was pub-lished. In their different ways, Fitzgerald and Hemingway each possess a 1920s worldliness that Thurber does not. His fiction is confined to flat domestic American scenes of urban rooms and suburban homes stricken by a sense of fear. Once confident of its central place in American life, the middle class has begun to suffer a crisis of identity. Driven inward upon themselves, Thurber's white-collar men experience awful doubts of their adequacy, and can barely cope. This sense of diminishment, of the anxious presentiments of an entire social class, has the mark of the Great Depression. If Thurber is an extremely private rather than politically engaged writer, his work nevertheless gives an underlying sense of a 1930s malaise.

Thurber has particular affinities with John O'Hara and Nathanael West, who emerged in the 1930s and evoke a sense of disintegrating values of the time partly through an emphasis upon male sexual vulnerability. O'Hara's first novel, *Appointment in Samarra* (1934), is specifically a Depression work, set in that time and concerned with a middle-class breakdown of identity. Julian English can no longer find any meaning in his existence. The social advantages he has been given by his emotionally distant doctor-father come to seem to him spurious, and he has no inner strength to fall back upon. Deprived of understanding and love, and unable to believe in himself as an adequate man and husband, he experiences inner terror and disorientation, and finally takes his life. His breakdown occurs during the Christmas holiday, but rather than a Christian God smiling down on him one has the sense of an inscrutable and even-malignant one claiming Julian's life almost whimsically, making him an exemplary case of a terror felt by countless others on a subterranean level at the height of the depression.

O'Hara dramatizes the loss of sustaining values and personal breakdown in his other novels of the 1930s, in *Butterfield 8* (1935) and *Hope of Heaven* (1938); but his obsession with a breakdown of identity, particularly as it is linked with an anxiety of male sexual inadequacy, continues to be felt in his social chronicles of the late 1940s and 1950s. Sidney Tate in *A Rage to Live* (1949), for example, cannot deal with his wife's infidelities when he is confronted by them; feeling alone and defenseless, he cannot act. Joe Chapin in *Ten North Frederick* (1955) becomes a study of isolation within marriage. He lives to see all his ideals destroyed and is, in effect, castrated by the women closest to him—his dominant, gubernatorial mother and his strong-minded wife. On whatever social level they are placed, O'Hara's characters are thwarted and reminded of their incompleteness and inadequacy. They are constantly humiliated by life and mocked by sexuality, which rather than bringing release exposes their vulnerability. The atmosphere of O'Hara's stories, particularly of the 1930s, is one of suffocation, of narrow rooms, of lives mysteriously stunted and filled with subterranean fear. O'Hara did not possess Thurber's special sense of fantasy, but their common emphasis upon constricted and frightening worlds in which power and effectiveness have been withdrawn from the male gives them a period affinity.

Nathanael West, whose brief career spanned the 1930s, has still closer ties with Thurber and shares his interest in fantasy. His first novel, *The Dream Life of Balso Snell* (1931), is a malignant modernist dream of impotence. No love exists in *Balso Snell*, merely biological and sexual drives that can lead to no fulfillment. In the novel, Balso Snell's whole life becomes an empty dream that is stalked by grotesqueness and a sense of helplessness from which he cannot escape. West's second novel *Miss Lonelyhearts* (1933), a work Thurber particularly admired, has a comic-strip quality, employing characters who have a cartoon dimension and inhabit a comic yet terrible world. Miss Lonelyhearts longs to play a heroic role but is instead a victim, quailing before the sexual threat of women. Fay Doyle, a huge, assertive woman who might have strayed out of a Thurber drawing, is so sexually voracious that she annihilates Miss Lonelyhearts's already tenuous sense of manhood. Like Thurber's dreamers, Miss Lonelyhearts cannot bring inner and outer worlds together. Their collision results merely in his death.

Of the two, West is the more radical in his alienation.

Anguish and fear in *Miss Lonelyhearts* and *The Day of the Locust* reach a pitch of hysteria beyond anything in Thurber. Yet both describe American social reality in terms of an unbearable bleakness that denies the individual the possibility of an integration of the self and the world, that strips him of identity and his life of meaning. Without outward confirmation of his identity, his existence becomes unreal. West's protagonists are driven inward into the theater of their minds to become self-dramatizing fantasists, and something of a similar nature happens to Thurber's characters. The further Walter Mitty's hold on reality weakens, the further he escapes into garish fantasy heroics. Mr. Bruhl comes to live wholly in self-dramatizing fantasy as a notorious gangster.

West and Thurber are alike in the sense they give of an extreme privacy and isolation, of nerves that are delicate and easily tortured. One of the most impressive features of their writing is the eerie depths of psychic fear that they are able to project. In West this acute sense of threat to the self, of violation of integrity, is almost religious in nature and seems connected with his consciousness of himself as a deracinated Jew. In Thurber it arises from the depths of some unheard-of innocence that cannot easily be labeled. In either case it creates an alienation so profound that it cannot be ameliorated.

Thurber's work involves more, of course, than his period affinities. His intellectual playfulness takes in writing of many different kinds and exhibits a startling versatility. White remarked that there "are at least two, probably six Thurbers,"[16] and one might almost think there are a dozen. Urbane reportage mingles with reminiscences of Ohio eccentrics; spare and poignant stories like "The Wood Duck" and "The Departure of Emma Inch" appear alongside grotesque tales like "The Greatest Man in the World" and "You Can Look It Up"; light humor pieces alternate with stinging fables that, with apparent satisfaction, foresee the end of the human race.

In our conversation, Scott Elledge referred to the

schizophrenic aspect of Thurber, and it is true, without wishing to use the word "schizophrenic" in any clinical way, that Thurber does split off in many different directions in his various voices and manners, and that his work suggests the slipping away of the real world into fragmented perceptions of it from odd, private angles. The frequent alternation of manners derives partly, one would think, from Thurber's natural gifts as a mimic and love of dramatic performance. His portraits of individuals are inherently dramatic, not only in their shaping but also in the empathy with which Thurber enters into their natures. Yet his very preference for many different voices and manners also implies a rejection of any systematic approach to life, a greater trust in spontaneity and impulse than in consistency.

If there is a figure in the American literary past Thurber most resembles it is not so much Henry James as Mark Twain. He writes at times in Twain's cadences and with something of his clarity and vigor; and like Twain he is a natural raconteur. Twain's prose, which lends itself to being read aloud, is particularly effective in its transitions from standard English to dialect and vernacular speech; and Thurber, too, is a keen listener to American speech and can switch suddenly and with striking effect to the parlance of ordinary or vulgar people. Thurber is like Twain, too, in his volatility, in his mood swings from innocence to wrath, from idealism to excoriating pessimism. Gregarious and outgoing in some ways, they were also introverts and skeptical moralists. Both espouse freedom and the individual, yet write at times with such a grimly deterministic outlook that it undermines the individual's importance. Both learned the craft of humor as reporters for newspapers and contributors to magazines, becoming celebrated writers whose American quality was savored abroad. Each was a renowned humorist and at the same time a serious literary artist with a deep strain of melancholy. Each suffered from highly strung nerves and from an early wounding—in Hannibal, Missouri and Columbus, Ohio—from which they never recovered. In *The Ordeal of Mark Twain,* Van Wyck Brooks ascribed "Twain's wound," his unappeasable anger, to a lifelong protest against his small-town-frontier origins, with its Puritan ethic and stark cultural impoverishment that stood in opposition to creative expression and imagination. Columbus was less forbidding than Hannibal, but it was here, clearly, that Thurber endured the trauma of being a half-blind misfit, a crisis in his inner life that did not subside even with vast success and international fame.

Significant differences, at the same time, exist between them. Twain does not have Thurber's sense of fantasy, and the spaciousness of Twain's America is absent in Thurber. Instead of mythic raft journeys down the Mississippi, one finds white-collar men who are seized by a sense of terror in the constriction of their anonymous lives. Fear invades their small, routine existences, and hallucination creeps up on them. In this respect, Thurber is a father figure to a line of modern writers, including John Cheever, who are absorbed by the thin line between reality and fantastic estrangement in the experience of representative middle-class Americans. Eponymous middle-class couples appear again and again in Cheever's short stories just as they do in Thurber's; and they are also likely in their isolation to experience hallucination—to see, as in a dream, a nude young woman in the window of a swiftly passing commuter train, or to swim through a series of neighbors' swimming pools to discover truths about their lives so horrendous that they have been unable to face them. Not only in the short stories but increasingly in Cheever's novels fantasy becomes a means of apprehending reality.

Thurber produced no works of great length to ensure his reputation. He was limited to minor forms, and even in these briefer modes leaves out much of human experience. There is, for example, very little love in Thurber's work, or perhaps none at all. Robert Morsberger has enumerated other absences in the writing—no proletarian or working conditions, nor political life, nor treatment (except in para-

bles) of death, war, or religion.[17] Yet despite these limitations, Thurber remains one of the essential writers of his
period, particularly in the field of humor. His great contri-
bution was in transforming humor into a form of moral
awareness that by destroying a strict rationalism restores
the sense of certain nineteenth-century writers of the un-
fathomable mystery beneath the floor of individual consciousness.

In *The Wound and the Bow: Seven Studies in Literature*
(1941), Edmund Wilson developed the thesis that the Phi-
loctetes myth of Greek literature illustrates the inseparable
connection between maiming and genius, between mal-
ady and the artist's invincible bow. In the cases of Dickens
and Kipling particularly, he shows the effect of intense
unhappiness in childhood upon their mature artistic creation. Thurber clearly belongs among this group of writers
who were maimed severely in childhood (in his case left
literally half blind) and whose imagining of life in maturity
is partly shaped by this experience. Thurber never quite
grows into adulthood, retaining a child's imagination. His
drawings were sometimes mistaken by those unfamiliar
with them as being the work of a child, and his protagonists are almost unaccountably innocent, having a
child's recourse to daydreams and experiencing childlike
terrors in which, unlike adults presumably, they are alone
and utterly helpless. These child-men are very small and
the outer world is very large and often filled with threat.
Later in his career, Thurber withdraws into a child's world
of fables in which animals are able to converse, and fairy
tales containing dragons, castles, marauding giants,
witches, spells, and metamorphoses. In these fairy tales
good and evil confront one another directly, as in a child's
imagination.

One of the most impressive features of Thurber's work
is his retention of what the child's experience feels like. His
resentments, which have a child's obstinacy, are remembered forever. Had Thurber been more "adjusted," had his
retention of the child in him been more diluted by adult

experience, he would not have been able to envision life as he had. His power as a literary artist depends absolutely on his ability to draw from mysterious inner sources that enable him to project wonder and fright pristinely, and to imagine life from odd, childlike angles. His early wounding was inseparably connected to his "invincible bow."

T. S. Eliot has remarked that Thurber's

is a form of humor which is also a way of saying something serious. There is a criticism of life at the bottom of it. It is serious and even somber. Unlike so much humor, it is not merely a criticism of manners—that is, of the superficial aspects of society at a given moment—but something more profound. His writings and also his illustrations are capable of surviving the immediate environment and time out of which they spring.[18]

It is a humor that is complex and as Eliot says "even somber," both disarmingly naive and extremely sophisticated, and having the stamp of a powerful originality. Thurber began his career in an age when American humor writing flourished, and rose to be its chief practitioner. Although afflicted in many ways in his personal life, his achievement was impressive. He wrote some of the finest and most haunting stories of the century, and excelled all of his contemporaries as a satirist and parodist. A poet of anxious psychological states and a fantasist of genius, he was, quite simply, inimitable.

Notes

1. James Thurber: The Life and Career

1. Information concerning Thurber's life and career has been drawn from a variety of sources, including Charles S. Holmes's *The Clocks of Columbus: The Literary Career of James Thurber* (New York: Atheneum, 1972), Robert E. Morsberger's *James Thurber* (New York: Twayne, 1964), and Burton Bernstein's *Thurber: A Biography* (New York: Dodd, Mead, 1975). My primary source, however, has been Bernstein's comprehensive biography. On October 22, 1985, I also held an interview with Bernstein at his office at the *New Yorker*, and certain subsequent footnotes refer to these conversations.

2. Elliott Nugent (1899–1980) made his stage debut at four when he joined his parents in their vaudeville act, and had frequently been on the stage before attending Ohio State University. After a short period in the US Navy, he made his Broadway debut in Kaufmann and Connelly's *Dulcy* (1921), and with his father, J. C. Nugent, wrote and appeared in a series of other Broadway plays in the 1920s. He not only collaborated with Thurber on *The Male Animal* (1940) but also played the starring role of Tommy Turner when the play was presented on Broadway. Nugent later adapted the play for the screen, and recreated the role of Tommy Turner when the work was revived on Broadway in 1952. After extensive work in the New York theater, Nugent went to Hollywood, where he became a prominent writer, actor, and director. His film career collapsed in the early 1950s, however, when he began to suffer from mental illness. His autobiography, *Events Leading Up to the Comedy* (1965), describes his years at Ohio State and association with Thurber as friend and collaborator. For further details of Nugent's career see the *Oxford Companion to the American*

Theatre, 512–13; *Notable Names in the Theatre*, 1021; and *The Film Encyclopedia*, 867.

3. Quoted in Bernstein, 133.
4. Ibid., 123.
5. Charles S. Holmes, *The Clocks of Columbus*, 72.
6. Bernstein, 147.
7. Of the Algonquin Round Table circle, those who contributed to the *New Yorker* by the late 1920s and early 1930s included Robert Benchley, Alexander Woollcott, Dorothy Parker, and Ring Lardner. The Algonquin group consisted of Ross, those just named, Franklin P. Adams, Heywood Broun, George S. Kaufmann, Marc Connelly, Deems Taylor, Donald Ogden Stewart, Robert E. Sherwood, Laurence Stallings, and Edna Ferber, among others. For books on Ross, the Algonquin Round Table, and the early years of the *New Yorker*, see: Dale Kramer, *Ross and the New Yorker* (Garden City, New York: Doubleday, 1951); Margaret Case Harriman, *The Vicious Circle: The Story of the Algonquin Round Table* (New York: Rinehart, 1951); Corey Ford, *The Time of Laughter* (Boston: Little, Brown, 1967); Jane Grant, *Ross, the New Yorker and Me* (New York: Reynald & Co., 1968); and Brendan Gill, *Here at the New Yorker* (New York: Random House, 1975).
8. For books on White, see Edward C. Sampson, *E. B. White* (New York: Twayne, 1974) and Scott Elledge, *E. B. White: A Biography* (New York: W. W. Norton, 1984). Elledge's biography should be consulted especially for its account of White's relationship to Thurber and their early association at the *New Yorker*. Letters exchanged between Thurber and White are included in Helen Thurber and Edward Weeks, ed., *Selected Letters of James Thurber* (Boston: Little, Brown, 1981) and Dorothy Lobrano Guth, ed., *Letters of E. B. White* (New York: Harper & Row, 1976).
9. Dorothy Parker, "introduction" to Thurber, *The Seal in the Bedroom and Other Predicaments* (New York: Harper & Brothers, 1932), viii, x.
10. Quoted in Holmes, 148.
11. Quoted in Bernstein, 219.
12. Thurber's close friends in Bermuda were Jane and Ronald Williams, whose various houses, such as Felicity Hall, where Harvey Allen composed *Anthony Adverse*, were liter-

ary centers. Ronald Williams was a seafaring Welshman who founded *The Bermudian*, to which Thurber contributed and was a shareholder. His friends included Kipling, Harvey Allen, Sinclair Lewis (whom Thurber met at the Williamses' home), and Joseph Hergersheimer, as well as artists and actors such as the Fredric Marches. Jane Williams was an upper-class American woman from upstate New York, whom men, including Thurber, found extremely attractive. Thurber wrote *The 13 Clocks* in Bermuda, drawing the princess's name from the Williamses' young daughter Sara Linda. Bernstein makes some cursory mention of Thurber's friendship with the Williamses, but I have learned of them more fully from the novelist Brian Burland, who grew up in Bermuda, and was introduced to Thurber by the Williamses. In the late 1950s, Burland also knew Thurber in New York.

13. Quoted in Holmes, 183.
14. Ibid., 184.
15. Peter De Vries, "James Thurber: The Comic Prufrock," *Poetry*, 63 (December 1943): 150–59. Reprinted in Charles S. Holmes, ed., *Thurber: A Collection of Critical Essays* (Englewood Cliffs, New Jersey: Prentice-Hall, 1974), 37–43.
16. Holmes, 244.
17. Quoted in Bernstein, 368.
18. Quoted in Holmes, 8.
19. Quoted in Bernstein, 464. Letter to Bernstein by Edmund Wilson.
20. In this regard Bernstein quotes White as saying: "After the *Atlantic* series, we were all up in arms, but now *The Years with Ross* just seems distasteful, not awful. I objected to the distortions in the book, the sex—just Jim showing off—and the payments for the writers. Also, Jim exaggerated his own administrative duties. He never, as far as I know, scheduled the magazine or attended art meetings regularly. When the book came out, I didn't write Jim about it, and it was the only book of his he never inscribed to us" (463).
21. Information concerning adaptations of Thurber's work into other media is contained in Bernstein, Holmes, and Morsberger; but I have been particularly indebted to Morsberger, *James Thurber*, 154–59. *A Thurber Carnival* is the best

known of the adaptations of Thurber onto the stage, but there were a number of others, drawn particularly from the fairy tales. *Many Moons* was made into a play in 1946 for school and children's theater audiences by Charlotte Barrows Chorpenning; and *The Thirteen Clocks* was staged by the Barter Theatre of Virginia in 1953. Another version of *The Thirteen Clocks* by a touring company was also presented on the 1953 summer circuit with Leonard Bernstein's *Trouble in Tahiti*. In 1955 three related one-act plays, based on Thurber's Mr. Monroe stories and entitled *Three by Thurber*, was produced at the Theatre de Lys in Greenwich Village. *The Beast in Me*, an adaptation of Thurber's fables by James Costigan, was produced on Broadway at the Plymouth Theatre, on May 16, 1963, but closed after only four performances. Another musical, planned by Jule Styne and Cy Coleman, an adaptation of the fairy tale *The Wonderful O*, never materialized because the producer was unable to obtain Peter Ustinov to play the part of Black the pirate.

22. Film adaptations of Thurber's work were of varying quality, often diluting or altering the original conception. The screen version of *The Male Animal*, produced by Warner Brothers in 1942, was a reasonably successful production but sentimentalized the play's ending. It was written by Julius J. and Philip G. Epstein, directed by Elliott Nugent, and starred Henry Fonda, Olivia de Haviland, and Jack Carson. Having acquired full rights to the property, the studio made use of it again as the inspiration for a meretricious musical set on a Midwestern campus, *She's Working Her Way through College*, which starred Virginia Mayo and Ronald Reagan. MGM's adaptation of "The Secret Life of Walter Mitty," which was released in 1947 and starred Danny Kaye, had only a marginal relation to Thurber's story. Instead of a nagging wife, Mitty was given a nagging mother (played by Fay Bainter), and was able to find romance with an attractive young woman (played by Virginia Mayo).

Thurber's "The Catbird Seat" was sold to MGM in an arrangement by which Thurber himself would do the screenplay. But he was dissatisfied with the screenplay he wrote, returned the advance, and canceled the project.

"The Catbird Seat," however, was later made into an English film, entitled *The Battle of the Sexes*, which was written and produced by Monja Danischewsy, and starred Peter Sellers and Robert Morley. The film received favorable reviews, and Thurber himself was satisfied with it. An ambitious film adaptation of Thurber pieces, in the form partly of live drama and partly of animated cartoons, and tentatively entitled *The Thurber Carnival*, was planned but was eventually dropped. UPA (United Productions of America), however, did produce an animated cartoon version of Thurber's fable "The Unicorn in the Garden."

23. A number of adaptations from Thurber, particularly his short stories and fairy tales, appeared on television during the 1950s. A version of "The Catbird Seat" was performed on television in July 1952; and in December 1953 a dramatic version of *The Thirteen Clocks* was presented with Basil Rathbone as the Duke, Cedric Hardwicke as the Golux, John Raitt as Prince Zorn, and Roberta Peters as Princess Saralinda. "The Remarkable Case of Mr. Bruhl," adapted by Tad Mosel and starring Elliott Nugent, was presented on the "Omnibus" series in 1954. "Playhouse 90" produced a version of *The Male Animal* on March 13, 1958, which starred Andy Griffith, Ann Rutherford, and Edmund O'Brien; a dramatization of "One Is a Wanderer," starring Fred MacMurray, was presented on the "G. E. Theater" on September 28, 1958; and *The Last Flower* was dramatized on "Camera Three" on October 12th of the same year. In June 1959, the "Goodyear Theater" dramatized material from Thurber in a program that was called "The Secret Life of James Thurber" and starred Arthur O'Connell as "Mr. Monroe." Adaptations have appeared since Thurber's death, but with less frequency.

24. Adaptations as opera and children's opera have been produced chiefly on college campuses. *The Thirteen Clocks* was made into a children's opera, with music by Mary Johnson and libretto by Mary Johnson and Maritza and Norman Morgan, and was performed at Hunter College. An opera version of "The Secret Life of Walter Mitty" by Charles Hamm was produced at Ohio University, and won the university's 1953 opera workshop award. An adaptation of "The Unicorn in the Garden" as a one-act opera by Russell

Smith was produced at the Hartt College of Music in Hartford, Connecticut on May 1, 1957.

Thurber's work also inspired several ballets. Doris Humphrey produced a ballet based on the picture parable "The Race of Life," and in the 1950–51 season Charles Weidman presented a ballet version of "The Unicorn in the Garden." The Charles Weidman troupe also presented a ballet based on "The War between Men and Women" at the YMHA's 1954 Summer Dance Festival. *The 13 Clocks*, a favorite source for adaptation into various media, was performed as a ballet on television's "Wonderful Town," with Fay Emerson narrating off camera.

25. During my interview with him, Bernstein told me that he had himself seen the production of *A Thurber Carnival*, and its generally favorable notices notwithstanding had found it disappointing. He said that he doubted if Thurber's special kind of imagination could be transferred intact into other media. The English production of *A Thurber Carnival* ran for only three weeks and received crushing reviews.

26. Bernstein, 480.

27. E. B. White, "James Thurber," *New Yorker*, 21 (October 27, 1945): 91–94.

28. Quoted in Bernstein, 502–3.

2. Thurber's Dreamscapes: The Drawings and Illustrations

1. Quoted in Bernstein, 196.

2. Ibid., 29.

3. Charles Holmes, 68. The column cited appeared in the *Columbus Dispatch* of May 20, 1923.

4. Ibid.

5. Quoted in Bernstein, 184.

6. E. B. White, "A Note on the Drawings in this Book," in Thurber and White, *Is Sex Necessary? Or Why You Feel the Way You Do* (New York: Harper and Brothers, 1929), 189–90.

7. Dorothy Parker, introduction, Thurber, *The Seal in the Bedroom*, viii.

8. Quoted in Morsberger, 166.

9. Quoted in Bernstein, 118.

10. Ibid.
11. Ibid., 298.
12. Ibid., 194.
13. See Holmes, 115–45, and Morsberger, 161–71.
14. Morsberger, 169.
15. Holmes has commented on the similarity, remarking: "There is no doubt that Thurber's treatment of family life in *My Life and Hard Times*, for example, owes something to the combination of farcical slam-bang, sharp observation of the domestic scene, and excursions into the realm of fantasy he found in his favorite comic strips." Holmes, 69.
16. E. B. White's personal collection of Thurber's drawings are included with the Thurber-White correspondence in the E. B. White Collection at the Cornell University Library, Department of Rare Books. The drawings include eight splendid pencil profiles of White and numerous other drawings on eight-by-eleven-inch paper. Among them is the "Embrace Series," a sequence of twenty-five pencil drawings under the general title "La Flamme and Mr. Prufrock—A Story," which Thurber gave to White on the occasion of his marriage in 1929. The series deals with a frustrated tryst between Mr. Prufrock and his ladylove. In the final drawing Prufrock lies in his bed smoking a cigarette, thwarted in his quest for sex. Thurber's naming of his protagonist is interesting, since it implies that Thurber was entirely conscious of Eliot's antihero as a father figure to his own "little" men.

    A number of the drawings—with such titles as "April," "May," and "The Stirring of Spring"—show nude men and women dancing and frolicking. In one, a man's arms and legs are swung wildly about as if made of rubber. His hands and feet are like flippers, his eyes are closed, and his face wears a stupid expression. The nude woman in "April," her arms flung out giddily and a flower gripped in one hand, is grotesquely heavy. She romps with full face to the viewer, her belly large, her breasts pendulous. Her primitively sketched face seems devoid of intelligence. "The Stirring of Spring" shows a nude man holding a nude woman, his large, moundlike back and buttocks facing the viewer. A courtship drawing entitled "The Months: August," depicts a man in a canoe with a woman as he serenades her on a ukulele, his mouth wide open as he sings. The woman sits in the canoe stonily and without expression, her eyes closed. Both figures in this summer idyl seem idiotic.

Some of the drawings are sacrilegious. "The Hotel Irving Madonna" shows a shepherd with his staff at night, with a star overhead in the sky. Nearby a cow looks with a goofy expression at a baby in swaddling clothes held by a woman with an unintelligent face and wearing a dress that silhouettes her heavy bosom and hips. In "Moses in the Bullrushes," an infant, looking like a bald-headed little man, looks from a clump of bullrushes at a woman on her knees before him. She wears a sack dress, her arms extended out in amazement, while the infant Moses stares at her irritably. Another drawing travesties the father of our country, George Washington, who is depicted grotesquely in a military uniform and holding a sword. A cloud of long, loose-flowing hair flies back from his head, which is turned in profile to the left. He has an enormously long nose and a face that is blank except for an eye having an insane expression. The caption for the drawing reads: "Geo. Washington at the time he was kicked out of the Virginia Military Institute. (couldn't learn)."

17.   Bernstein interview. Bernstein said that the face was that of Thurber's mother, but partly too of Aunt Margery Albright. Charles Thurber was, in fact, surrounded by his wife's assertive and eccentric female relatives, multiplying the effect of matriarchal domination.

18.   E. B. White, "James Thurber," *New Yorker,* 37 (November 11, 1961): 247.

19.   W. H. Auden, "The Icon and the Portrait," *Nation,* 150 (January 13, 1940): 48.

3. Ordeal in Fantasy: Thurber's Fiction of the 1930s

1.   Oddly, Charles Holmes is less impressed by Thurber's contributions than White's. "White is more likely to be discursive," he remarks, "while Thurber is generally more dramatic, casting the material in the form of a scene, with characters, action, and dialogue. But stylistically, White

has more variety, subtlety, and range than Thurber. One can see why Thurber took him as a model." Holmes, 116.

2. E. B. White, introduction, Thurber, *The Owl in the Attic and Other Perplexities* (New York: Harper & Brothers, 1931), xi.

3. Leslie A. Fiedler, *The Return of the Vanishing American* (New York: Stein & Day, 1968), 91.

4. Joseph Kramm's play *The Shrike,* presented on Broadway in 1952, deals with a somewhat-similar situation of a man reduced to helplessness by his wife, who is in effect his castrater. Having attempted suicide, he is confined to a mental hospital and has the choice either of being institutionalized indefinitely or of being released under his wife's supervision. A later work dealing with this female type is Ken Kesey's *One Flew over the Cuckoo's Nest* (1962), in which Nurse Ratched has a lobotomy performed on the unruly McMurphy, thus castrating him in a sense. These women, although presented in the guise of realism, are evoked as witch figures, possessing an ominous power over the male.

5. Bernstein, 311.

6. Morsberger, 178.

7. Bernstein, 31.

8. The comic-strip influence on the stories is discussed by Holmes, who observes: "This picture of the American household may owe something to the comic strips. [Thurber] was a lifelong admirer of such cartoonists as Clare Briggs, Cliff Sterett, and Sidney Smith, whose speciality was the humorous treatment of the domestic scene, and the great stereotype with which they all worked invariably cast the husband in the role of weak protagonist and the wife as strong antagonist." Holmes, 122.

9. Morsberger, 45.

10. Ibid., 47.

11. In "Some Notes on Miss L.," West remarked that while writing *Miss Lonelyhearts,* he conceived of it as a comic strip: "The chapters to be squares in which many things happen through one action. The speeches contained in conventional balloons. I abandoned this idea, but retained some of the comic strip technique: Each chapter instead of going forward in time, also goes backward, forward, up and down in space like a picture. Violent images are used to illustrate commonplace events. Violent acts are left al-

most bald." Nathanael West, "Some Notes on Miss L.," in Jay Martin, ed., *Nathanael West: A Collection of Critical Essays* (Englewood Cliffs, New Jersey: Prentice-Hall, 1971), 66.

12. Otto Friedrich, "James Thurber: A Critical Study," *Discovery*, 5 (January 1955): 170.

13. Robert H. Elias, "James Thurber: The Primitive, the Innocent, and the Individual," *American Scholar*, 27 (Summer 1958): 361.

14. This point has been made by Helen Batchelor Petrullo in her unpublished doctoral dissertation "Satire and Freedom: Sinclair Lewis, Nathanael West, and James Thurber" (Syracuse University, 1967).

15. Carl M. Lindner, "Thurber's Walter Mitty—The Underground American Hero," *Georgia Review*, vol. 28 (1974): 283.

4. The Further Range: Thurber's Other Stories

1. Quoted in Morsberger, 158.
2. Ibid.

5. Portraiture and Reminiscence: From *My Life and Hard Times* to *The Years with Ross*

1. Malcolm Cowley, "James Thurber's Dream Book," *New Republic*, 112 (March 12, 1945): 262–63.

2. Charles Holmes, 148.

3. Quoted in Bernstein, 407.

4. Morsberger, 149.

5. Wolcott Gibbs, *Season in the Sun* (New York: Random House, 1951), 92.

6. Bernstein, 459. Bernstein points out that Thurber had considered ending the book with an epilogue that would consist either of a collection of short pieces by friends of Ross (commissioned by Thurber) or an overview by Thurber of changes that had taken place in the *New Yorker* since Ross's passing. The second would undoubtedly have afforded Thurber the opportunity to comment, as he had done in interviews and elsewhere in the 1950s, on the decline of humor in the magazine. He wisely decided, however, to

end the book with Ross's last years and death, a conclusion that is affectionate and moving.

7. Brendan Gill, *Here at The New Yorker* (New York: Random House, 1975), 29.

8. Quoted in Bernstein, 464.

6. Humor Pieces, Parodies, and Reportage

1. Professor Walter B. Pitkin was the author of numerous popular books on the attainment of happiness that appeared from the 1920s onward through the 1950s. In making him the butt of his satire, Thurber was broaching terrain recently explored by Nathanael West. Thurber points out with some irony that Pitkin's book *The Secret of Happiness* was published in the black year 1929, but West appears to have made Pitkin the target of more savage satire in one of his depression novels. In *A Cool Million* (1934), West's hero Lemuel Pitkin is a naive believer in the American myth of happiness. A young wanderer across America in the depression, he is shorn of every vestige of hope and is at last dehumanized and destroyed. Especially by comparison with West's sharply focused novel, Thurber's foolery seems groping and tentative.

2. James Thurber, "A Visit from Saint Nicholas," *New Yorker*, vol 3 (December 24, 1927): 17–19.

3. James Thurber, "Recollections of Henry James," *New Yorker*, vol 9 (December 17, 1933): 11–13.

4. Quoted in Morsberger, 157.

5. The "Where Are They Now?" series, written by Thurber under the pseudonym Jared L. Manley, appeared in the *New Yorker* between 1936–38, with twenty-five profiles in all, included in seventeen separate columns. They consist of the following: "Boy from Boston"/"Most Popular Personage," vol 12 (April 18, 1936): 23–27 (on Joseph Killion [Jake Kilrain] and Gertrude Ederle); "Glory Be and What Ho!"/"Promising Lad," vol 12 (April 25, 1936): 20–23 (on William Sulzer and Wilber Huston); "The Little Tailor"/"The Lady in Fox Street," vol 12 (May 23, 1936): 22–25 (On Jacob Maged and Charles G. Pease); "Izzy and Moe"/"An Honest Man," vol 12 (June 6, 1936): 18–20 (on

Izzy Einstein and Moe W. Smith, and Santo D'Amico);
"Little Johnny"/"Crusader," vol 12 (July 4, 1936): 19–24 (on
John Joseph Hayes and Kitty Marion); "The Glorified Tug,"
vol 12 (August 15, 1936): 21–24 (on the *Macom*); "Eight Men
in a Boat," vol 12 (September 5, 1936): 20–25 (on Richard
Pearson Hobson); "Finnigin"/"The Erg Man," vol 12 (Oc-
tober 31, 1936): 19–21 (on Strickland Gillilan and Howard
Scott).

"Invitation to Dinner," vol 12 (December 5, 1936): 29–33
(on Andrew Summers Rowan); "The Santa Claus Girl," vol
12 (December 19, 1936): 22–25 (on Virginia O'Hanlon); "A
Sort of Genius," vol 12 (January 23, 1937): 21–27 (on the
Hall-Mills murder case and Willie Stevens); "41313 NY," vol
13 (March 27, 1937): 22–25 (on the Herman Rosenthal
murder case); "500,000 Copies," vol 13 (June 26, 1937): 26–
29 (on Edward Streeter and *Dere Mable*); "April Fool!," vol 13
(August 14, 1937): 22–26 (on William James Sidis); "Prod-
igy"/"The Banana Boys," vol 13 (December 25, 1937): 23–25
(on Edward Rochie Hardy, Jr, and Irving Conn and Frank
Silver); "Death of a Dog," vol 14 (August 20, 1938): 24, 26,
30, 32 (on Caleb E. Norris and Albert Payson Terhune's
collie Sunnybank Jean); "The Hoosier Cyclone," vol 14
(September 17, 1938): 51–52, 54–57 (on Amos Rusie).

Three of the pieces were later included in Thurber's book
collections. They are: "A Sort of Genius," in *My World—and
Welcome to It* (1942); "Death of a Dog," in *Thurber's Dogs*
(1955); and "41313 NY," in *Alarms and Diversions* (1957).

6. Although Thurber does not refer to it, F. Scott Fitzgerald
    drew from the Rosenthal murder case as part of the back-
    ground of *The Great Gatsby*. When Nick Carraway has lunch
    with Gatsby and Meyer Wolfsheim in a Times Square res-
    taurant, Wolfsheim reminisces about his friend "Rosy"
    Rosenthal, a gambler and shady figure who was shot to
    death in front of the Hotel Metropole. The allusion links
    Fitzgerald's theme of the debasement of the ideal and won-
    drous with New York's pervasive corruption.

7. James Thurber, "Where Are They Now?," *New Yorker*, vol 12
    (January 23, 1937): 23.

8. Quoted in Morsberger, 184.

9. Edward Stone, "James Thurber's 'Four Pieces,' " in his *The*

Battle and the Books (Athens: Ohio University Press, 1964), 163–86.

10. Thurber discussed James's *The Ambassadors* with Mark Van Doren on the CBS radio series "Invitation to Learning." *The Ambassadors* was one of Thurber's favorite books, and he claimed to have read it "four times in the last thirty-five years." In the broadcast, Edward Stone notes, Thurber corrected Van Doren on details of the publication history of the book. It was James's scenario, he pointed out, and not the manuscript of *The Ambassadors* that the reader for *Harper's* rejected in 1903; and the rejection, moreover, pertained to the work as a serial in *Harper's* magazine, not as a book under the Harper imprint. Edward Stone, *The Battle and the Books*, 168.

11. Otto Friedrich, "James Thurber: A Critical Study," *Discovery*, 5 (January 1955): 175.

12. Bernstein interview.

7. The Fables and Fairy Tales

1. In 1940, Thurber cited William March as one of the writers he was then reading (Morsberger, 185). Later, in an unpublished letter to E. B. White of April 16, 1956, Thurber called March the best of the "dead" American fable writers. William March (1893–1954), whose actual name was William March Campbell, was an executive for the Waterman Steamship Corporation of Mobile, Alabama who, following a period of "hysterical blindness," discovered his second vocation as a writer of fiction in his thirties. His first novel, *Company K* (1933), based on his combat experiences, is one of the classics of World War I literature. Other novels and short-story collections include: *Come in at the Door* (1934), *The Little Wife and Other Stories* (1935), *The Tallons* (1936), *Some Like Them Short* (1939), *The Looking-Glass* (1943), *Trial Balance* (1945), and *The Bad Seed* (1954), the last of which was adapted as a Broadway play by Maxwell Anderson in 1954 and made into a Hollywood film in 1956.

   March published his fables in little magazines and newspapers in New York in the 1940s, later revising them in the early 1950s, but they were never collected in book form during his lifetime. March's *Ninety-nine Fables,* edited by William T. Going, was published posthumously in 1960 by the University of Alabama Press. The fables are written in the tradition of Aesop, but suggest an extremely urbane imagination. Many of them treat the cruelties or aberration from reason of mankind, and some attack the hypocrisies of religion. Highly polished and ironic, they are masterful compositions of comparable stature to Thurber's fables, and resemble them in their deep skepticism.

2. Quoted in Holmes, 296. Letter to Thurber, March 21, 1956.

3. In *The Art of James Thurber,* Richard Tobias has discussed *The White Deer* and the other fairy tales with very little sense of their containing inner complexities at all. Rather than recognizing that each is different from the others, he has regarded them as being all the same. All of them, he believes, tell the same story of a redemption from a wasteland by a figure, often slighted at first, who stands for imagination and romance. In this way, the fairy tales constitute Thurber's testament of faith in life achieved in the later period of his career. Tobias's interpretation breaks Thurber's work down into period categories that are astonishingly inapplicable. "The writing of the 1930's," he asserts, "create a kind of *Inferno,* the writing of the 1940's a *Purgatorio,* and the writing of the 1950's a *Paradiso.*" How Tobias could claim that the writing of the 1950s, much of which is pessimistic or misanthropic, constitutes a *Paradiso* is difficult to imagine. The *Paradiso* is illustrated for Tobias in the romantic and "optimistic" fairy tales, but to read such tales as *The Thirteen Clocks* and *The White Deer* as being unambiguously romantic is to be guilty of critical blindness.

4. Edmund Wilson, "Books," *New Yorker* vol 21 (October 27, 1945): 89.

5. Unpublished letter, c. 1945, from White to Thurber. E. B. White Collection, Cornell University Library.

6. Unpublished letter to E. B. White, June 30, 1950. E. B. White Collection, Cornell University Library.

7. Unpublished letter, c. 1945, from White to Thurber. E. B. White Collection, Cornell University Library.

8. Conclusion: Thurber in Context

1. Walter Blair, *Horse Sense in American Humor: From Benjamin Franklin to Ogden Nash* (New York: Russell & Russell, 1942; rev 1962); Walter Blair & Hamlin Hill, *America's Humor From Poor Richard to Doonesbury* (New York: Oxford University Press, 1978); Norris W. Yates, *The American Humorist: Conscience of the Twentieth Century* (Ames, Iowa: Iowa State University Press, 1964).
2. Robert Morsberger, 18.
3. Quoted in Holmes, 280.
4. Scott Elledge, *E. B. White: A Biography* (New York: Norton, 1984), 132.
5. Ibid., 130.
6. These early casuals of White's, many of them suggesting Thurber's influence, have been donated by Elledge to the Cornell University Library, Department of Rare Books. There are four boxes of this material in all.
7. Elledge, 131.
8. Quoted in Bernstein, 29.
9. Ibid., 212.
10. Ibid., 202.
11. Edward C. Sampson, *E. B. White* (New York: Twayne, 1974), 67.
12. Thurber, "E. B. W.," in his *Credos and Curios* (New York: Harper & Row, 1962), 141.
13. Norris Yates, *The American Humorist*, 320. Norris Yates has remarked: "At home in both the country and the city, White helped the *New Yorker* to combine small-town informality with cosmopolitan breadth and refinement. The prose and some of the poetry . . . suggest a neighbor leaning on the fire escape to talk to his neighbor. His main *persona* is the urban white-collar man attempting to recapture the 'sanity and repose of nature.' "
14. Ibid., 288.
15. According to Bernstein, Thurber claimed that "given any two consecutive lines of *The Great Gatsby*, which he had read only once, he could state on what page the lines occurred—and approximately where they were placed on the page." Bernstein, 40.

226 James Thurber

16. E. B. White, quoted in James Thurber obituary, *New York Times* (November 3, 1961): 35.
17. Morsberger, 199.
18. Quoted in "Priceless Gift of Laughter," *Time*, 58 (July 9, 1951): 94–95.

Bibliography

I. Books by James Thurber

Is Sex Necessary? Or Why You Feel the Way You Do (with E. B. White). New York: Harper & Brothers, 1929.

The Owl in the Attic and Other Perplexities. New York: Harper & Brothers, 1931.

The Seal in the Bedroom and Other Predicaments. New York: Harper & Brothers, 1932.

My Life and Hard Times. New York: Harper & Brothers, 1933.

The Middle-Aged Man on the Flying Trapeze. New York: Harper & Brothers, 1935.

Let Your Mind Alone! and Other More or Less Inspirational Pieces. New York: Harper & Brothers, 1937.

Cream of Thurber. London: Hamish Hamilton, 1939.

The Last Flower. Harper & Brothers, 1939.

The Male Animal (with Elliott Nugent). New York: Random House, 1940.

Fables for Our Time and Famous Poems Illustrated. New York: Harper & Brothers, 1940.

My World—and Welcome to It. New York: Harcourt, Brace, 1943.

Many Moons. New York: Harcourt, Brace, 1943.

Thurber's Men, Women and Dogs. New York: Harcourt, Brace, 1943.

The Great Quillow. New York: Harcourt, Brace, 1944.

The Thurber Carnival. New York: Harper & Brothers, 1945.

The White Deer. New York: Harcourt, Brace, 1945.

The Beast in Me and Other Animals. New York: Harcourt, Brace, 1948.

The 13 Clocks. New York: Simon & Schuster, 1950.

The Thurber Album. New York: Simon & Schuster, 1950.

Thurber Country. New York: Simon & Schuster, 1953.

Thurber's Dogs. New York: Simon & Schuster, 1955.

Further Fables for Our Time. New York: Simon & Schuster, 1956.

The Wonderful O. New York: Simon & Schuster, 1957.

Alarms and Diversions. New York: Harper & Brothers, 1957.
The Years with Ross. Boston: Little, Brown, 1959.
Lanterns and Lances. New York: Harper & Brothers, 1961.
Credos and Curios. New York: Harper & Row, 1962.
A Thurber Carnival. New York: Samuel French, 1962.
Vintage Thurber. 2 vols. London: Hamish Hamilton, 1963.
Thurber and Company. New York: Harper & Row, 1966.
Selected Letters of James Thurber. Ed. Helen Thurber & Edward
      Weeks. Boston: Little, Brown, 1981.

II. Books on James Thurber

Bernstein, Burton. *Thurber: A Biography.* New York: Dodd, Mead,
      1975.
Black, Stephen A. *James Thurber: His Masquerades.* The Hague:
      Mouton, 1970.
Bowden, Edwin T. *James Thurber: A Bibliography.* Columbus: Ohio
      State University Press, 1968.
Holmes, Charles S. *The Clocks of Columbus: The Literary Career of
      James Thurber.* New York: Atheneum, 1972.
————, ed. *Thurber: A Collection of Critical Essays.* Englewood
      Cliffs, New Jersey: Prentice-Hall, 1974.
Kenney, Catherine M. *Thurber's Art of Confusion.* Hamden, Con-
      necticut: Archon, 1984.
Morsberger, Robert E. *James Thurber.* New York: Twayne, 1964.
Tobias, Richard C. *The Art of James Thurber.* Athens, Ohio: Ohio
      University Press, 1969.

III. Other Criticism and Comment

Auden, W. H. "The Icon and the Portrait," *Nation* 150 (January
      13, 1940): 48.
Blair, Walter. *Native American Humor.* New York: American Book
      Co., 1937.
————. *Horse Sense in American Humor: From Benjamin Franklin to
      Ogden Nash.* Chicago: University of Chicago Press, 1942.
———— and Hamlin Hill. *American Humor from Poor Richard to
      Doonesbury.* New York: Oxford University Press, 1978.
Brandon, Henry. "Everybody Is Getting Very Serious" (inter-

view), *New Republic* 138 (May 26, 1958): 11–16. Reprinted more fully as "The Tulle and Taffeta Rut," in Brandon, *As We Are*. Garden City, New York: Doubleday, 1961.

Cooke, Alistair. "James Thurber in Conversation with Alistair Cooke" (interview), *Atlantic* 198 (August 1956): 36–40.

Cowley, Malcolm. "James Thurber's Dream Book," *New Republic* 112 (March 12, 1945): 262–63.

————. *The Literary Situation*. New York: Viking, 1954.

De Vries, Peter. "James Thurber: The Comic Prufrock," *Poetry* 63 (December 1943): 150–59.

Eastman, Max. *Enjoyment of Laughter*. New York: Simon & Schuster, 1936.

Elias, Robert H. "James Thurber: The Primitive, the Innocent, and the Individual," *American Scholar* 27 (Summer 1958): 355–63.

Friedrich, Otto. "James Thurber: A Critical Study," *Discovery* 5 (January 1955): 158–92.

Gill, Brendan. *Here at The New Yorker*. New York: Random House, 1975.

Herrmann, Dorothy. *S. J. Perelman: A Life*. New York: G. P. Putnam's Sons, 1986.

Kramer, Dale. *Ross and the New Yorker*. New York: Doubleday, 1952.

Nugent, Elliott. *Events Leading up to the Comedy*. New York: Trident, 1956.

Plimpton, George, and Max Steele. "The Art of Fiction" (interview), *Paris Review* 10 (Fall 1955): 35–49. Reprinted in Malcolm Cowley, ed., *Writers at Work*. New York: Viking, 1959.

Sayre, Joel. "Priceless Gift of Laughter," *Time* vol 108 (July 9, 1951): 88–90.

Stone, Edward. *The Battle and the Books*. Athens: Ohio University Press, 1964.

Updike, John. "Indignations of a Senior Citizen," *New York Times Book Review* (November 25, 1962): 5.

Van Doren, Mark. *The Autobiography of Mark Van Doren*. New York: Harcourt, Brace, 1958.

Weales, Gerald. "The World in Thurber's Fables," *Commonweal* 55 (January 18, 1957): 409–11.

White, E. B. "A Note on the Drawings in This Book," in Thurber & White, *Is Sex Necessary?* New York: Harper & Brothers, 1929.

————. "James Thurber" (obituary article), *New Yorker* 37 (November 11, 1961): 247.

————. "Introduction," reprinted edition, Thurber & White, *Is Sex Necessary?* New York: Delta, 1963.

————. *Letters of E. B. White,* ed. Dorothy Lobrano Guth. New York: Harper & Row, 1976.

Wilson, Edmund. "Books," *New Yorker* 21 (October 27, 1945): 91–94.

————. *The Fifties: From Notebooks and Diaries of the Period.* New York: Farrar, Straus and Giroux, 1986.

Yates, Norris. *The American Humorist: Conscience of the Twentieth Century.* Ames: Iowa State University Press, 1964.

Index